Robert Bryan

ROBERT BRYAN

The Flying Parson of
Labrador and the Real
Story Behind Bert and I

ROBERT BRYAN

Down East Books

CAMDEN, MAINE

Down East Books

An imprint of The Rowman & Littlefield Publishing Group, Inc.
4501 Forbes Blvd., Ste. 200
Lanham, MD 20706
www.rowman.com

Distributed by NATIONAL BOOK NETWORK

British Library Cataloguing in Publication Information Available

Library of Congress Cataloging-in-Publication Data
Bryan, Robert, 1931–
  Robert Bryan : the flying parson of Labrador and the Real Story behind Bert and I /
Robert Bryan.
    pages cm
  ISBN 978-1-60893-276-4 (cloth : alk. paper) — ISBN 978-1-60893-662-5
(paperback) — ISBN 978-1-60893-277-1 (electronic) 1. Bryan, Robert, 1931–
2. Côte-Nord (Québec)—Biography. 3. Dodge, Marshall, 1935–1982 Bert and I.
4. Air pilots—Québec (Province)—Côte-Nord—Biography. 5. Clergy—Québec
(Province)—Côte-Nord—Biography. 6. Episcopal Church—Clergy—Biography.
I. Title.
  F1054.S3.B79 2014
  629.13092—dc23 [B]   2014032508

∞™ The paper used in this publication meets the minimum requirements of American National Standard for Information Sciences—Permanence of Paper for Printed Library Materials, ANSI/NISO Z39.48-1992.

Printed in the United States of America

This book is dedicated to the families of the Quebec Lower North Shore who inspired me then and continue to inspire me now.

Contents

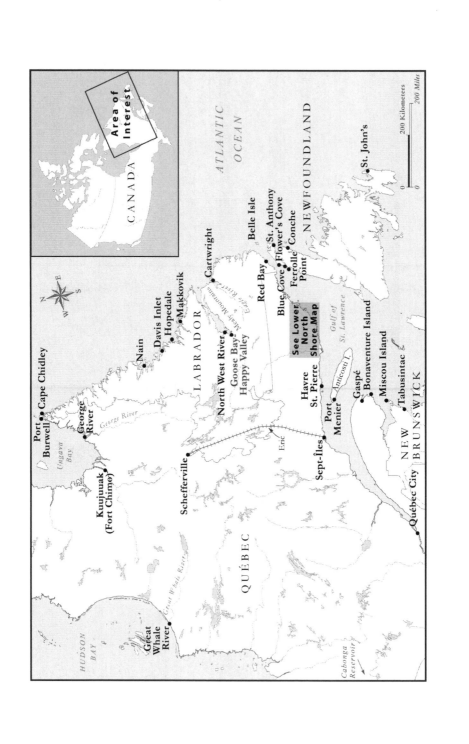

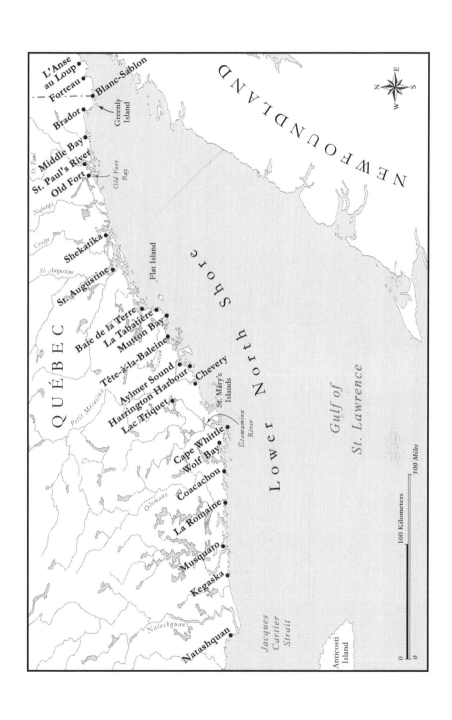

Foreword

I S HE BERT OR IS HE I? Either one, we'd say. We'd smile, thinking of our father and my sister's godfather, making themselves laugh as they ran through takes on the reel to reel tape recorder. My sister, whose bedroom was just above the small room where they'd sometimes record, remembers hearing their low, steady drone as she fell asleep, then, rocketed awake by the likes of "Give a blast of the horn, Bert!" *Blaaaaaaaaaaaaaah!*

Our father created *Bert and I* with his great friend and Yale classmate Marshall Dodge. All these years later, we still hear the iconic Maine phrase, "You can't get there from here."

But that is only part of Dad's story, of our story. Though we were residents of Massachusetts, our hearts were also far to the north along the North Shore of the Gulf of St. Lawrence, held fast by the people and communities of a hard, beautiful landscape. Early in the 1960s, our father, with our mother, Faith Lamb Bryan, by his side, founded the Quebec Labrador Foundation. QLF programs entailed bringing volunteers—known as "students"—to isolated communities in Quebec, Labrador, Newfoundland, and Maine to run summer activities and environmental programs.

Our parents came to the Quebec Labrador region with their young family, and fell in love with the people and the place. They were an irresistible couple, fun loving and friendly and genuinely interested in the lives of everyone they met. They were a team with Dad as the pilot, adventurer, and catalyst, and Mum, equally adventurous, as the home and the hearth. She raised three children while immersing herself in the life of an isolated fishing community. When we flew as a family across great reaches of sea and untracked land, our mother was co-pilot and navigator. Our father honored Mum and their teamwork in his tribute to her in a graduate school paper about the coast: "With love to my intrepid wife Faith, who shares the deep love of the Labrador."

With a floatplane as our primary mode of transportation, we saw the world from an avian perspective, flying over massive icebergs and mosaics of moving ice in the Gulf of St. Lawrence, over herds of caribou, wolves, black bear, and humpback whales.

We counted rafts of black ducks, and watched puffins, gulls, kittiwakes, and murres circling their rocky nesting sites. We landed in pristine lakes, hooking robust trout and salmon on fly rods. I once tied a Mickey Finn to an old knotted leader on an alder branch and caught a three-and-a-half-pound trout.

When the fog swept in, we'd pitch a tent and pull out the survival gear—which usually included expired freeze-dried food—until the weather cleared. In winter we rode on dog sleds, marveled at the seal catch, and snow-shoed on "raquets" made by First Nation neighbors to check rabbit snares. We broke ice to dip drinking water from a roof-fed cistern before electricity and running water came to the coast.

As part of the Bryan family my sisters and I had the time of our lives. We made wonderful friendships across all generations and were welcomed in every home up and down the coast. We listened to stories late into the night, in kitchens warmed by wood cook stoves. We took wise counsel from elders, faces lined by the maps of their lives, living close to the sea. When I talk with old friends on the coast about QLF's summer programs in their heyday, they too speak of having the time of their lives. In coastal vernacular: "We had *some fun!*"

Dad's passion for his work, his energy and charisma, and his desire to do purposeful work for the people and the places he loved created a magic that endures today.

At age 87, Dad still dreams of flying over Anticosti Island to the Quebec Lower North Shore, dipping his wings at the boats he knows below, flying down coast over Kegaska, Wolf Bay, St. Mary's Island, Chevery,

Harrington Harbour, and points north, turning east over the Strait of Belle Isle to northern Newfoundland, skimming back across the Gulf of St. Lawrence to Harrington, circling the island, cranking down the flaps, reducing the throttle, and splashing down for a landing. He slowly taxis toward the shore of the place he has known for so many years as home.

I hope that by reading this book you may get a sense of the particular beauty and indelible charm of this place and time, and of these incredible people and communities along the "Coast of the Labrador."

—Kerry Brokaw

Introduction

I WAS TWENTY-FOUR years old, still two years short of graduating from Yale Divinity School and three years shy of being ordained, when I found my parish for life on the North Shore of Quebec. In the middle of the twentieth century, that section of Canada was among the most sparsely populated sections of North America: so cold, rocky, and windy that the trees were stunted. It was remote, inaccessible, and distant even to Canadian government officials. I fell in love with the purity of the wilderness, the remote stretches of muskeg, and the intricate coastline of ancient land formations untouched by the influence of man. I also fell in love with the strong, stoic, and exceptionally kind people of the North Shore.

This memoir will touch on many moments from my fifty years as a flying minister on the Quebec and Labrador coasts. It will focus on the early years, particularly the 1960s, when I first moved to Harrington Harbour as the official parish priest for five small villages scattered along 150 miles of the Quebec Lower North Shore. The 1960s was a decade of turmoil, of social and civil discord, and of revolutionary change in much of the world, particularly the United States. Old traditions, expectations, and practices were turned upside down. Change came more slowly to the North Shore, but it eventually arrived here. Technology and innovation brought welcome relief from some of the harshest aspects of living in a subarctic climate, but it also brought more fundamental changes to the culture and lifestyle, more I suspect than anyone ever imagined.

My role as a parish priest in the early 1960s very quickly expanded far beyond the spiritual because of my experience as a bush pilot and a succession of floatplanes and ski planes, all painted a distinctive bright yellow, that allowed me to move from village to village and fly deep into the farthest parts of Labrador. I introduced some change into this region, change that I hope improved the quality of life. I created the Quebec Labrador Foundation to provide recreational and educational opportunities for youth and children and to foster a new generation of leaders. It eventually evolved with the times into an organization dedicated to the environmental and cultural stewardship of this rare piece of earth.

When I was an undergraduate at Yale, the chaplain for the Episcopal students was John Gillespie Magee, who achieved considerable fame as the courageous missionary who stayed behind during the Rape of Nanking by the Japanese military in 1937 and recorded the atrocities with a camera at great personal risk in order to provide to the world undeniable proof of those horrific war crimes.

By the time I met him, John was living a very quiet life. He died in 1953, while I was still a student. His son and namesake, John Jr., had enlisted in the Royal Canadian Air Force instead of enrolling at Yale in order to fight the Nazi menace before the United States entered the war. John G. Magee Jr. tragically died in a mid-air collision during a training exercise over Britain in 1941. Young John was not only a pilot, he was also a poet. Just months before his death at the age of nineteen, he wrote a poem called "High Flight." I have recited that poem countless times at the funeral services of pilots.

> Oh, I have slipped the surly bonds of earth,
> And danced the skies on laughter-silvered wings:
> Sunward I've climbed, and joined the tumbling mirth
> Of sun-split clouds,—and done a hundred things
> You have not dreamed of—wheeled and soared and swung
> High in the sunlit silence. Hov'ring there,
> I've chased the shouting wind along, and flung

My eager craft through the footless halls of air . . .
Up, up the long, delirious, burning blue
I've topped the wind-swept heights with easy grace,
Where never lark, or even eagle flew—
And, while with silent, lifting wind I've trod
The high untrespassed sanctity of space,
Put out my hand, and touched the face of God.

Every pilot understands the sentiment expressed in John Jr.'s words, bush pilots perhaps the most, because we fly in smaller, more exposed aircraft that make the experience of flying a far more intimate experience with the clouds, sky, and weather. As my bush plane carried me into the heavens, I found spirituality through the connections I built with my ministry. The people of the Lower North Shore opened their homes and hearts to me. We shared our lives in good times and bad. We mourned together, and we also laughed a lot. They enriched my life and my faith, and for that I am eternally grateful.

It is my hope that these stories from the Lower North Shore will give readers some insight into an extraordinary place and people.

The Venerable Robert A. Bryan
Cookshire-Eaton, Quebec, Canada
June 2014

The Call of the North

CRASHING SURF and high winds wore down and smoothed away the harsh edges of the granite of the Quebec North Shore over the course of thousands of years. That weathered lichen-encrusted rock has become as familiar to me as the face of an old friend. During a ministry that stretched more than fifty years and seemed to pass in a blink, I logged thousands of hours as the pilot of a series of small floatplanes and ski planes. Each plane carried a tail number ending in "69E" and came to be known to friends and family as "Six-Nine-Easy." I had each plane painted bright yellow with a black nose and a black stripe.

The airplane color, a splotch of sunshine even on a foggy day, was 69Easy's distinctive signature for my parishioners. I was the first Anglican priest to use a floatplane to make the rounds on this remote stretch of the Quebec Diocese back in 1959 and the early 1960s. Those durable small planes and my growing experience as a bush pilot expanded my duties beyond the routine spiritual responsibilities of a cleric. The change occurred in an organic manner. I picked up sick patients and carried them to hospital in an emergency, delivered lobsters, tossed mail and messages from the air, fished in remote lakes and hunted in the bush, and visited the simple homes of my parishioners in isolated villages and outposts in one of the most remote sections of North America. I also had great adventures in that treacherous region, flying over and around fog, dodging fierce storms, and landing in precarious settings. During my years on the Quebec North Shore, I had the privilege of fulfilling my ministry to bring comfort and connection to an isolated people. The location also indulged my love of flying and my passion for the wilderness. I not only survived; I also had a wonderful time.

Today, the bird's-eye view of the Quebec North Shore and Labrador looks much as it did on my first exploratory flight in 1959, when I flew with my wife Faith from Tabusintac, New Brunswick, up the Matapedia Valley, across the St. Lawrence Gulf to Trinity Bay, and then on to Sept-Iles in a Cessna 170. At the time, my day job during the academic year was chaplain at the Choate School in Wallingford, Connecticut, but I had arranged for a most unusual summer job through the Anglican Diocese of Quebec. Like the Episcopal Church in the United States, the Anglican Church dates back to the Reformation in England. My ordination in the Episcopal Church, routinely accepted by the Anglican Bishop of Quebec, led to a summer ministry providing vacation relief for the clergy stationed in one of the harshest and most sparsely populated sections of Canada. When I first arrived, there was no electricity, no running water, no telephone, and no indoor plumbing. There were no roads. Life was difficult; winters were long, dark, and bitterly cold. Most residents survived by fishing for cod from May through September. They hunted seals in December and January. During the coldest months of the long winter, they hunkered down, not unlike the first human inhabitants, the Maritime Archaic people who migrated to the area eight or nine millennia earlier. I loved everything about it.

While the region still looks as it always did from the air, much has changed. The population has dropped to fewer than 5,000 in the entire Lower North Shore of Quebec from Kegaska to Blanc Sablon. Even then there were precious few people willing to live in an area that was so forbidding for eight months of the year. Those who did stay were hardy fishing families who had built up a level of resilience and developed a fierce independence over the course of many generations. As the twentieth century wore on, many young people left the isolated little villages for larger towns with better services. Others left the region in search of economic opportunity. There was always a job in the mines or construction in places such as Schefferville. The migration for work continues to this day; many leave the region seasonally to work in western Canada, going to places such as Fort McHenry, near Calgary, for work on the oil rigs.

The region has also changed in fundamental ways: climate change has affected the mix of wildlife and fauna. Man has nearly wiped out the caribou and cod. Progress and modernity have arrived in the form of snowmobiles, electricity, satellite telephones, and other conveniences of modern life. After the collapse of the cod fishery, the economic mainstay of the area, the Canadian government introduced unemployment benefits that provided some relief to the region but also contributed to an irreparable change in a culture of stoic independence.

The North Shore gave meaning and purpose to my ministry and also defined my adult life. While change is an inevitable part of every life, I found change had both positive and negative consequences for this land that barely showed the influence of man for thousands of years but in the space of my lifetime in the mid-twentieth century changed more than any of us could have imagined. Although the geography has kept the area physically isolated and remote, a traditional way of life has shifted before the torrent of modern convenience and progress. There is much that is unfortunate about that change because it threatens to undermine a way of life that bred a nobility of spirit, pride, tenacity, and instinct for self-sufficiency and survival that I deeply admire. In this book I hope to re-create a special moment in time that in my mind remains so magical and special.

In 1955, four years before that first exploratory flight, I married Faith Lamb, who shared my sense of adventure. Beautiful and vibrant, she had been my younger sister Hazel's classmate at the Green Vale School, an independent school in Old Brooksville, New York—where I had been four grades ahead. She went on to attend Vassar College where her mother and grandmother had matriculated. I had just finished my first year at Yale Divinity School. My classwork included a requirement to conduct a summer research project. Many of my classmates signed up to work in psychiatric hospitals. At that time, there was growing concern about the mentally ill, warehoused in large public institutions that were beginning to come under severe and justifiable criticism. But I wanted to do something different and yearned to return to the northern wilderness I had visited the previous summer with three friends from Yale. So I came up with the idea of conducting a survey in the remote parts of Quebec province to assess the spiritual needs of the Protestant workers. My adviser at school, Liston Pope, the Dean of the Yale Divinity School, was bemused by my attraction to the wilderness, but he allowed me to pursue it.

The previous year my friends and I reprised a trip inspired by an article we'd read in *Collier*'s magazine called, "We Did it Without a Guide," about a group of canoeing enthusiasts who had taken a northern adventure by themselves. I drove north with Yale friends Peter Crisp, Nat Reed, and Ed Meyer with two stacked canoes strapped to the roof of our car. We crossed the Canadian border and drove to a town in northern Quebec called Senneterre, 41 miles northeast of Val-d'Or, or Valley of Gold, near the spot where gold was discovered in 1923. We boarded a train at Senneterre and traveled east on the Canadian National Railway to the whistle-stop of Bourmont and began our journey down the Capitachouane River, a marvelous pristine river with enough twists, turns, rocks, and rapids to more than satisfy our youthful yearning for adventure. The river drained into the Cabonga Reservoir, located in the heart of a massive wilderness area in northern Quebec called the La Verandrye Game Reserve. As we spotted dozens of moose and fished for walleye and northern pike, it was eminently clear that we were far from New Haven. I nearly destroyed one of our aluminum canoes when I hit a rock, ripping a gaping hole in the aluminum. We pried the canoe off the rock and patched it with some tough glue carried by Nat Reed. The canoe was still bent and bulged out ominously at the repair site, but we had days left in the trip. Every time we paddled, we heard a "kabunk-bonk, kabunk-bonk." We eventually became utterly lost for several days because the portages were covered by water. Our map did not inform us of the latest developments—that the Cabonga Reservoir had been recently flooded so only the tops of trees showed above the waterline. We had a compass but could not find the egress. We spotted a few signs sticking out of the water saying "Pas de Fumer" (French for "No Smoking."). We paddled for miles to no avail and spent the night in our canoes. Then we heard the sound of woodcutting, the first sign of any human contact in days. We found a solitary man harvesting wood from tree stalks in the flooded waters. He agreed to tow us back the ten miles to the road for a small sum and put us back on the path to civilization. It was a great feeling to lie back in the canoes and be pulled along by someone who knew where he was going.

Faith and I followed essentially the same route the next summer, though I took precautions to avoid getting lost again. We thoroughly enjoyed ourselves despite several thunderstorms that left us soaked to the bone and crouching for cover from the lightning strikes. I probably spent more time fishing and paddling than I did working on my school project. But I did seek out English-speaking Protestants at the railroad stops and the lumber camps and questioned them about their religious needs. Although Roman Catholics outnumbered the Protestants by an overwhelming margin in Quebec, a tradition dating back to the French roots of the area, the handful of English-speaking Protestants, mainly Anglicans, in these remote and isolated logging camps remained faithful to their religion. However, they did feel disenfranchised. They could not take part in the Roman Catholic services and wished that someone from their church could visit them once in a while. I found their faith heartening, and their lonely plight put the germ of an idea in my mind.

It was extraordinarily beautiful country and fortunately my wife accepted the rough terrain and frequent soakings with good humor. Faith grew up in a family that loved the outdoors as much as I did and she had an innate sense of fun and adventure. As we made our way back south, we stopped in Quebec City, both looking a bit disheveled and worse for wear after three weeks in the woods. I had grown a beard. Faith tucked her hair up under a red kerchief. We wandered through the ancient Cathedral of the Holy Trinity, the first Anglican cathedral built outside the British Isles. It is a lovely gray stone structure constructed in the British Palladian Style around the turn of the nineteenth century in the heart of the old walled city of Quebec. The church was empty when we arrived and its silent majesty so awed us that we nearly tip-toed through the hushed shadowy building. Tattered and torn historic flags hung listlessly from the balcony; the cavernous quiet building felt lost in time. I found a pamphlet on a table by the church entrance describing the work of the Anglican Diocese of Quebec. As a priest in training, I was curious about how my Church ministered to those in the wilderness. The diocese covered 250,000 square miles, almost as large a landmass as the state of Texas, and stretched 700 miles east of Quebec City to the Strait of Belle Isle and included the eastern townships the Gaspé, the Magdalen Islands, and the interior of Quebec north to Schefferville. My eyes fixed upon a phrase: "It makes no difference how few and far between they are: we will be there somehow, sometime with the gospel and the ministrations of the Church." I thought of those faithful souls in the remote lumber camps who rarely, if ever, saw a minister. The phrase deeply moved me, burned itself into my mind, and became a touchstone throughout my own ministry.

As we left the cathedral, I told Faith that I wanted to learn more about this diocese and its work. We ran into an elderly gentleman who was passing through the churchyard and asked him if he knew where we might obtain more specific information. He sent me to the residence of Archbishop Philip Carrington on D'Auteuil Avenue. I recognized the name—Archbishop Carrington was a world-renowned New Testament scholar. We set off to find him.

After a few long rings on the bell, the door opened a crack. A severe and elderly housemaid dressed in a starched gray and white uniform peered suspiciously at us through the tiny opening. We did not present an impressive sight after three weeks of camping and canoeing. As she began to close the door, doubtless thinking we were panhandlers looking for a handout, Archbishop Carrington appeared behind her. I blurted out my mission and explained I was a Yale Divinity School student conducting a survey on faith among the people of north central Quebec.

He welcomed us in and we were soon sitting in front of a silver tea service in a gracious parlor. I told the Archbishop about my love of the outdoors and attraction to remote areas. He launched into an explanation of the work of the Anglican Church on the Quebec North Shore. I suspect Archbishop Carrington immediately recognized in me a potential recruit. He offered to show us some home movies he took during his last visit to the most eastern section of the diocese that he reached by mission boat traveling from St. Augustine to Bradore, near the Strait of Belle Isle. He pulled out an ancient Bell and Howell silent projector and showed the mission boat *Glad Tidings* pitching and rolling in the sea from Old Fort Bay to Bradore as it inched through a deep fog and passed icebergs and drift ice. I was enthralled.

The brittle film stuttered and snapped as it rattled through the worn projector. The Archbishop stopped each time the film broke to make repairs on an ancient splicing machine. I had some experience working with similar films with my father and grandfather. I offered to help and he was delighted when I enthusiastically spliced more than a dozen breaks in his 300-foot roll from the trip and even repaired several other films stored in a nearby closet.

We spent three hours with him and by the time Faith and I left the residence, we were fully determined to return some day and work in a place where it made no difference "how few and far between they are." The following winter, Archbishop Carrington visited Berkeley Divinity School, the Episcopal seminary next to Yale Divinity School, in New Haven. He remembered me from my visit and called to ask if I would attend a film and lecture he was presenting to the Berkeley students. He had an ulterior motive, and asked if I would stand by in the event the film broke. It did, repeatedly. Once again, I spliced and repaired the film at least six times while he continued his lecture as if nothing had gone amiss. Afterward, I walked him back to the guest room where he was staying. As he said farewell, he added, "Please come and be with us some day. We want you on the lower North Shore." I did not need any more encouragement.

My adult life on the North Shore was a world away from the privileged world in which I grew up. But my connection to the natural world was always present and nurtured by what was then the wildness of Long Island. I was the sixth of seven children, born two years after the 1929 stock market crash that wiped out the fortunes of my grandfather Bryan and my father. Before the Crash, my grandfather, Benjamin B. Bryan, had co-founded what had become the largest stock and grain brokerage firm in the United States, Logan & Bryan, with more offices at its peak than any other brokerage house in the country. The company even operated a small office aboard the train that ran between New York and Chicago and in grand hotels, such as the Château Frontenac in Quebec City, and established the first private wire to California from New York and Chicago. My father, James Taylor Bryan, had joined him as a partner.

Because I was born after the Crash, I never experienced the flush years and the difficult economic stresses of those years seemed "normal" to me. Yet I was acutely aware that the family faced financial difficulties. I remember workmen coming to the door for their overdue payment after doing tree maintenance or lawn work on the twenty-acre parcel that held the brick mansion my mother's parents had built for our growing family back in 1928. The house perched on a ridge and overlooked a freshwater pond called Beaver Dam. A causeway separated the pond from a saltwater creek and meadow. It was an idyllic setting and a fascinating environment for children. My parents probably should have sold that house and found us something smaller and more affordable, but my father was optimistic and hopeful that his fortunes would shift again. It was not to be. Grandfather Bryan invested the little he had left after the crash in oil wells in California and silver mines out West. Both enterprises failed. An old family 16-mm black-and-white film captures an image of my grandparents waiting expectantly for oil to spout from a well in which they had invested. The film shows clear disappointment on their faces as they slowly turn away while water gushes from the ground instead of the promised black gold.

My father was essentially broke, but we tried to carry on much as before. Three of the five full-time house staff stayed on for room and board but no pay. There were precious few jobs, particularly for household help, during the Great Depression, so the agreement worked for both parties and was not as unusual as it sounds today. My mother's father, Ferdinand William Lafrentz, had survived the Crash reasonably intact with his insurance and auditing business, and was able to help out with some expenses. Our parents, particularly my formidable mother, did not want to compromise for their children. We lived in an affluent area on the north shore of Long Island, where private school and boarding school were the norm. While our parents did their best, I was very aware that my parents could not afford as much as some of the parents of my friends. There were extracurricular activities with fees that our family simply could not afford. The needs of seven active growing children imposed real constraints on spending, but we made do. Mother urged my sister Joy to ride her bicycle a considerable distance to sailing lessons at the Seawanhaka Yacht Club on Centre Island in Oyster Bay. While Joy's friends ordered lunch at the club, Joy snuck into the changing room to eat the sandwich she had brought from home in a brown paper bag. After lunch, she rejoined her friends, and after her sailing lessons, she commuted home on her bicycle. My younger sister Hazel often reminded me that I was away at boarding school during the lean years so I received a hero's welcome every time I came home and was spared the day-to-day difficulties. She remembers the pantry being bare and the struggle to feed the family and the unpaid staff living with us. Joy has also written about those years. She recounts an occasion when our athletic mother rigorously mowed the lawn before preparing the tea service and dashing upstairs to change into a formal tea dress to welcome old Mrs. Vanderbilt, who arrived in a chauffeur-driven car for afternoon tea.

Many families in our area experienced similar financial strains. One country club reduced or eliminated the fees for the longtime members and some of the private schools extended scholarships to many of us in those years. During the flush years, Father had donated the money for a swimming pool to his alma mater, Hotchkiss: the first swimming pool at one of New England's Independent Schools. He had provided scholarships out of his own pocket to many outstanding students. When the time came for his sons to attend prep school, Hotchkiss welcomed my older brother Bill with a full scholarship (financial aid). All that said, I still grew up in a far more comfortable world than many other Americans in those difficult Depression years. Moreover, the great care and love of our parents was bottomless, and I never suffered for lack of love, affection, and guidance in a loving, close family.

My father, affectionately known as "Prof," never became embittered by the career and financial reversals. Instead, he simply adjusted his priorities from work to family. He was filled with joy and relished every day of his life. He loved to wrestle and play with his children. When he visited me at Hotchkiss School, my classmates would play tricks on him and knew he would enjoy the joke as much as they did. His distinctive wheezing, sucking laugh made everyone around him dissolve into helpless fits of laughter. He loved everyone and was notorious for his tardiness. But he was always late for a particular reason: because a conversation could not be cut short, or a stranger needed a helping hand. To me, he remains to this day an enduring example of a true gentleman.

My mother also had a wonderful sense of humor and joined in all the family games, often as the biggest prankster of all. She loved gathering family and friends together, and when I was at Hotchkiss, she and my father would arrive on my birthday in late April with steamer blankets and picnic baskets for a "Bryan Picnic" at the boathouse on the lake. They invited all the boys on my hall. My old friends still remember those birthday picnics.

I probably inherited my sense of adventure from mother's father, F.W. Lafrentz. He was a remarkable man. He came to the United States from Germany at the age of sixteen, and by the time he was nineteen in 1878, he was teaching at the Bryant Stratton Business School in Chicago. Later he became a professor of auditing at New York University. He headed west as a young man as the business manager of the Swan Land and Cattle Co. and spent a lot of time out on the range with the cowboys, eating from the chuck wagon, and riding in the roundup. He became great friends with Charles Marion Russell, the noted artist who painted cowboys, Indians, and landscapes of the American West. My grandfather thrilled me with tales of cattle rustlers being strung up for stealing. My mother was born in Ogden, Utah, during that time. While living out west, he served on the territorial legislature and presented the petition for Wyoming statehood to the U.S. Congress on February 7, 1887. When he returned to the East, he made his fortune as head of the American Surety Co., then one of the leading bond insurance companies in the country. The company was located at 100 Broadway, the second skyscraper built in New York City, and now an historic landmark. My first paying summer job when I was an undergraduate at Yale was at an insurance brokerage firm. I absolutely hated it. I wanted to be outdoors and recoiled at being cooped up in an office.

My grandfather wrote a book called *Cowboy Stuff* that was published by G. P. Putnam's Sons in 1927. He had a special edition of the book bound in exquisite high-grade leather to raise money for construction of a dormitory at Lincoln Memorial University in Harrogate, Tennessee. My grandfather was a member of that remarkable generation of American entrepreneurs who established the economic foundation of the still young country at the time of the Industrial Revolution. He came up to New Haven to speak to my Western American History class at Yale and told us stories about the West and what it meant to him to be an American. The old cattle man received a three minute standing ovation. He died at the age of 95 in 1954 when I was still at Yale. I was fortunate to have his influence and example in my life.

A desire for adventure fused with my love of the outdoors seemingly from infancy. In my childhood, the section of Long Island where we lived was still largely rural with pastures and scrub forests. The housing developments that now pepper the island were built on farmland later, after World War II. Fishing and shooting ducks and other waterfowl were a daily part of life in those early decades of the twentieth century. My two older brothers—Jim, who was fifteen years older than I, and Bill, who was ten years older—taught me how to kick a football and hit and catch a baseball. They always included me in their games when they came home from school or later on leave from the military during the war. Jim served on the aircraft carrier USS *Yorktown* (CV10) as an ordinance officer during World War II. He was later the prime mover in turning the ship into a museum ship at Patriot's Point, Mount Pleasant, Charleston Harbor, South Carolina. Bill continued to work with young people with patience and passion throughout his entire life. He was Director of Admissions at Colby College and athletic director at Hotchkiss, and worked on the admissions staff at the University of Maine.

Skating was my favorite sport in the winter. As soon as the weather became cold enough to freeze the dog dish, Bill took my sisters Ruth, Joy, and Hazel, and me out to neighboring fields to find frozen puddles on which to skate. Eventually, Beaver Dam, the pond near our home, froze enough to support skaters. We walked down a hill and across a three-acre field, crawled over a fence, and cut through a neighbor's property to reach the pond. The whole trek took six minutes. Music was played on a phonograph by the Beaver Dam Skating Club, usually waltz records and other recordings favored by skaters. We would skate all day long and into the night when lights illuminated the glistening ice, music filled the air, and a big fire burned brightly on the nearby shore to take off the chill during rare breaks from skating. After I saw photographs in the Sunday newspaper of ski jumpers at Bear Mountain in New York, I wanted to do the same. I built ski jumps on the hill in front of our house, or on our neighbor's steeper and more open hill, by taking firewood from the woodpile and then covering the logs with as much snow as I could scrounge.

My desire to explore nature was fulfilled each summer at Tunk Lake in Maine. My grandfather Benjamin Bryan began fishing in Maine around 1912 in the mountain area of western Maine near Rangeley Lake. He fished up through Eustis and the Dead River area up near the Canadian border. He learned about Tunk Lake on a trip to an estate near Bar Harbor. Tunk Lake is a large, pristine body of crystal clear water just north of Bar Harbor in Hancock County. One of the deepest lakes in Maine, it is four miles long and two miles wide and is flanked by 1,100-foot mountains. The lake is only 200 feet above sea level; its most southern end is just 5 miles from the saltwater in Frenchman Bay. Benjamin Bryan discovered that the fishing, particularly for landlocked salmon and lake trout, was excellent. Every October, up to 10,000 black ducks stopped at Tunk Lake as part of their fall migration from the Maritimes. In the mid-1920s, just a few years before the Crash, my grandfather decided to build a sporting camp and lodge on the lake to cater to families. He set up a corporation with about twenty colleagues, mostly Wall Street friends, called the Wickyup Club. *Wickyup* is an Indian term for a shelter in the forest. My grandfather Lafrentz, my mother's father, was also one of the members. Tunk was perfect for swimming, boating, hunting, and fishing. The plans called for each member to build a camp on five-acre lots. They planned eventually to build a golf course and tennis courts for all of the families to use and enjoy.

Grandfather Benjamin B. Bryan built the lodge and our family camp, The Boulders. Clifford Hemphill, a New York investment banker, was building the second camp when a messenger arrived waving a telegram on October 30, 1929, shouting "Stop!" It was the day after the Crash. The carpenters walked away, leaving behind their tools and building supplies.

The Crash effectively ended further development at the lake. By 1931, the only visitors to Tunk Lake were the Bryan family. Eight years after the Crash, the state seized the Wickyup Lodge for back taxes and sold it to polar explorer Admiral Richard E. Byrd. Our family, however, managed to hang onto our camp. The Byrd children were close in age to my older brothers and sisters and they became fast friends. Admiral Byrd wrote his book *Alone: The Classic Polar Adventure* while floating in his rowboat on the lake. Often I would hear a call from Admiral Byrd while I was playing at The Boulders. He called when he got stuck on the rocky shore. I would run and push him off the rocks and back onto the lake.

Our summer visits to Tunk Lake were among the high points of my boyhood. My first visit to the lake took place when I was an infant, only six or seven weeks old. My parents were worried about a diphtheria epidemic in the New York area and moved the whole family north for the summer to minimize the risk of infection. By the time I was two years old and toddling after my older siblings, the magic of Tunk Lake had captivated me. I did dread the long ride to get there. It took us two full days in two cars—1928 Packards, and later Ford coupes—to transport the family from Long Island. We invariably arrived after midnight on the second day, exhausted and depleted from the long ride. Of course, within minutes, the long ride and fatigue would be forgotten. All winter long I daydreamed about summer and Tunk Lake. The very idea of missing a summer trip was almost too much to bear. We were unable to go for two summers during World War II when fuel shortages and rationing made the long ride impossible. I remember being devastated.

Tunk taught me about the wilderness. I loved nothing more than roaming through the woods, swimming in the refreshing lake water, fishing from a favorite rock, hiking, mountain climbing, hunting, and exploring nature in all its glory. The stock market crash ended my grandfather's vision of the Wickyup Camp but ironically protected Tunk Lake from further development. The area remains as beautiful and untouched today as it did then and is one of the most treasured natural sites in the state of Maine.

In my youth, Long Island was the cradle of American aviation. Small airplanes constantly buzzed overhead and I found them all enthralling. I studied and memorized the markings of small aircraft the way other boys memorized baseball statistics. I cut pictures from aviation magazines and hung the plane photos in a special place in the playroom. My brothers and sisters were skeptical when I looked up at the sky and immediately identified a speck in the clouds as a stagger-winged Beechcraft or a Stinson Reliant. They said I could say anything I wanted because they could not disprove me. But I did know. I knew the models, the engines, the horsepower, fuel capacity, useful load, and gross weight of every one. In fact, my grades at school suffered because of my infatuation with airplanes. I still have the frayed paper, framed by my mother, that I wrote when I was just seven years old. It is dated December 5, 1938, and signed by Bobby Bryan. It was laboriously printed in pencil. This is what it says, complete with misspellings:

I love to fly in a airapane. Wood you like to ride in a airaplane? Some men fly miles and miles in airaplane. They fly way out over the water.

It gives a sense of how enamored I was with planes from the earliest age.

At one point, there were about seventy different airfields on Long Island, including Roosevelt Field where Charles Lindbergh had embarked in the *Spirit of St. Louis* for the first solo flight across the Atlantic Ocean in 1927. Our home in Mill Neck was about twelve air miles away from Roosevelt Field, the busiest civilian airfield in the United States at its peak in the 1930s. Two major aircraft manufacturers were just minutes from our house: Republic Aviation and Grumman Aircraft. During World War II, almost half of all the American fighter planes, including the famous Grumman F6F Hellcats and the Republic Aviation P47 Thunderbolts, were constructed on Long Island. The airplanes constantly flew overhead. We saw prototypes of the fighter planes that became famous during the war passing over our house as early as 1935.

I was most thrilled by any aircraft that could land and take off on water. Pan American Airlines purchased the first of the 314 series of flying boats from the Boeing aircraft company in 1939. It was an extraordinarily huge plane weighing 30 tons with a wingspan of more than 200 feet. It was the largest flying boat in the world. Although the aircraft was built in Seattle, Washington, much of the training took place in Long Island Sound near Port Washington, the primary eastern base for these great clipper ships. I would sit on the beach on the shore of Long Island Sound, three miles from my house and watch the pilots train, taxiing back and forth across the water at take-off speed. Every day we watched those giant flying boats go up and down Long Island Sound on the water. They seemed to defy nature. I marveled at the sight of the 314 passing over our house on its way to the marine terminal at LaGuardia Airport. You could hear the roar of the four engines long before spotting them overhead. The Clipper Ships were so big they blocked out the sun. The American flag painted on the bottom of each sponson was clearly visible

When I was about six, I invited my big sister Joy, who was nine, to come to my room and admire my artwork. I had drawn an airplane in crayon across an entire wall with cockpit seats for Joy and myself. When Joy explained that writing in crayon on wallpaper was a bad idea, I tried to clean it up with a wet washcloth but only succeeded in making a bigger mess. My mother was horrified but I suspect also secretly amused by my fascination. On May 6, 1937, I went with my mother into New York City on a shopping expedition. Paulie Gotwald, one of the household staff who lived with us during the Depression in return for room and board, put on his chauffeur's cap and drove us. As we crossed the East River on the 59th Street Bridge into Manhattan, I looked down the river and saw the great German airship, the LZ 129 *Hindenburg*, heading toward us. The *Hindenburg* was in its second year of commercial service and en route to a landing site at Lakehurst, New Jersey. The pilot diverted from his course to make a brief swing over Manhattan because of reports of bad weather in Lakehurst. I remember seeing a policeman stop and look up as ground traffic came to a standstill all around him. Like those motorists, I was mesmerized by the sight of the enormous airship, which had made 26 successful trips over the Atlantic in 1936. It was not more than 500 feet off the ground and so big that I found it hard to imagine how it stayed in the air. Twice in 1936 it flew at a very low altitude over our house in the early morning. The swastika on the tail fin was huge and clearly visible. A visiting friend of our German maid flung open her window to shout "Heil Hitler!" at the sight. My father ordered the woman out of the house.

When we returned home from our shopping trip that night, we turned on the radio to hear that the *Hindenburg* had exploded while coming up to the mooring mast at the airship base in Lakehurst. The entire family gathered around the radio to listen to reports of the explosion and subsequent inferno that killed 35 of the 97 people on board. One of the passengers, named Belin, was a friend of my brother Jim. The friend was returning from a year of study in Germany. His parents were waiting to pick him up and when they saw the fireball and dramatic crash, they were certain their son had died. Bereft and shocked, they turned to return home when they heard the familiar family whistle. Their son had jumped out as the gondola crashed to the ground and miraculously escaped.

I had another connection to that tragic day in aviation history. Max Pruss, the second in command of the *Hindenburg*, suffered serious injuries in the crash and was taken to a major hospital in New York City for treatment. Young Trubee Davison, the best friend of my big brother Bill, was in the same hospital gravely ill with childhood leukemia, at that time nearly always a fatal disease. Trubee's father, F. Trubee Davison, had been a World War I aviator who founded the First Yale Unit, a group of Yale-educated pilots, and then served as the Under Secretary of the Army for Air and later became director of personnel at the Central Intelligence Agency. He visited Max Pruss in the hospital and Pruss, as he recovered, returned the favor and visited young Trubee's room. He presented the sick boy with a salvaged piece of fabric from the emblem on the tail of the *Hindenburg*.

Young Trubee died, leaving Bill devastated. The Davison family gave my brother the piece of fabric as a remembrance. Bill treasured that scrap of material for forty years and then honored me with the gift because I was the pilot in the family. When Trubee's older brother, Cottie, became chairman of the board of the Quebec Labrador Foundation, joining me in my life's work, I was pleased to cut that storied piece of fabric in half and present it back to a member of a wonderful family.

I yearned to fly and was distressed that most of my friends had already been in an airplane when I entered first grade. I formed a boy's flying club with some of my friends in the late 1930s. We visited airports in the area on weekends and sometimes went to LaGuardia to watch the DC-2s and DC-3s take off. The Douglas DC-3 was then the largest passenger airplane in the United States.

I finally got a chance to take my first flight in 1943 when I was twelve years old. My flying club friends and I went to the Grumman Aircraft plant to ride in a Grumman A21 Goose, the next size up from the G44A Widgeon in the amphibious series. We were to fly in a blue airplane complete with military identification. We were told to go to the door and wait at the bottom of the air steps. As we looked up, a woman's head popped out the door. She was dressed in pilot's garb and could not have weighed more than a hundred pounds. She was not much bigger than we were. I thought she might be the attendant, but she introduced herself as the pilot.

I was a little disappointed. I thought I would be flying with a hero of Grumman Aviation. The gender roles were pretty clear in those days. But it turned out this woman was a hero in her own right. She was one of the many female test pilots who helped develop the Grumman fleet during World War II. After I got over my initial disappointment, I became excited again and strapped in for the flight. The pilot flew us over Long Island Sound and over my house. It was thrilling to finally be up in the clouds looking down at the countryside I knew so well. I spotted Mr. Callahan, the man who taught me to swim at the beach we frequented, and later that day asked him if he remembered the plane. I proudly told him I had been on board. During that virgin flight, I did not feel a trace of discomfort or fear. I was meant to be up there floating through the clouds.

I was an active boy, spending most of my time outdoors hunting, fishing, trapping, or playing sports. Inside, I devoted hours to making model planes or cutting photographs of airplanes from magazines. My schoolwork suffered. I had little patience for homework or studies. But my older brother Bill was able to get me to sit still for the stories he told us about the most northern reaches of the planet. He called them wolf stories. The stories were about woodsmen, explorers, adventurers, and trappers who used dog sleds and snowshoes to cross desolate barrens from log cabin to log cabin. They were tales of brave lonely men willing to test their mettle against the worst Mother Nature could fling at them. They battled snow, ice, bitter winds, and ferocious wild animals, and they always prevailed. Joy, Hazel, and I were mesmerized by these wildly fanciful tales of the wilderness, and I dreamed that one day I would visit the vast untracked wilderness of the North myself.

After finishing one of his stories one day, Bill said we ought to take a trip up there. The suggestion electrified us. For the next six months, Joy, Hazel, and I planned for a visit to all the places Bill had described. We planned and plotted and collected equipment for the trip and looked forward to heading off on our great northern adventure. We pestered him relentlessly about when we would go. Bill finally realized he had to do something about it.

One summer day Bill came into the breakfast room and announced, "Okay, we are going to go. We are going to start out on this trip." I don't think I slept a wink the night before our departure. We woke early the next morning and got in the car. Bill drove us to the Mill Neck Railroad station on the Oyster Bay Line of the Long Island Railroad. Taking everything we could carry—skis, snowshoes, canteens, and knapsacks— we boarded the train full of commuters heading to work in New York City and drew some curious glances. But we were very excited and had a wonderful time riding the train. After about twenty minutes on the train, Bill announced a slight change in plans. We got off the train at Sea Cliff and there was Paulie wearing his chauffeur's cap, waiting for us. Paulie put his coat collar up and pulled his hat down. He pretended to shiver in the warm summer air. "Brrr . . . it's cold," he said. Although I shed some tears of disappointment, my big brother Bill was irresistible and had an alternate plan that caught our fancy. He took us to Roosevelt Field and after watching all the airplanes for a few minutes, we were distracted and let go of our plans to conquer the wilderness. Later that day, he took us fishing at Beaver Dam to see if we could catch some fish for supper. By the time we caught some yellow perch, the three of us were exhausted and hungry and ready to go home for a nap. Bill continued to tell us wolf stories and I knew that someday I would visit the wonderful distant North.

Besides reinforcing my fascination with the North, the wolf stories gave me an inveterate love of storytelling. I grew up during the golden age of radio. Before television, families gathered around the radio to listen to the news or music. The radio was the prime source of entertainment. There was something for everyone. The broadcasts were all live and included drama, comedy, shows developed from the comic strips, and adventure serials with heroes like Jack Armstrong. My favorites

were *The Lone Ranger* and *Captain Midnight*. I listened to them reli-
giously and never missed an episode. In fact, I begged my mother to
buy Ovaltine, a well-known malted milk flavoring which I did not even
like, so that I could send in the container tops to qualify for a cardboard
periscope offered by the *Captain Midnight* show.

During my summers at Tunk Lake, I heard my first Down East Maine
stories from Simon Bunker, the caretaker for my family's log cabin. He
and his wife Mabel also ran a lodge on the lake. Simon was born in 1866
and Mabel five years later. Neither of them got past the eighth grade in
school, not unusual back then. There was no one like Simon. He had a
genius for finding the perfect fishing spot, running an outboard motor,
and kindling a campfire in any weather. We followed him as if he were
the Pied Piper. He was a natural raconteur. His stories were based upon
his personal version of what had happened in town since our last visit the
prior summer. They were funny but dry descriptions of the adventures
and misadventures of local people. He would tell the tale of a man scheduled to appear before the judge on some criminal matter who arrived late
to the courthouse. He was late because he had a peg leg and as he crossed
the wooden bridge spanning the Union River, his peg leg slipped into a
knot in the wood and got stuck. He kept walking in a circle round and
round until finally he got free. I remember being fascinated by these stories as early as age six. I would beg Simon to tell me one more. These dry,
often lengthy stories sometimes pitted the laid-back but clever Mainer
against the fast-talking outsider who was invariably outwitted or told
some life lesson. A braggart, for example, insisted he was so smart and
knowledgeable that he could identify every single rock on Tunk Lake.
As he regaled a captive audience in his boat about his incredible skill, he
drove his boat directly into a rock and announced, "There is one now!"
There were stories of motorists encountering bears on the road and living to tell the tale. The famous peg-leg man used his peg leg to fill a hole
in his boat to keep out water when he hit a rock. Simon had a wonderful
raspy voice and a full head of brilliant white hair. He had real presence.
His wife Mabel also told stories of her own on the domestic side, providing endless amusement to my mother.

I began to do imitations after meeting the loveable Joe Bossé, a
French Canadian from Old Town, Maine, who worked at Tunk Lake

during the summer. Joe was a builder and specialized in making log cabins from the local forest. Just as Simon was a natural genius at surviving in the outdoors, Joe was a genius builder. He could take trees and transform them into beautiful cabins complete with log beds and chairs, split log tables, and even birch-bark picture frames.

He built Wickyup, the largest log cabin in the state of Maine at that time, and The Boulders, my grandfather's cabin. Joe was hard of hearing, almost deaf. So anytime anyone addressed him, he would reply, "What say? What say?" in a very loud voice. I could replicate his accent and tone perfectly and entertained family and friends with my Joe Bossé stories. We loved Joe, so the impressions fell into the category of "imitation being the sincerest form of flattery." My early introduction to the ancient art of storytelling proved to be an important influence in my life.

Bert and I

THE STORYTELLING tradition is as old as mankind. Before the written word, narrative and song were the only ways to transmit history, culture, values, and traditions from one generation to the next. Fables and myths that became classics are rooted in the oral tradition. In remote places where there are few people and limited opportunities for fun, storytelling remains an important form of entertainment. My friend Tim Sample, the Maine humorist, says that Maine humor grew out of the struggle for survival in a beautiful yet unforgiving place of sea and forest. The geography of Maine affects its culture and people. It is the farthest point east in the United States and the farthest north in New England. Ninety percent of the state is covered by forest and the coastline is rocky, with few of the sandy beaches of southern New England. In Tim Sample's words: "Maine humor comes from the harshness and reality of life in Maine. The occupations of fishing, logging, and farming are dangerous, hard, backbreaking occupations. The winters are long and harsh; the pay minimal; the rewards few. Out of this comes a unique way of looking at the world, of surviving. In traditional Maine humor we are often, quite literally, laughing in the face of adversity."

When I was a boy, telling a tall tale was a popular way to pass a cold winter evening. I discovered the same tradition on the Quebec North

Shore. In the late 1950s and throughout most of the 1960s, there were few other outlets for amusement on the North Shore. There were no televisions and no movie theaters, and residents made sparing use of the battery-operated radio. Those living in such isolated communities were starved for the company of others and eager for news of the outside world. We would tell stories to one another day and night. After heading back to school from my summer vacations in Maine, I regaled my friends with Maine stories and impressions. That led to a partnership with my friend Marshall Dodge, known as Mike to his friends, and the creation of *Bert and I.*

Marshall Jewell Dodge III was four years younger than I. He was a classmate of my younger sister Hazel at the Green Vale School on Long Island and a member of a prominent New York family. He was not a playmate when we were children because a four-year age difference is enormous to the very young. But I knew him because of his friendship with Hazel, and his cousins, the Pratt boys, were my friends.

There was a tradition at Yale University of playing tricks on the innocent incoming freshmen. When I was a senior, Marshall came to Yale as a freshman. I went to his dorm room to explain that he needed to purchase his radiator if he wanted any heat that winter. (This was a standard trick and surprisingly effective at fooling gullible freshmen.) I recognized him from childhood right away and afterward ran into him on campus from time to time. After I graduated from Yale and began graduate studies at Yale Divinity School, I heard that Mike was telling Maine stories in a campus theatrical production. Mike had never been to Maine but he learned Maine stories at St. Paul's School, a private preparatory school in Concord, New Hampshire, and he had a natural gift for mimicry. He and a group of St. Paul's friends taped these stories with a conventional tape recorder. Years later his classmates told me that they gathered for taping sessions in the Sixth Form upper bathroom because the tiled cavernous bathroom had great acoustics.

Not long after learning Mike shared my interest in storytelling, I met him by chance in the middle of campus on a beautiful New England day. We started to tell one another our favorite Maine stories. Before too long, we were in hysterics laughing at one another. A great partnership was born. We routinely got together to tell one another stories, particularly Maine stories. I belonged to a senior society at Yale that had included many creative and talented members over the years, including Cole Porter, Calvin Trillin, Gary Trudeau, and the famous pediatrician Benjamin Spock. I recommended Mike for membership and was delighted when he was tapped. His father had been a member. It became another connection we shared.

One day we amused a group of friends with our stories during my summer work at Squam Lake in New Hampshire. Our stories featured two laconic fishermen who went out of Kennebunk harbor to fish in a boat called the *Bluebird*. The stories revolved around the various adventures of the two fishermen as they encountered nature, the Bangor Packet, and various tourists. One of our best known stories was called "Which Way to Millinocket?" In that story, a Mainer is asked by a tourist how to get to Millinocket, a small lumbering town in the northern part of Penobscot County. The Mainer goes on and on about various ways to get to Millinocket before concluding with the now-legendary "Come to think of it, you caahn't get theyah from heah!" The story has its roots in an old nineteenth-century Arkansas troupe but has come to define Maine humor. Our friends made us promise we would record the stories in time to present the recording to them as a Christmas present. We used the Yale audiovisual studio to record a ten-inch vinyl record and had fifty copies made for our friends. By Christmas the first fifty copies of *Bert and I* were gone and we had friends and friends of friends clamoring for more, so we ordered fifty more copies. We then recorded a twelve-inch record of *Bert and I* stories that sold pretty well at the Yale Co-op and at the old Cutler's record store on Broadway in New Haven.

Encouraged by the reactions of our friends, I carried a copy of the record to Cecil Steen, the President of Records Inc., in Boston to see if he would be interested in helping the recording receive broader distribution. To put it mildly, Cecil was not impressed. Cecil was quite a character. He had a tremendous barrel in the corner of his office filled to the brim with rejected twelve-inch vinyl records. Our record came in a plain white cover without colored art. The cover consisted of little ink sketches by our friend, the painter Nelson C. White, of Waterford, Connecticut, and the recording itself featured two guys telling stories in exaggerated Maine accents without a note of music. Cecil was polite but all business and left me with the clear impression that I was wasting his time and our record was destined for that oversized barrel of rejects.

At the time, I was working as an assistant—a standard two-year stint before formal ordination to the priesthood—at Christ Church in Cambridge, a lovely old church overlooking Cambridge Common with roots that precede the American Revolution. I had convinced some individual record-store owners in Harvard Square to take some copies of our record, and the record enjoyed brisk and steady sales. We were fortunate that comedy albums were becoming enormously popular at that time. In the 1960s comedy albums routinely beat out legendary singing stars like Frank Sinatra and Tony Bennett for album of the year. Vaughn Meader, coincidently a native of Maine, did a wildly popular parody of President John F. Kennedy and his family called *The First Family* in 1962.

Because of the popularity of comedy albums, other record-store owners were willing to take a chance on a comedy album even by two obscure young guys pretending to be Maine fishermen. In Harvard Square, one owner kept a stack of our records next to the cash register, where it became a popular impulse buy. Cecil Steen was a savvy businessman. He noticed. He also listened to our record. Less than two weeks after my visit, Mr. Steen called me. He wanted to talk again. He paid a visit to the rickety old house where Faith and I were living in Cambridge. To reach our apartment on the third floor, he and his secretary had to pass through the church Sunday school. A class was underway so we went into the kitchen to talk. He told me that he loved the album and had decided to take us on as a client. He handed me a check for $2,700. It was more money than I had ever seen. In fact, it was quite a windfall for the times. The minimum wage was then only $1 an hour and the median income for an individual amounted to a scarce $2,600 a year. Mr. Steen proposed a deal: 90 cents an album with a guaranteed sale of 1,000 albums a month. He offered us a better royalty on mail order sales, $1.66 per album, which worked out well for us because that is how we ended up selling most of our records.

Mr. Steen made an agreement with Decca Records to distribute the albums nationally. Although I had a vocation as an Episcopal priest and was committed to that career path, I took enormous pleasure in *Bert and I*. Mike and I eventually set up our own company, Bert and I, Inc., with Faith as our manager. Faith skillfully managed and directed the company as a mail-order business for forty years. During our twenty-year partnership with Mike, we produced a few books and more recordings, eventually selling more than one million copies. We periodically reunited for public performances, often to raise money for a good cause, and sometimes just to tell one another stories and laugh into the night. Mike was godfather to my daughter Sandy. The entire family was delighted whenever he stopped by the house for dinner. He not only kept the family in stitches with his stories and accents, but he also had a quality of listening intently that conveyed his deep respect for others.

Mike died unexpectedly in Waimea, Hawaii, on an extended vacation in January 1982. He was bicycling, another favorite activity of his, when he was struck by a hit-and-run drunk driver. His death was a shocking loss to me and many others. I suspect one is never prepared for the death of a friend, especially a friend who is younger than oneself: Mike was only 47 years old. I presided over his memorial service on February 1, 1982, at Trinity Church on the Green at New Haven, where our partnership had begun 27 years earlier. While Mike was best known as a raconteur and storyteller, he was a true philosopher who opened his mind and heart to people, experiences, and ideas. He spent years writing a philosophy book. He radiated gentleness and kindness and his presence never failed to fill a room. A natural abundant affection flowed freely back and forth between him and his friends. He was brilliant and zany and inventive.

I recalled the time he used a beach umbrella rigged to a kayak to sail the fifteen miles from Vinalhaven to Rockland, Maine. While Mike had never even visited Maine when he began telling his Maine stories in high school, he had settled in the state permanently by 1973 and became as accepted as a native in a place where natives make a clear differentiation between the native born and anyone who is "from away."

Mike once said, "Stories are the core of all art, and all art is basically stories. You can probably tell everything about a culture from its stories. They're a perfect window into its soul. When you see what a culture laughs at, you can more easily understand it." He was absolutely right about that. I still smile when I think of him and still feel his presence when I hear the sound of a foghorn or clatter of a boat motor roaring to life. His amazing ability to replicate the stutter of a single- and double-cylinder boat engine or deep honk of a fog horn was one of the elements that made the *Bert and I* albums so special.

I met a young grief-stricken mourner from Maine at the memorial service. Tim Sample, a storyteller from Boothbay with a strong and natural Maine accent, was then 31 years old. He had recorded his first humor album three years earlier and Mike Dodge wrote the liner notes. Mike and Tim worked up an act together and the previous summer they had been performing night after night to delighted crowds all across Maine. They had just begun work on a comedy album when Mike was killed.

Out of our mutual grief at losing a dear friend, a great friendship and new partnership was forged. I invited Tim to visit me at my home in Ipswich, Massachusetts, some months later. We sat in the garden on lawn chairs swapping stories and remembering our friend on one of those rare New England spring days that hold the promise and warmth of summer after the long chilly winter. Tim went on to record four albums and a video for the Bert and I company. He was a regular essayist on *CBS News Sunday Morning* for years and we collaborated on the book *How to Talk Yankee* and two television specials, *Out of Season* and *Maine Humor Behind the Barn*. I met with Tim in 2013 in a studio in Portland to record some of the old stories and a few new ones, including a brand new version of the *Bluebird II*. We dedicated the recording to the memory of our friend, Marshall Dodge, and only wished he had been around to laugh with us.

Meanwhile, my childhood obsession with airplanes had never abated. As I watched the airplanes and test planes buzzing over my boyhood home on Long Island, I vowed that one day I would be a pilot and take to the skies myself. My limited finances in those years as well as a busy schedule frustrated any chances of actually learning to fly. But I would not be deterred. The impetus pushing me to finally sign up for lessons was a film.

In April of 1957, *The Spirit of St. Louis*, a movie based upon Charles Lindbergh's Pulitzer Prize–winning autobiography, was released. The film starred the iconic actor Jimmy Stewart. Jimmy Stewart was then in his 40s but his natural talent and boyish charms allowed him to easily portray the 25-year-old Lindbergh, who made the famous and daring cross-Atlantic flight. The movie was not a box-office smash, but it did earn an Oscar for special effects the following year. Those special effects captivated my imagination. I felt as though I was in the cockpit with the Lone Eagle himself.

I loved every second of the movie, which chronicled Lindbergh's struggle to prepare for his flight and then fly the historic route to Paris. The next morning the images of that courageous and dedicated young aviator still played through my mind as vividly as if I were still watching the movie in the theater. I felt I had waited long enough to take to the skies as an aviator. It was time for me to fly. In 1957 I was just graduating from Divinity School. The Yale Flying Club had negotiated a special $5 an hour rate from the local airport, Tweed New Haven Regional Airport on Burr Street in East Haven, to rent a Piper J3 Cub, the standard training plane. I paid a flight instructor $15 an hour to teach me to fly, so I could become a pilot at a total hourly rate of $20. A flight-training program required about eight hours of instruction with a licensed pilot before a fledgling pilot is allowed to take a solo flight. I completed the program in just over seven hours.

My training went quickly and easily because I'd had indirect tutelage for years from three relatives who were pilots. I had paid scrupulous attention to them and learned a lot simply by proximity and osmosis. My sister Hope's husband, Edward C. Oelsner, had a profound effect upon me because he had a floatplane that he kept in front of his house in the village of Centre Island in Oyster Bay on the north shore of Long Island, New York. He used that plane to commute to his office, a shipping business called U.S. Navigation Company, on Whitehall Street in the financial section of Manhattan, not far from the Staten Island Ferry Terminal on the East River. Ed had the most amazing commute I have ever seen. He left home in his floatplane, a Cessna 170B, and flew to Port Washington, where he picked up a second pilot at the Ventura Air Service. He would then fly to Wall Street, hop off, and walk to his office while the pilot flew the plane back to Port Washington. Ed tried to tether the floatplane to a wharf on the East River during his workday, but the rough waters and winds whipped up by the Manhattan skyscrapers nearly wrecked the plane on the wharf. At the end of his workday, Ed met his co-pilot, flew the floatplane to Port Washington, dropped off the pilot, and continued back home. From the perspective of my starry eyes, this was the perfect way to travel.

When I worked at my brother Jim's insurance brokerage firm, Dunn and Fowler, and a second firm, The Royal Globe, in Manhattan during summers as an undergraduate at Yale, I would hope and pray that the weather would be clear and Ed would be flying to work so I could tag along. I learned a lot about flying as his passenger.

My two brothers-in-law, Lawton and Gordon Lamb, were also pilots. Gordon, who was a year older than I, was a professional pilot who enlisted into the Naval Air Service and flew jets off aircraft carriers after he graduated from Princeton in 1952. Lawton, a year younger than I, earned his flying license at the age of 16. His mother would pick him up and drop him off at Deer Park, Long Island, airport in her car because he did not have a license to drive a car at the time. The three of us talked aviation all the time.

Although I felt prepared to take over the controls for my first solo, I was still a bit nervous. I took off from Tweed and did three takeoffs and landings while an instructor stood in the grass by the runway. Once I took off, I relaxed, the nerves disappeared, and everything was fine. Flying felt natural to me.

I felt a bit of pressure to get my license because my time in New Haven was drawing to a close. I would be graduating from Yale Divinity School that spring and I had a strong feeling that ministering to the people of the Quebec North Shore would be facilitated by my ability to fly to each distant outpost. I was anxious and eager to get on with my life and my ministry and like many young men in a hurry, felt I had no time to waste.

As soon as school ended that spring, Faith and I and our new baby, Sarah, headed back home to Long Island. My first stop was Ventura's Air Service in Port Washington, which was owned by the George F. Baker family. I told them I wanted to learn to fly a floatplane. Although I had spent only about eight and a half hours in the air in a wheel plane at that point, they were happy to put me in a Piper PA11, just a little bit more powerful than the J3s used in my training at Tweed. After about ninety minutes of practice, they let me solo. I am sure they told me to fly around the bay and get a little bit of practice, but in my excitement, I never heard the instructions. Flying a floatplane was so much easier than flying a wheeled airplane. I took off and immediately flew down Long Island to fly over my parent's house and then fly over Faith's family house. I went to the swim club where I had spent so many happy summer days as a boy, landed out in front by the beach, and went in for a hotdog. I finally returned the plane some time later. The manager of the air service, John O'Neill, rushed out of his office in a rage. He was so angry that he was literally shaking with fury. They were all convinced I had crashed somewhere and were relieved to see me alive. I had no idea I had caused such consternation. I learned a lesson that day.

I had another memorable and influential flying experience that summer. We headed up to Squam Lake, New Hampshire, where Faith and I had signed up to be counselors at a family camp called Rockywold-Deephaven. Straight away, I searched for a floatplane in the area and located one about an hour's drive away in Wolfeboro, New Hampshire. I drove down and spotted it sitting at the end of a dock. The owner was Merwyn Horn, a great pilot and instructor and a delightful character. He greeted me in his bedroom slippers. I spent about thirty hours training in his Taylorcraft floatplane that summer and Merwyn proved to be an excellent teacher.

Bush pilots are a special breed. They fly into the most remote and least hospitable parts of the world where there are few airstrips and the countryside still falls under the auspices of Mother Nature. Pilots need to be equipped to take off and land under almost any circumstances aided by floats, skis, or extra big tundra tires. Bush flying took hold in Canada after the late 1930s and was initially used for exploration of the remote reaches of the North Country, to spot forest fires, and to get to natural resources located far from the population centers. In some places, particularly the furthest reaches of Canada, the Outback of Australia, and Alaska, bush flying is still the principal method of transportation. Merwyn provided my first real introduction to the art of bush flying.

I suppose a fanciful person would wonder if flying made me feel closer to God. I believe it did because flying filled me with euphoria and made me feel closer to God's natural world. Bush planes tend to fly below the clouds and not far above treetops, giving a real bird's-eye view. Flying that close to the ground gave me a rare perspective of the wilderness and the creatures living there. Most bush planes are small so there is little protection from wind or snow and rain. On a flawless day, soaring above the ground through the brilliant blue sky, I would feel at one with the universe.

A formative experience the summer after my senior year at Hotchkiss School reinforced my love of the outdoors and adventure and my admiration and respect for people from all walks of life. My Hotchkiss friend and classmate Tom Keresey invited me to join him working that summer in Montana in the lumber division of the Anaconda Copper Mining Company. Tom's grandfather, Cornelius F. Kelley, was a mining legend. Mr. Kelley, who was called Con by his friends, was chairman of the company and known as "Mr. Anaconda" for his formative role in the firm's growth and prosperity. He was born in Nevada and his first job had been as a water boy carrying water to the miners on Butte Hill in Montana. He eventually became a lawyer and guided Anaconda into becoming one of the world's dominant mining companies. He died in 1957 at the age of 82. Just as his grandfather had worked in modest jobs as a teenager and young man, Tom wanted to do the same and spend the summer working in a lumber camp in a remote region just east of Flathead Lake, Montana.

Tom and I drove across the country in late June in the Keresey family car and checked into the lumber division office in Bonner, a short distance from Missoula. We would be working with about 75 other workers in the lumber camp that was a 90-minute drive to the nearest town, and would live in little camps that held 10 workers and use the 5-holer outhouses. This was a distinctly new experience for me. We were swampers, an unskilled position, responsible for clearing the branches off the trees felled by the saw teams with a double-edged axe. In 1949, there were no chainsaws to speed up or ease that tedious chore.

Cornelius Francis Kelley was a god in Montana. There are few individuals who have had as much impact on life in Big Sky Country. We did not want to be treated as special so Tom kept his family connection a secret and told the lumber camp workers that his father was a car salesman. I told them that my father was a lobster fisherman. Our false identities allowed us to fit into camp life. Life as a lumberjack in an isolated camp mixed hard work and routine. We rose at daybreak and went to the mess shack and sat at long tables for enormous filling meals of pancakes, bacon, sausage, and eggs. Meals were almost completely silent. If you wanted eggs, you simply pointed at the platter. Tom and I sat next to one another but did not speak. Then we lined up with our lunch pails and packed them with sandwiches we made ourselves and filled our thermos bottles with milk. We also filled a water bag with about a gallon of cold water.

After breakfast, a school bus carried us up a dirt trail to the log loading area. Then we worked our way up the hill to where the cutting was taking place. The saw teams, often father and son, cut tamarack, ponderosa pine, and Douglas fir. Periodically, the sawyers would call out "Down the hill!" We had to be careful we were not in the path of the crashing tree. Once the tree came down, we jumped on the trunk and went to work. The Douglas fir were the most difficult because they had the most branches. Every hour or so, a caterpillar tractor with cables attached to the rear would pass by and a worker known as a choker setter would loop the cable like a noose around the log and drag it down the hill to a loading area.

Thunderstorms frequently swept through the mountains in the afternoon. When the workday ended, the sawyers would lay down their saws and we were expected to carry them down the hill. More than once, we made our way down a hill with huge cross-cut saws on our shoulders with flashes of lightning cutting through the skies over our heads. Back at camp, there was nothing to do until supper. Again, there was no conversation during the evening meal, but the food was incredible because the workers insisted upon the finest cooking. At one meal considered subpar, the lumberjacks threw the food at the cook as he stood by the door. They were tough guys!

On weekends, the lumberjacks headed into town for fun. Not all owned cars so each car had six men piled into it by the time it roared toward Missoula for the weekend. They clearly had wild times considering the condition they were in when they returned to work on Monday morning. Tom and I were too young for the Missoula revelry so we went to his grandfather's lodge, the largest log lodge in the northwest, on Swan Lake. We would arrive near the end of supper each Friday night and Con stood up and announced, "Here come the lumberjacks!" He was very proud of us. We spent our weekends fly-fishing, water skiing, playing tennis, and relaxing. On Sunday night, we returned to camp.

The lumber camp closed for a two-week construction holiday, but we wanted to keep working so we went to a spot about fifty miles away where the company had recently closed a logging camp and a railroad track. For the first week, our job was to tear up the railroad track. We used six-foot long pries that weighed more than fifty pounds each and enormous wrenches to take the rusted bolts off the fish plates. We lived in a wheel-less boxcar with bunks inside.

While working on the railroad bed one day, a considerable thunderstorm swept through the area and lightning struck a tree about half a mile from our location. I saw a puff of smoke. That summer of 1949 was a bad year for forest fires in Montana. I ran toward the fire with a shovel to dig a trench around it and prevent it from spreading. Tom took off to sound the alarm. After a half hour, the first pickup trucks from the Blackfoot Forest Protection Association arrived with better tools. They snuffed out the fire in no time but gave me a lot of praise for starting to put it out. They wrote down my name and several months later, I received a check for $27.50 in the mail as a thank you.

During our second week, we helped electricians rewire another camp. The experience was a useful and in-depth primer on circuits and electricity. After that two-week interval, we went back to the logging camp and our job as swampers.

As the summer ended, we congratulated ourselves on our successful masquerade as two unknown guys from the east who came west desperate for work. We headed to Con's Kootenai Lodge one last time. I took part in a tennis tournament. As I crossed the road in my tennis togs, an electrician who had worked with us earlier that summer was working on top of a utility pole. When he saw me, he nearly fell off. By the time we returned to the logging camp for our final week of work on Monday, everyone knew Tom was Con Kelley's grandson. The men were incredulous that anyone would voluntarily choose such backbreaking work. We took great pleasure that we had been able to prove ourselves as hardworking young lumberjacks before anyone made the connection between us and the highly regarded iconic boss. We headed home and decided to drive back without stopping. We took the northern route through Montana, North Dakota, Michigan, Ontario, and Niagara Falls before reaching New York State and working our way down to Long Island. Con Kelley returned to his home in Manhasset, Long Island, in his own railway car that he kept in Kalispell for the summer.

This excellent adventure only whetted my appetite for more camping, more time in the woods, and more adventures in the remote reaches of the north. I had some dues to pay first, however. I had to repeat Grade 12 at Hebron Academy in Maine after my four years at Hotchkiss. I had spent more time on sports and extracurricular activities than on my studies. I was disappointed in myself at not being able to go directly to Yale with my friends but I spent a marvelous year at Hebron Academy, located on the eastern edge of the White Mountains. It took me longer than most to get serious about my studies. But it was better late than never.

My religious vocation came to me organically. It evolved gradually over time as I matured. Church and religion played an important role in our family. I vividly remember hearing a scratch on my bedroom door each night as my father quietly made a sign of the cross on the door of each of his precious children to bless us as we drifted into sleep. The Bryan family attended church each Sunday at St. John's of Lattingtown, a beautiful granite church in Locust Valley, just fifteen minutes away from our home in Mill Neck.

While church attendance and religious faith were fundamental parts of our life, I did not prove to be a very good student of religion. I was the only boy in a class of eight preparing for confirmation at the age of thirteen. We had to memorize passages of the Bible related to the sacrament. I could memorize the passages but had no clue as to what they meant. At the time, I was distracted by sports, my infatuation with airplanes, and the other interests of my boyhood. I flunked the final test and had to ride my bicycle to the church for remedial lessons with the Reverend Rush Sloane before I could be confirmed with my classmates.

During my years at Hotchkiss and Yale, the inspirational ministers I met had a profound influence on me, particularly the Reverend Sidney Lovett of Yale and Bill Spurrier of Wesleyan. I was enthralled by their sermons and lessons and thought I might also aspire to be a minister, but the idea was not fully formed until my senior year at Yale, when I was asked by Reverend Charles "Kelly" Clark to help him and his wife Pricilla run a church school for faculty children. I loved working with the children. I had found my vocation, or, as sometimes happens in life, my vocation found me. That experience convinced me to apply to Yale Divinity School halfway through my senior year at Yale. I was accepted.

I loved the liturgy of the Book of Common Prayer, but it was the pastoral side of the ministry that most interested me. My studies at Yale Divinity School were captivating and showed me the relevance of academic studies to my future work. I focused on my studies with an intensity that I had previously devoted to planes, fishing, hunting, and sports. The Divinity School was a professional school and I fully realized that I was preparing myself to go out into the world for my life's work. I gave up many of the extracurricular activities I enjoyed as an undergraduate and continued to help with the church school and other church-related activities. I was as drawn to pastoral work, particularly working with young people, as I had been drawn to my boyhood avocations.

After graduation, two years as the assistant at Christ Church in Cambridge, and my ordination, I was ready to face my future. I had finished my pilot training at Hanscom Field in Bedford, Massachusetts, a 25-minute ride from Cambridge. The *Bert and I* recordings had added unexpected and welcome income to our tight budget. The spring after Mr. Steen agreed to sell the *Bert and I* album in 1958, I enrolled in a summer graduate program at the Munson Institute of Maritime History at Mystic Seaport in Connecticut. Faith and I had budgeted to live off the pittance I was receiving from the church as a new clergy member. With *Bert and I* selling like hotcakes and Faith managing our books and handling the mail orders, the record money provided an extra bonus. One day I visited the local airport and spotted a beautiful old Aeronca 7AC airplane on floats for sale. It cost $2,500. It seemed to be destined, and I bought my first floatplane.

My first official role as a minister was as the chaplain at the Choate School, in Wallingford, Connecticut, but my ambition to work in the wilderness still burned brightly.

CHAPTER 3

Early Flying Days

THE CHOATE SCHOOL, then an all-boy preparatory school in Wallingford, Connecticut, hired me to be their chaplain in my first official job as a priest. In what became a pattern in my life, my job stretched beyond the spiritual. I taught history and comparative religion, and coached the varsity crew, co-coached the junior varsity hockey team, and was player-coach of the faculty hockey team, called the Wobblies. It was a near perfect job for me; not only did I do gratifying work with young people but I also remained engaged in competitive sports, which I always found invigorating and great fun. Another distinct advantage of this position was the flexibility of the academic year. During school holidays and the summer, I would be able to pursue my other interests. I wasted no time in doing just that.

The Quebec North Shore beckoned. After Faith and I flew north to Sept-Iles and the Mingan Islands on our initial exploratory flight in 1959 in the 130-horsepower Cessna 170 B that I had bought to replace the $2,500 65-horsepower Aeronca 7AC "Champ," I longed to return. I searched for an opportunity and Bishop Russel Brown, the bishop who replaced Philip Carrington as leader of the Diocese of Quebec in 1960, gave me my first assignment on the Lower North Shore. My summer job was to replace the Reverend Alex Stringer, incumbent minister at All

Saints Sept-Iles, while he went on vacation with his family. I was scheduled to arrive in Sept-Iles during the third week in June. After working in Sept-Iles through July, I would move onto Harrington Harbour to fill in for the Reverend Percy Graham, who would take his holiday for the month of August. Percy, a Newfoundlander, was in charge of Kegaska, Harrington Harbour, Mutton Bay, La Tabatiere, and fifteen outpost settlements of one to five families in between Kegaska and La Tabatiere. Bishop Brown said he was excited about me taking on this temporary duty because I would be the first priest to use an airplane to move around the diocese. Needless to say, I was excited, too. I was heading north, this time in a more powerful Cessna 180, and had been offered an opportunity to minister to the families who lived in this remote area.

Bush planes had become more and more important as a mode of transportation in Canada in the years after World War II and they were in high demand by the dawn of the 1960s. After only three weeks of flying out of Rapide Lake, five miles north of Sept-Iles and the major bush pilot and seaplane base on the Quebec North Shore, my new friends, the Blanchette brothers—Valmond, Gaby, and Adrian, who ran Sept-Iles Air Service—asked for a favor. Their aircraft operation was growing and one of their accounts involved running the food service for Air Canada flights between Sept-Iles and Montreal. The Vice-President of Air Canada came out from Halifax one day to discuss building a hangar next to the Sept-Iles Air Service hangar. The Blanchettes needed the hangar space and wanted to close the deal. To curry favor with the Air Canada rep they offered to take him and his son sixty miles north to Ouapatec Lake for some trout fishing. But all their aircraft were either out on long trips or in maintenance, so they were short a plane to take their special guests to the lake. They asked me to take the trip for them.

I was reluctant. I had never flown in to Ouapatec Lake and my experience flying on the North Shore was then limited. I also felt intimidated by the Air Canada official. What if he were a pilot? What would he think of flying into the Canadian bush with a rookie pilot from Long Island, New York? However, the Blanchettes had welcomed me to Sept-Iles and had already helped me so much that I agreed to do it. The plan was for me to fly Valmond and the Air Canada vice president up to the lake and then return to Rapide Lake to pick up the man's teenage son. We loaded up at the wooden dock on Rapide Lake. Adrian, Valmond, and Gaby stuffed the Cessna from floor deck to overhead with fishing gear, camping equipment, an outboard motor, and other essentials. The Air Canada rep sat up front next to me. Valmond took position atop a butter box filled with food in the rear.

We took off and climbed slowly to about 5,000 feet to clear the hills behind Sept-Iles before moving slowly over the bush country. It was a beautiful day and the bush, with its tangle of trees broken by the occasional sparkle of a stream or lake, was an entrancing sight. I followed the Moisie River for guidance and came to a fork that led to the lake. Valmond pointed out a landing spot, a thoroughfare between two lakes where the Blanchette family maintained a camp. On our first pass over the lake, we spotted trout rising, a sight that excited my passengers. After landing, we emptied the plane quickly and I headed back to Sept-Iles to fetch the Air Canada rep's son.

The wind had picked up quite a bit so I kept the floatplane at a lower elevation, at about 3,000 feet over the Moisie River. I hung on tightly as the plane bounced around but the turbulence grew worse and the plane began to shudder. I worked the ailerons hard and could barely control the aircraft when the plane hit a sudden down draft and bounced so violently my head struck the overhead dome light in the Cessna despite my loosely belted seatbelt and shoulder harness.

I saw stars and was dazed for several seconds. I felt something wet on my forehead—blood. I had cut my scalp on the light. Nothing like this had ever happened to me before. I wondered whether the wind would get worse. Would the plane shake so badly that there would be structural failure? I did not have enough experience to know what the plane could endure. I had only one option: keep flying. I plugged on, prayed for strength and protection, and eventually arrived back at Rapide Lake in one piece.

As I taxied into the dock, I brooded about returning to Ouapatec Lake with the Air Canada representative's son. I debated whether it was prudent to fly any more that day given the turbulence and my lack of experience. But I considered the two men I left on the lake, one waiting for his boy to appear. If I did not show up, he would worry. There was no way to communicate with anyone at Ouapatec Lake; they did not have radios at the camp. They might think I had crashed. The imagination can be far worse than reality.

The Blanchettes immediately noticed the dried blood on my face and expressed concern. But I assured them that I would be fine after a short rest. After eating and taking a nap, I did feel better. I was apprehensive, yet I could not shun my responsibility to the men I brought up to the lake. We refueled the plane and I took off, leaving the boy behind because it did not seem safe enough to bring him with me. By late afternoon, the wind had died down a bit. I climbed higher to get on the windward side of the highest mountains. As I approached the lake and passed overhead, I could see the two men standing on the shoreline and could only imagine how my long delay had upset them. When I landed, I told them what had happened and the Air Canada executive fully understood my decision not to bring his boy. Finally, they could relax and do some serious fishing. Within a half hour, they filled a basket full of trout. We loaded it on the plane and headed back to Rapide Lake before sundown.

While I was shaken by that experience, it did not deter me from flying in the bush. Within a few days I was flying my Cessna 180 300 miles north, up along the railroad tracks to Schefferville, a Quebec town near the Labrador border in the heart of Innu territory. The town had been established in 1954 by the Iron Ore Company of Canada to support mining in the area. It is a straight shot from Sept-Iles to Schefferville, and, if the weather is good, a pilot need only follow the railroad tracks of the Quebec North Shore and Labrador Railway. The Iron Ore Company uses the railway to carry the iron ore from Schefferville to Sept-Iles on the Gulf of St. Lawrence. I recruited a passenger for this trip, a major in the Royal Canadian Air Force whom I had befriended during church services at the radar station in nearby Moisie. The radio station was part of the Pine Tree Line system, the first coordinated system to detect Soviet bombers, established early in the Cold War by the United States and Canada. The major was not a pilot but he was an avid fisherman and he readily agreed to join me as soon as I told him about the superlative fishing spots en route to Schefferville.

We took off at 5 a.m. and landed within 3 hours at Squaw Lake, the floatplane base for Schefferville and Knob Lake. I sought out the resident Anglican clergyman, the Reverend Bill Clinton, and some Sept-Iles parishioners who were working on maintenance assignments for the Iron Ore Company at the Schefferville mines. My visits went well but I learned of a serious problem when I returned to the plane.

I had asked the floatplane base lineman to top off my fuel tanks but when he did, he broke the latch on the plane's left fuel tank filler cap, making it impossible to lock the cap. He did not have a replacement part and his mechanic was away on a three-day holiday. We tried to jam in the cap so it was flush, but it continued to leak even after we hammered shivs in the side and stuffed in rags. I knew the plane could not make it back to Sept-Iles before dark, so we planned to stop at Lac Joseph, a large lake about 123 miles from Schefferville and 40 miles east of the railroad tracks. All would not be lost. We could do some fishing on the stop.

Fuel washed over the trailing edge of the wing as we flew south toward Lac Joseph. I realized I would have to replug the tank if I was going to get all the way back to Sept-Iles. I spotted a beach with a beautiful river flowing out, the perfect place to pitch a tent and enjoy some fishing. As I circled, I looked down and saw a lone man standing at the edge of the forest on the beach. He looked up at us and stood absolutely motionless. We were in the middle of the wilderness, miles from the nearest logging camp or any human habitation. Who was he? How did he get here? What were his intentions? Was this a friend or foe? I puzzled over the difficult choice. I was hesitant to land and taxi up to the beach because I did not know how he might receive us. On the other hand, I could not fly straight towards Sept-Iles because the sun was beginning to set and we were rapidly losing fuel.

He disappeared on my third turn around the beach so I decided to land. We pitched our tent on the beach, lit a cooking fire, and set up our rods. About forty minutes of light was left to the day and the trout were enormous and almost leaping out of the lake. Every fish I hooked broke my leader the minute it hit. But the major had a spinning rod and lure and he caught a four-pound fish that we cooked for our dinner. When I unpacked the plane, I took my survival rifle, a .32-20 Winchester, into the tent. I was still uneasy about the stranger I had spotted from the air.

We cooked supper, cleaned up our gear and crawled into our sleeping bags. It was quiet except for the occasional howl of wolves and the call of loons. Yet I slept fitfully. I heard some twigs snapping nearby in the middle of the night. I grabbed my flashlight and turned the beam into the darkness. I did not see anyone but when I climbed outside the tent I spotted footprints leading from the woods and circling our tent. I was ready to take off right then and there but it was beginning to rain and it was still dark. I retreated into the tent to wait for first light—which came about 3:30 a.m. in mid-July. I spoke to the major and he readily agreed that we ought to get out of there as soon as light allowed. With the first hint of dawn, we loaded the plane and prayed the engine would start. It did.

Because of the rain, the ceiling was low. The tank still siphoned fuel and we had forty miles of bush and muskeg to cover before reaching the railroad tracks that would guide us back to Sept-Iles. The rain came down harder; I flew just below the 400-foot ceiling level. Visibility was maybe a mile and a half. It was a white-knuckle trip. We finally reached the railroad tracks, turned left, and started toward Sept-Iles. I kept one wary eye on the gas siphoning out of the tank and over the wing. I fixated on the railroad tracks, our iron compass to safety. We likely burned fourteen gallons of fuel flying from Squaw Lake to Lac Joseph and lost another ten gallons from the broken cap. I was sure we would never make it back to Sept-Iles on the fuel left in the tank. I looked at the map and estimated we could reach Eric, a railroad maintenance station at mile 138 on the railroad track. There was a narrow lake next to the tracks where railroad workers had a camp. We could land there, possibly procure some fuel, and regroup.

At the lake, I spotted a group of men working on the tracks and, not far away, their campsite, a couple of boxcars at the end of the lake. I landed in front of the camp and taxied back to where the men were working. There was a large embankment obscuring the group of men so we could not see them from the water. It turned out they could not see us either. I had no sooner hooked my line to a tree to anchor the plane when I heard a whistle blow. I instinctively knew we were in trouble. Seconds later, a huge blast threw a shower of boulders and rocks into the air. Stones and rocks of all sizes rained around us, some large ones landing close to the plane causing geysers of water to spray into the air. I raced up the embankment to the surprise of the railroad workers. The ten men, unaware we had taxied just a few hundred feet from where they were working, had set off a large charge of dynamite. We could not safely fly any longer that day so they invited us to join them at their camp. We spent two nights swapping stories and enjoying hot meals prepared by the camp's cook.

As soon as the weather cleared, we thanked the workers for their hospitality and went searching for a fuel cache left behind by helicopter crews working for the Iron Ore Company. We found several 45-Imperial-gallon drums, the equivalent of 55-gallon U.S. drums, stuck in the muskeg and were able to recover about 20 gallons of fuel.

We cut a bung from a tree to better plug the fuel filler hole. The bung was a slight improvement over the previous arrangement, but fuel immediately began to siphon as we got into the air, just not as badly as before. I calculated we would make it back to Rapide Lake with a few gallons to spare. When we came over the trees and touched down on the lake, the fuel gauge indeed showed empty. As we taxied toward the dock, the engine started to sputter and we were forced to draw on the auxiliary fuel pump to get to the dock. At that point, the plane was totally empty of fuel.

Those few days of flying in the bush left me wondering if I was in over my head as a bush pilot. I questioned whether I had the experience and flying time necessary to fly safely in that part of the world. However, I was not about to give up. I realized that the only solution to my shortcomings as a pilot was more flying and more experience. I was finally doing what I had always dreamed of doing, and to quit so early made no sense. While experienced pilots can help train others, there is no substitute for flying in real-life conditions in the bush. I would only learn and hone my instincts and judgment by flying, and I learned every time I took the Cessna into the air. In a report to Bishop Brown at the end of the summer I wrote:

I believe that the airplane was of great assistance in my work this summer. In emergencies, it is unsurpassed. On one occasion, I carried a child with a broken arm from Kegaska to the hospital at Harrington Harbour. The time en route was 45 minutes. A small boat makes the trip in two to three days. Throughout a full year, an airplane would have limitless possibilities. It is, perhaps, even more practical during the winter when boat travel is curtailed.

The climate of the Quebec North Shore and Labrador is hostile to both man and machine. Miles of granite shore are bereft of trees because of the relentless wind. The ferocity of storms, year round, is legendary. The seas of the Atlantic and Gulf of St. Lawrence are notoriously rough. Weather conditions can change in an instant.

When I began my work on the North Shore, I was still young, a couple of years shy of thirty, but I had a growing family—a wife and two daughters, Sarah, born in 1956, and Kerry in 1958. Our youngest daughter, Sandy, would arrive in 1961 to complete our family. (A fourth daughter, Mary, was born prematurely in 1972, and died within hours. Although she was born in Beverly, Massachusetts, we buried her in Harrington Harbour.) I not only had a responsibility to my wife and children but felt a strong obligation to the people of the North Shore as well. The climate and topography of the region, however, created an ongoing challenge to me as a pilot. I constantly had to balance my need to reach a parishioner in crisis or an ailing resident who needed to be transported to hospital against the level of threats posed by weather, errant winds, and a forbidding landscape.

The best aviation instructors constantly remind their students to be on guard for engine failure. Merwyn Horn, owner of the Lakes Region Airport and floatplane base in Wolfeboro, New Hampshire, harped on that theme during the time I spent with him early in my flight training. Merwyn took me through the most vital hours of floatplane instruction in the transition to floatplanes from the Piper J-3 Cub in which I learned to fly. Merwyn had an innate understanding of the wilderness. He explained to me the types of trees that would be most comfortable for a forced landing. A young hardwood, he said, would spring over from the impact of an aircraft and with luck might result in an "off airport" landing causing little or no damage to the plane. The best trees were stands of young maple, birch, and poplar because they had "give" with flexibility and would provide the best deceleration rate. His forced-landing lectures concluded with a commentary on the perils of pine trees, endemic in the north. "Pine branches break, snap, puncture, rip, and tear the wings and fuselage . . . try to avoid the pine," he warned.

Once, during training with Merwyn, we were on a dual cross-country flight from Wolfeboro to Naples, Maine. Merwyn enjoyed going to Naples because his friend Clarence Irving, a pilot, owned a grocery store featuring the best cheese in Oxford County. Clarence kept the cheese on display under a great glass cover. We would fly to Naples, land, refuel, pick up some cheese, and fly back to Merwyn's base at Lake Winnipesaukee. One day we were flying at 1,500 feet under a 2,500-foot overcast sky. As we approached Kezar Falls, a small village in Oxford County, Maine, we flew over forest, mostly pine, with no lakes in sight. I turned to Merwyn and said, "Merwyn, if the engine quits now, what do we do?" He shook his head and said, "We'd just have to pick the pine."

Merwyn drilled into me a discipline and attitude. For example, he told me that I should always expect an engine to quit on takeoff. His wisdom helped save my life years later. On September 18, 1967, I was taking off from Hood Pond in Topsfield, Massachusetts, when the engine of the Helio Courier suddenly went deathly quiet. My passenger that day was Philip Nadeau of St. Paul's River, Quebec, the first scholarship student of the Quebec Labrador Foundation. Philip was returning to the Choate School for soccer practice at the beginning of his senior year. When the engine failed, I had less than ten seconds before the plane would hit the ground. For the first second or two, I vainly tried to restart the engine. I thought of turning back toward the lake. But I knew there was not enough time or room for a safe landing. The laws of gravity, the loss of altitude, and the turn would cause me to strike the tops of the trees at the shore of the lake. If I reached the water, I would be out of control when I hit. Merwyn's words came back to me: Land straight ahead, in control, and you will be OK, no matter how rough the landing area.

A grove of trees lay ahead of me with uniform tops stretching about 200 feet. It was a perfect landing area. However, they were pines and I remembered Merwyn's admonition about landing on pine. There were no maple, birch, or poplar trees. The few rugged hardwoods off to the side would likely entangle and upset the aircraft. I went toward the pines and touched down on the tops, telling myself, "I just have to pick the pine." I assured Philip, "We'll be OK." As we touched down on the treetops, pine branches swept by my side window, like the brushes in an automated car wash. Trees uprooted ahead of us as we gently settled to the ground. There was no sense of deceleration or jab from the seatbelts and shoulder straps.

On the ground, I instinctively opened the left door and heard a terrified red squirrel chattering in protest nearby. I instructed Philip to get out and move away from the airplane. We scrambled fifty feet to one side and waited. There was no explosion, no sound at all, and we returned to the aircraft, which was intact and at rest on the forest floor.

Although statistics show that engine failures are rare and cause less than 1 percent of all aviation accidents, I have a very different feeling about landing conditions over water. I feel safer flying over forests at 300 feet, passing over heavy stands of timber and rock outcroppings in search of a spot for an emergency landing, than I do when flying over the Atlantic Ocean or the Gulf of St. Lawrence. I spent years flying over the Gulf of St. Lawrence, where weather and sea conditions vary with the hour and day. There are days when the gulf appears smooth and calm enough to paddle a canoe from New Brunswick's Miscou Island eighty miles to Anticosti Island, and other days when the seas are so rough that the waves would break over the bow of an ocean liner. Even if I landed safely on smooth water, a rescue by boat or helicopter would be difficult. The location of a downed aircraft constantly changes on the sea. In the event of an electrical failure, it would be impossible to radio a location. Any Coast Guard search would not begin until three hours after I was overdue at my flight plan arrival site unless I had high frequency (HF) capability to maintain voice contact. I knew that a landing in the gulf could mean drifting around for three or more hours before a search even began and if the crossing were in the evening, I would spend the night out there. Wave action or any breeze over ten knots would require abandoning the floatplane and retreating to an inflatable raft. The risks are high: hypothermia, rough seas, and equipment failures. If the fuselage gets submerged because a float strut collapses on impact with the sea, it might be difficult to open the doors because of water pressure. It is critical to have a marine quality, heavy-duty life raft aboard, and survival equipment.

I developed a safety drill and periodically reviewed each step in my mind. Crack open doors before ditching and wedge them open with clothing or any other item available to allow water to fill the cabin quickly to equalize pressure, and maintain a firm grip on the life raft. While flying over long stretches of water, I constantly scanned my instruments. I looked at the oil temperature and oil pressure gauges every fifteen seconds and kept the fuel gauge in the corner of my eye. Pilots develop a sensitivity to the most subtle changes in engine sounds. It is called "automatic rough." The smallest change in engine sounds can signal the first intimation of a sick engine. I felt the slightest tingle in the balls of my feet and in my toes when my ear caught some variation from the smooth purr of the engine. I carried two separate inflatable life rafts for flights across the Gulf: a four-man raft with canopy and survival gear and a two-man raft. I always carried survival equipment while operating in the bush. While I was fortunate to not need it in a crisis, I used the gear quite often after getting fogged in and required to overnight unexpectedly. I packed warm sleeping bags, enough food for a month, a tent, saw, ax, flares, and a portable radio transceiver. High frequency radio communication was the single most important safety tool while flying in the bush. Better to carry extra survival equipment than be stranded in the wilderness for two weeks without food or shelter. I knew many bush pilots who had close calls and some who died while awaiting rescue.

For my first lengthy stay on the North Shore, I went to the outdoor specialists, L.L. Bean, to stock up on the gear I would need for the sixteen-month stay. One of my favorite Christmas presents in 1943 at age twelve was a copy of *Hunting, Fishing and Camping*, the no-nonsense guide to the great outdoors by Leon Leonwood Bean, the founder of the Maine L.L. Bean store. The Bryan household had been receiving the L.L. Bean mail order catalogue for many years. I devoured each one and spent hours looking over the sports and camping equipment for sale. But this new guide took it all to a different level. The book was a how-to written by the master himself: L.L. Bean, a native of Greenwood, Maine, who created the first hunting boots out of necessity and turned his rubber-soled boots with the leather uppers into the start of a fabled company. In his introduction, he wrote, "I am a firm believer in the conservation of all fish and game and the strict enforcement of all game laws." He offered an encyclopedic description of hunting, fishing, and camping, complete with details on the proper techniques. Illustrations graced every page. The final five chapters of the book were designed to be cut out "to keep on your person." Those chapters included how to dress a deer, how to hang up a deer, signals for hunters, how to use a compass, and how to find a lost hunter. For years, I carried the L.L. Bean book with me whenever I was off on a wilderness expedition. Then in March 1963 I came face to face with the man himself, L.L. Bean, in Freeport, Maine.

At Choate School there was a free-day rule that gave faculty members a day off. I had a Thursday free day, and took off from the Meriden Markham Municipal Airport in the Cessna 185 and flew to Portland, Maine, where I transferred to a taxicab and arrived at Freeport at about 9 p.m. The L.L. Bean flagship store was famous for being open 24 hours a day, 365 days a year. It was located in a two-story wooden structure and I remember the treads of the stairs were worn by the feet of thousands of visitors.

I mounted the stairs and found myself the only person in the store except for an elderly gentleman. I was bowled over to recognize the founder himself: L.L. Bean, then ninety years old. He was the only person working that night, and he shuffled along in his bedroom slippers. We became friends right away. He was fascinated by my intent to spend sixteen months on the Quebec Labrador Coast. My departure was then two and a half months away. I bought survival kits, emergency flares, fishing equipment, .30-06 rifle cartridges and 12-gauge shotgun shells. Mr. Bean found everything I needed and then said in his distinctive Maine accent: "I want to give you a few supplies I am sure you might use."

He packed up a folding sled, which easily fit in the Cessna. He added a light ax in a scabbard and a collapsible reflector baker. L.L. Bean was smiling and shaking his head as I left in the taxi for the airport in Portland with all that gear to fly the Cessna back to Meriden.

Ten years later, and six years after the legendary founder died at the age of 94, I walked up the same steps at the Freeport L.L. Bean store to deliver 24 copies of *Bert and I* records to Leon Gorman, L.L. Bean's nephew, who had become the CEO of L.L. Bean. He not only agreed to sell *Bert and I* records and books, but he agreed to subsidize students from the Quebec North Shore who attended Hebron Academy with the profits. Thousands of records were sold by L.L. Bean; those record profits helped educate many young people from the North Shore.

Radio communications improved dramatically in my time as a pilot. I was flying the Helio Courier from the hospital in St. Anthony to Harrington Harbour in August of 1976 with Rick Bullock, a great friend and fellow pilot; R.L. Smith, then a summer intern; and a nurse who worked for the International Grenfell Association. We ran into dense fog thirty miles east of Harrington and had to turn off course. For ninety minutes, I tried every trick to find a way around the fog to return to Harrington. Finally, I proceeded north up the Etamamiou River and landed by a little log camp I had built at Lac Triquet (also known as Ocean Pond) in 1962. The camp is only twenty air miles from Harrington Harbour, but with pea soup fog it might as well have been one hundred miles away. The high frequency radio was not working properly, so I could not inform those in Harrington that we would be spending the night at Lac Triquet. I knew they would worry, and this upset me because I know what it is like to worry about a missing aircraft. I tuned into the emergency frequency with line of sight capability of VHF 121.5 and said, "Any aircraft monitoring frequency 121.5, please come back to Helio N369E." Not three seconds later, a loud and clear Germanic voice replied, "N369E, this is Lufthansa 738, 35 miles east of Cartwright at 41,000 feet." We told the Lufthansa pilot of our predicament and asked him to radio Gander Radio so the Gander Radio staff could make a telephone call to Harrington Harbour. Within four minutes, Lufthansa reported back that the message had been relayed. Our family and friends received word we were safe in Lac Triquet. It was amazing. We radioed 250 miles to the Lufthansa crew, who radioed 200 miles south to Gander Radio, who used the telephone microwave system to call Laurie Cox's house, 20 miles from our position.

Rick Bullock became an important member of the Quebec Labrador Foundation team and history. For years, he flew for QLF and developed his own friendships with many people on the coast. Every time he flew from his home base in Gardner, Massachusetts, in his twin engine Aztec and later a King Air turbo prop E90, he brought along a few bags of fresh produce from a local farm. His many friends in the North looked forward to the fresh corn on the cob, juicy ripe tomatoes, and crisp green beans picked just hours before.

Floatplanes were particularly well suited to the severe climate of the north. It was far easier to find a landing spot in a lake or pond in a heavily wooded area devoid of a single man-made road or open field. Like many pilots, I paid close attention to any innovation in floatplanes and traded up over the years as finances allowed and need demanded. The Cessna 170B that replaced my first plane, the Aeronca 7AC, quickly proved inadequate for long flights over the North Country. In September 1959, I traded up to a Cessna 180, which had a more powerful 230 horsepower engine. John O'Neill, the manager of Ventura Air Service, where I had learned to fly floatplanes, offered me the 180, which had had limited service as a commuter plane flying daily to 23rd and Wall Street on the East River. I bought it for $15,000, a great deal at the time, and traded it in for a Cessna 185 a few years later. Those two airplanes, the 180 and 185, became the workhorses of the Cessna line, particularly in the North.

My infatuation with the Helio Courier, a short takeoff and landing (STOL) aircraft, was not exactly love at first sight, but it became one of my favorite airplanes. The Helio Courier, a lightweight all aluminum plane designed in 1949, proved to be particularly adept at takeoffs and landings in confined spaces, and a pilot could maintain control of the aircraft at speeds as low as 27 miles per hour. My experiences flying in the North demonstrated the importance of an aircraft that could adapt to the difficult flying conditions. A Helio demonstration pilot gave me my first ride in a Helio Courier in 1958. He was flying from Hanscom Field in Bedford, Massachusetts, down to New Bedford on the south coast of Massachusetts to deliver a movie projector, and he let me fly the plane. Although the weather was perfect that day, the crosswind gear of the Helio was unfamiliar to me and I found it distracting. With crosswind gear, the plane starts straight on the runway but the nose might be thirty degrees to the right. The test pilot showed me how the leading-edge slats operated and how the plane could fly at low speeds. I didn't give the Helio much more thought until my friend and longtime Helio owner Alan Bemis told me about his experiences with it. The Helio Courier was manufactured in Pittsburg, Kansas, but the company's administrative offices were at Hanscom Field in Bedford, Massachusetts, so I flew to Bedford to take a closer look.

My Cessna 185 was a mere three years old but I had put that plane through the mill and the shower of sparks ignition system on the fuel-injected Continental 260 horsepower engine was causing some problems. There were no Helios available at the airfield that day for a test flight, but after a long talk with the company president, Bob Kimnach, a review of brochures, and some back-of-the-envelope calculations, I decided to trade in my 185 and buy a new Helio. Bob was a terrific salesman. I suspect no one ever bought a new Helio Courier without a test flight before. When I asked Bob about the safety features, he replied, "Bob, the airplane is fool proof, but not damn fool proof."

The day my Helio was delivered to Hanscom Field, I had four hours for a check-out ride before I needed to fly back to Wallingford, Connecticut, with the new plane. Lou Drosti, the test and demonstration pilot, took me up to Nashua, New Hampshire, for my first flight. Within five minutes, I was questioning my impulsiveness in buying an aircraft I had never flown. I owned the airplane and I was having a hard time getting it under control.

As I began to take off, a little bit of a crosswind came from the left, 45 degrees at 10 to 15 knots. The aircraft seemed to want to go to the left. I applied the right rudder but could not stop it, the tail was up in the air and the torque was forcing the nose to the left. It felt as though the plane were about to do a ground loop. At a very slow speed, I gave a jerk and the airplane went into the air. The landing was bumpy and again I felt the problems with the right rudder. I tried it again, and this time I had better control and kept the nose of the aircraft straight down the runway on the takeoff.

Lou motioned me to come over to him on the runway after I had completed a second takeoff and landing. He said he had to get back to Bedford so I could take my new plane home to Connecticut. Three hours would be a short time for a checkout in a Helio Courier for a non-Helio pilot; I got my check-out ride in about thirty minutes. I did not feel qualified or comfortable in the Helio but if Lou said I was ready to go, I was.

On my way back to Wallingford, I landed on small fields and runways and took some extra time to get back. By the time I reached Wallingford, I felt so good about the airplane I wanted to take all my friends on rides to show them its features. The Helio's amazing adaptability and deft flexibility proved to be invaluable assets over the next fifteen years.

One year I was scheduled to participate in the Reading Air Show in Pennsylvania, but first had to stop at Thomas "Mac" Close's hangar and aircraft maintenance facility at the Gardner Municipal Airport in Massachusetts. Mac had extensive maintenance training in the U.S. Navy and was considered the best Helio mechanic in New England. Every autumn, it was necessary to switch the straight floats on the Helio to wheels and skis. We landed on the grass where Mac could hoist the plane onto a dolly and take it into the hangar for the changeover. In the spring, we returned to Gardner to switch from wheels to floats. I was scheduled to demonstrate a straight float landing and takeoff from the grass in Reading, Pennsylvania. A grass takeoff in a float, equipped aircraft had never been tried at Reading. I had performed a number of successful takeoffs at the Sterling, Massachusetts, airport fifteen miles south of Gardner, so I decided to try a grass takeoff at Gardner, fly directly to the Merrimack River for refueling and then go to Reading.

It was June 6, the start of summer in New England, but the morning was cold and there was frost on the grass at the Gardner Airport where the elevation is 1,000 feet. We moved the Helio to the end of the runway, lifted it off the dolly and put it on the grass. With the help of Mac and three others, I tried to take off. The Gardner airport soil is sandy, and sand did not provide enough of a slippery surface for the aluminum floats. The plane moved sluggishly for 100 feet and then came to a grinding halt. We tried it two or three times, but it was clear the plane would never move over the grass fast enough to take off. I was scheduled to appear at the Reading Air Show at 2:50 p.m. It was 6:30 a.m. and I knew I had to be in the air by 10 a.m. to make the trip with refueling stops at the Merrimack River and at Little Ferry, New Jersey.

Mac came up with an idea. He had two heavy, round tabletops that were five feet in diameter. He was sure that if he could find the heaviest casters made by a local furniture factory (Gardner was the furniture capital of Massachusetts for years), he could install four on the bottom of each tabletop and this would support the aircraft on the runway. I could accelerate on the takeoff and roll with the caster tabletops under each float until the plane reached airspeed and then be on my way.

By the time Mac returned and installed the casters, it was 9:30 a.m. He enlisted a crew to run alongside and help hold the plane straight down the runway until the air rudder took effect. I agreed to give it a try.

A takeoff roll was started and I had no problem keeping directional control. I decided I would not try to fly the plane until I was sure I had adequate flying speed so I would not topple off the tabletops. I reached at least fifty miles per hour before I pulled off. The airplane sprung into the air and I was exhilarated. But when I made a sharp bank to the right, I was dismayed to see the tabletops still moving at fifty miles per hour. As soon as the airplane weight came off, they tipped onto their sides and began to roll like hoops. Mac jumped out of the way as one headed toward him. It continued by the side of the runway for at least 1,000 feet. The other rolled into the tie-down area of the fixed based operations and halfway down the field on the right side. It narrowly missed planes and rolled into the parking area at a tremendous speed. Onlookers jumped out of the way and it kept rolling, past people, planes, and the administration building until finally ending up in a field where it stopped.

Mac pulled off another amazing feat in the summer of 1972. I was forced to fly the Helio with fuel that had been left behind by the military at Labrador coast airbases abandoned after World War II. I normally stored emergency fuel in caches in places up and down the coast, but on this occasion, my fuel cache in Cartwright had been invaded. The old fuel was not the correct octane for use in the Helio, but it would suffice in an emergency. John Pratt, a friend since childhood, pilot, and QLF associate, was with me, along with Mac, who had come to Canada for a visit. We flew toward Goose Bay when an approaching weather system forced us east of our intended route over the Mealy Mountains, an hour from Northwest River near Goose Bay. We began to lose power. We looked down at the ponds and lakes still full of ice remnants despite the July 15 date. The loss of power caused us to lose speed, but we were able to maintain altitude. One of the six cylinders had failed, but we thought we could make it to Northwest River on five cylinders.

Mac did not have his tool chest when we landed, but he borrowed dental tools from a dentist at the Grenfell Hospital. Mac removed the distorted valve that resembled a squashed tulip. He worked over the rough edges with the dental tools and somehow got the cylinder running again. We flew back to Harrington late in the afternoon. Mac's fix not only held for the two-and-a-half-hour trip back to Harrington but also through the nine-hour flight I took two days later to Beverly Airport also in Massachusetts, where a new cylinder was installed.

Mac once made a two-foot-long portion of a step section of our fiberglass Seamaster amphibious floats on the Helio from the leg of an old wooden piano stored at the Grenfell Hospital for fifty years. The piano fix worked so well I was able to postpone installation of a new section from the Seamaster factory to replace the broken one until months later.

My experiences as a bush pilot brought me into contact with other enthusiasts, and I enjoyed fly-ins and various convocations and organizations of seaplane pilot get-togethers over the years. It was always great fun to swap information and hear the experiences of other pilots. This led to a unique experience in 1966, when I was asked to make the first fixed-wing aircraft landing in Manhattan on Pier 26 on the Hudson River. The Federal Aviation Agency and the Office of Emergency Planning co-sponsored an experiment with the city of New York called Metro Air Support '66. The test was designed to prove that emergency supplies could be airlifted directly into New York City when all other transportation modes were out of commission. My task was to fly in from the west over the elevated West Side Highway, duck down, land, and then stop at the end of a 900-foot dock in the Helio. Anyone traveling on the West Side Highway and looking down on Pier 26 would think that 900-foot strip was much too short for an aircraft landing. In fact, my humorous father-in-law, Dana Lamb, called me the night before to suggest stacking mattresses at the end of the landing area to keep me from collapsing the West Side Highway if I overshot the landing.

At daybreak, I went out to LaGuardia airport with Ed Miller, a Choate School student who became a lifelong friend, and asked permission to make a series of takeoffs and landings at the intersection of runways 4-22 and 13-31. Permission was granted and we took off, circled, landed and took off again for fifteen minutes at one of the busiest intersections of any airport in the world. Within a very few years, it would have been impossible to practice takeoffs and landings in the middle of LaGuardia, even at 6 a.m.

When the time came to make the flight, we flew directly to the George Washington Bridge and then flew down river at 1,500 feet. I was startled when I looked out and saw a large twin-engine plane flying right next to me, wing-tip to wing-tip. "Miss Daily News" was painted on the fuselage of the Aero Commander, and a large photography door was open with a camera pointed straight at us. The next day in the November 6, 1966, edition, a photo of the Helio appeared in the tabloid newspaper with a story. The headline read: *The City's a Landing Stage / And Airlift Pilots are its Players.* The proximity of an airplane and cameras did nothing to calm my nerves, but I was reassured when the temporary tower on Pier 26 told me that there was a slight crosswind of nine knots at the pier. I decided to make the approach over the water. If the tail wind was under 15 knots, I could make a low approach and touch down the first 100 to 200 feet, relying upon friction and brakes to stop the plane before it reached the gaggle of photographers, reporters, and city and federal government officials waiting expectantly for the first landing of a fixed-wing aircraft on a pier in Manhattan. The landing went well. I sputtered to a stop to the clicking of newspaper cameras and cheers. It was with gratitude for a safely completed landing that I delivered the invocation for the official program.

Over the span of two days, the Metro Air Support '66 experiment entailed hundreds of missions to drop various items and supplies around Manhattan. The air drops included eight cartons of medical supplies on South Street, a telephone communications truck on East River Park, a generator at Bellevue Hospital, a Red Cross emergency canteen to Pier 42, and an amphibious truck to Pier 9. I made two more landings myself at two other spots that afternoon, at East River Park and the parking lot at the Bowater Paper Shed at the Williamsburg Bridge.

A grandstand full of various spectators, FAA officials, and company officials from aircraft manufacturing concerns gathered at East River Park. My assignment was to fly the commissioner of prisons for New York from Flushing Airport to East River Park. He noticed I was wearing a clerical collar when he boarded the plane and told me that although he was Jewish, he felt in good hands. But he was obviously nervous and lit up a pipe and began puffing furiously as we flew down the East River. I decided to make the shortest and best landing of the entire exercise. I slowed down the Helio to 45 knots and held the nose in the air as we approached over the and maple trees at the north end of the park. As soon as we cleared the trees, I pulled back on the power and let the plane settle. I misjudged. The airspeed fell to less than 30 knots and the Helio began to fall like a brick. I automatically reacted and applied power but was out of time.

The left wing started to dip so I applied full aileron deflection to bring the wing up. With the help of a ground effect and the grace of God, the left wing recovered and started back to level position a fraction of a second before we hit the ground. It was the hardest landing I ever experienced. The rattled commissioner of prisons dropped his pipe and it landed between the rudder pedals. I was relieved and amazed that we were on the ground and the landing gear was still in place. It was a near miss with worldwide media coverage. With the benefit of hindsight, I can now look back and see that those early escapades in the airplane honed my skills as a pilot and provided the type of practical experience I needed as a bush pilot for decades to come in the North.

I have always been tempted to land and take off Helio Couriers in impossibly small areas. The operation handbook for the Helio describes the STOL, or Short Take Off and Landing standard, as a 600-foot level surface with 50-foot barriers on either end. To meet these standards, an aircraft must be at full gross weight. But I found that by reducing the useful load and cutting the gross weight of the Helio from 3,300 pounds to the 2,700 to 2,800 pound range, I could operate well under the 600-foot standards.

My brother-in-law Ed Oelsner's family owned property on the end of Centre Island near Oyster Bay. The house, called Seacroft, was an impressive neo-Spanish design and acted as a landmark for sailors entering the Cold Spring and Oyster Bay Harbors. By the 1960s, Ed's youngest sibling, Jim Oelsner, and his wife Carol were raising their children in that house. The house featured a sloping lawn in the front bordering a pond less than 400 feet away. A swimming pool was next to the house and lawn. I flew over Seacroft many times on my way from Boston to LaGuardia. There were no trees around the pond and I was sure I could make a low approach to the less than 400-foot slope leading up to the house.

One summer day in 1977, I gave short notice to Jim and Carol Oelsner and secured their permission to land. As I approached over the sailboats at anchor at Seawanhaka Yacht Club at Centre Island, there was little wind. I made my approach ten to twenty feet over the pond and closed the throttle as soon as I knew I had the landing made. The Helio collapsed onto the lawn, the landing gear absorbing the shock, and I applied every ounce of pressure available on the brakes. The Helio rolled about 100 feet up the hill and stopped well before the swimming pool and porch of the house. I continued to taxi and made a turn at the edge of the pool. Carol Oelsner, customarily a calm and steady woman, was terrified, convinced she was about to witness a fatal crash. As I stepped out of the airplane, a Centre Island police car raced up the driveway. Jim Oelsner quickly assured the police not only that the landing had been authorized but also that an important air demonstration was underway. Jim had a way to convey authority that cut off any further inquiries.

I had no doubt I could land the plane, but taking off again was another matter. Carol, now recovered, offered me a sandwich and iced tea. I sweated out the next two and half hours worried about whether I would be able to take off on that slope. Fortunately, a draft of wind from the southwest appeared as the afternoon waned, promising to give me a boost during takeoff. I prayed for a stiff wind but had to be satisfied with ten knots. The ten-knot wind proved to be enough and I readied for takeoff, reigniting Carol's dismay. I put the tail wheel on the flagstone porch and jumped aboard, started the engine, and looked at the impossibly short runway ahead of me. With brakes full on, I applied full power to check the engine, sending off a blast of wind that scattered most of the Oelsners' porch furniture. The remnants of our picnic lunch whistled through the French doors leading into the house. The moment had come. I released the brakes, kept full power, and was astounded to feel the airplane lighten parallel to the end of the swimming pool, a mere fifty feet from my departure point. At another fifty feet, the airplane was ready to go. I held on and pulled back on the yoke. The Helio shot into the sky and I flew straight over the yachts at Seawanaka Yacht Club.

This remarkable airplane proved to be reliable and trusty as I became fully engaged with my ministry in the most remote section of the Diocese of Quebec.

The Quebec North Shore

W HEN I FLEW the Cessna 180 from Sept-Iles to Harrington Harbour for my second assignment of that first summer on the coast, it was like flying into an earlier time. At the start of the 1960s, modernity had not yet intruded upon the rural isolation of the Quebec Lower North Shore. The lifestyle of most people living in those small fishing villages was remarkably similar to that of their parents and grandparents. The only way to reach the area was by sea or air. There was not a single highway and there were no internal roads. To travel from one village to the next was only possible by air, boat, or (in the winter) dog sled and, later, snowmobile.

There was no electricity or modern refrigeration, no indoor plumbing or running water, no sewage systems, and no paved roads. There were none of the conveniences that came to be taken for granted in most of North America during the twentieth century. Harrington Harbour was only 362 miles away from Sept-Iles, but it was part of a region that remained insulated and distant from the rest of Canada. The physical isolation of one of the most northern and most eastern spots on the continent was compounded by the harsh climate. The Labrador Current, the cold surface current that runs through the North Atlantic Ocean from the Arctic all the way down past Cape Cod in Massachusetts, effectively keeps the Quebec North Shore in a colder ecosystem for much of the year. The North Shore "summer" is cool and short, about six weeks long, and is often marked by heavy fog. It was not unusual to have fog obscure the coast for at least part of every day for 25 days in July. On the good days during those more humid summers, the sun would burn off the fog by mid-day. Other summers, the days might be clear and windy for days on end. We used the aviation terms "zero zero" to signify a day of dense fog, and CAVU for "Ceiling and Visibility Unlimited" for a clear weather day. The weather on the North Shore is highly changeable and conditions can switch from calm and safe to stormy and dangerous within minutes. My travel schedule was ruled by the vagaries of fog, high winds, and winter snow.

When I first arrived, about 400 people lived in Harrington Harbour. The English-speaking people of the Quebec North Shore were mostly descended from the English-speaking fishermen of Newfoundland who had originally migrated from the British Isles. The Labrador Current that kept the region so chilly also brought extraordinary richness to the seas. The low temperature of the water slowed the growth of bacteria in plankton, which is found in extremely high concentrations in the North Atlantic. Plankton is the foundation of the ocean food chain. As a result, the Grand Banks southeast of Newfoundland is one of the most bountiful fishing grounds on the planet. Fishermen had come from France, Spain, Portugal, Ireland, and England since the sixteenth and seventeenth centuries. The earliest settlers from southwest England and southeast Ireland came to the region between 1750 and 1858. That arrival of English-speaking settlers came soon after Britain's defeat of France in "New France" (which became Canada) just before the American Revolution. At first, the fishermen essentially commuted to what is now the Quebec North Shore in the summer, returning to their homes in Newfoundland just before the ice arrived for the next winter. But autumn storms often caused them to lose their small boats along with the summer's bounty of fish, so they eventually moved with their families and set up permanent settlements near the fishing area. These hardy pioneering fishermen were the ancestors of my parishioners. Like the early aboriginal people who came to the region 9,000 years before them, the European settlers learned ways to survive in the challenging climate.

The English- and French-speaking fishermen picked up the use of dog teams and the komatiks (wooden sledges on runners) from the Inuit, who were already living in the area by the time the fishermen arrived. As the fishermen and their families adapted to the climate and conditions, they developed a distinctive culture that lasts to this day. Years of isolation made them extraordinarily independent, enterprising, and stoic.

The Atlantic cod, a white fish popularly used in cooking and the source of cod liver oil, has been an important commodity on the coast since the Vikings first fished in the area around 1000 AD and developed a way to preserve fish by salting it. Salted cod can be stored for several years, and it became one of the first and most important items in the trade between the old and new worlds. Fishing has always been back-breaking work; in the Gulf of St. Lawrence and the North Atlantic, it is also very cold and dangerous. The fishermen routinely spent long hours out fishing for cod, pulling in the nets by hand. When they brought the catch into shore, the entire family would be involved in gutting, fileting, salting and drying the fish. Today there are processing plants that handle much of the work; then, it was largely a family affair.

A commercial freight boat that also provided transportation brought in items that were in short supply to the coastal families. While the independent and resilient coasters built or made almost everything they needed, or simply did without, they eagerly awaited items like sugar, molasses, flour and tea. Boats would also bring staples such as eggs, cloth, and canned vegetables. The growing season was painfully brief and, like the pioneer families of old, the enterprising women canned and preserved cloud berries, which they called bakeapples, and lingonberries or mountain cranberries, which they called red berries or partridge berries. On many occasions, I was touched by families insisting that I share the last of their precious eggs. The last commercial boat would arrive in November or possibly early December if the harbor had not yet frozen solid. There would not be another boat visit until May, so families often ran out of fresh eggs and other basic food items long before the spring thaw.

There were no conventional refrigerators because of the absence of electricity, but there was a community icehouse. Each family, including mine, had its own clearly marked box nestled firmly into the ice and sawdust of the large icehouse. Family members periodically stopped by to pick up whatever they needed for meals that week.

Our family's lifestyle in Harrington Harbour was not different from those of others who lived there. Back in the 1960s, it cost about $300 to build the parsonage we lived in. The kitchen was the center of family life because it was always the warmest room in the house. A large wood-fired cook stove was used for heating and cooking. There was no plumbing system so we used a bucket with a toilet seat on top. It needed to be emptied every day. There was no dump until the late 1960s so waste was dumped out behind the house or into the sea. The rainstorms that signaled the end of winter washed everything away. The population was so low that the waste could be safely absorbed by the environment and did not create an environmental hazard as it would in a large city, though I recognize this was far from an environmentally appropriate disposal method. We used a recycled 45-Imperial-gallon fuel drum to store water. The water would be pumped up by hand from the basement cistern, which was filled with water hosed from a small pond on top of the island. A community hose was used to fill the cistern. After filling our drum, we passed on the hose to the next neighbor. Water was precious. We saved rainwater from the house gutters in a big barrel and were frugal with our use. Saturday was traditionally bath day and we filled the bathtub only once or twice for the entire family.

There is not a single tree on Harrington Harbour, but it is a pretty sight from the air, particularly in the summer when the green mossy ground cover of the coastal tundra provides a vivid contrast to the crystal clear blue of the ocean. Millions of years ago, glaciers carved and smoothed the granite shore. The entire coast is built upon the Canadian Shield, the ancient rock that underlies nearly half of Canada. The landscape is truly awe-inspiring, but what most impressed me from the very first moment I set foot in the village was the overwhelming kindness, generosity, and goodness of the people. As I taxied to a stop that first time, Uncle Sam Bobbitt, the warden of the church, and Uncle Fred Cox, the agent for the lighthouse keepers, greeted me. (All older people on the North Shore are called "aunt" or "uncle" as an honorific to acknowledge their age and experience and value to the community.) Uncle Sam reached out with his strong hand to help me and Faith and our little girls onto the wharf. As we walked to the parsonage located next to the church, people from the village appeared and hoisted our luggage from the airplane along with all the other items we brought for the summer. We had packed everything we would need for the entire summer in the back of that small plane with the survival gear. As I look back, it is quite amazing how well we managed without many of the conveniences we now find so essential.

My new parishioners crowded into the parsonage kitchen. We were a bit of a curiosity. There were few visitors to the town and they had never seen a minister arrive in his own airplane. The clergy had a reputation for lacking in practical skills such as carpentry, small boat handling, and engine repair, all skills that are essential to survival on the coast. Although I flew an airplane, which suggested some technical skill, I was no exception to the clergy rule. I had learned to sail as a boy but I tied my floatplane mooring with what coasters called a "minister's knot," a pathetic combination of grannies that secured the line but were almost impossible to untangle when time came to shove off. I suspect they found my lack of practical skills reassuring. I was not so very different from the priests who preceded me after all.

That Sunday I began what became an established pattern in my coastal ministry. We arrived on a Saturday and the next morning I conducted my first Sunday morning service. I announced I would fly that afternoon to the summer fishing village of Wolf Bay, thirty miles to the west, to hold services there as well. My floatplane allowed me to perform Sunday services in more than one community in a single day and I intended to do just that. Billy Bobbitt, one of the great characters of the North Shore, met me at the church door and asked if he could go along for the ride and help me. I was pleased to oblige this offer, unaware that Billy had very poor eyesight and many health issues. I later learned that he and his brother Don were delightfully eccentric. From the perspective of those who knew him, Billy was an unlikely candidate to sign up as a crewman for the plane. But we rowed out to the mooring in a double-ended pulling boat—called a canoe by the coasters although it resembled a rowboat more than a traditional Indian-style canoe. Virtually all of these boats were hand made on the coast. I climbed into the cockpit, prepared to start the engine, and asked Billy to tie up the canoe and cast off. Billy inadvertently hooked the painter onto the rear "after" cleat on the right float instead of the mooring, and then climbed into the right seat and shut the door. As we taxied away, the canoe trailed after us. As soon as I applied power, I felt a vibration and knew something was wrong. I closed the throttle and asked Billy to look outside. He opened the door, leaned out, peered back and shouted in his nasal voice "Oh, my God, the canoe!"

Needless to say, it was a singular introduction to coast life. The flying parson was initially enough of a novelty that most of the townspeople were standing by the dock to watch me take off. However, this huge local audience of Harrington Harbour residents never waved at me or gave a signal that something was wrong when I started to take off with the boat in tow. It was as if they all said to themselves: "He must know what he is doing; we won't interfere." To this day, that story is still told on the coast of the new priest and Billy Bobbitt who thought they could fly an airplane towing a canoe behind.

Harrington Harbour was distinctive from other villages on the coast because it had a small hospital built by the Grenfell Mission, an association established by Sir Wilfred Grenfell in the late nineteenth century, and later called the International Grenfell Association, or IGA. Sir Wilfred, a physician, medical missionary, and humanitarian from England, came to Newfoundland and the coast of Labrador to attend to the medical needs of the fishermen. The hospital acted as a lifeline and magnet for anyone in need of medical services for hundreds of miles.

When I arrived, Dr. Donald G. Hodd, a physician and native of Ontario, had been the medical officer at the hospital at Harrington Harbour since a year after graduating from medical school in 1926. He was the only doctor on the coast and traveled by the forty-foot hospital boat, *The Northern Messenger*, in the summer and komatik in the winter. He spent two full months each summer on the boat visiting every single community and fishing out port from Kegaska to Bradore. He was a man of quiet dignity with a gentle face and a healthy mane of snowy white hair. For 42 years, many patients traveled to see him by whatever means they could manage. The families not only relied upon him—they loved him. He said he came to the coast because he wanted to work where he would be needed. He was the quintessential family practitioner. He delivered babies, performed operations, set broken bones, stitched up cracked skulls, and did whatever was necessary. As someone on the coast might say, "He borned most of us." He had extraordinary practical skills. He was a plumber, electrician, and general all-round fix-it man, too. He did all the winter meat butchering for the hospital supply.

He had been on the coast so long that he developed an acute understanding of the variable weather. I often listened to the weather forecast on the battery-powered radio during the 11 p.m. news with Dr. Hodd. We would check the barometer and the wind speed indicator and Dr. Hodd would then do his own weather prediction, which invariably was far more accurate than the Canadian government's marine weather forecast. One December day in 1963, I stood with him on his porch watching the wind speed indicator during a storm. The fluid went right off the scale at 95. We tied five 45-Imperial-gallon fuel drums to the airplane on the harbor ice that night.

We had no telephone at our house in Harrington Harbour in the early 1960s, so if Dr. Hodd had a medical emergency that required a plane, he would stand outside my window in the middle of the night and call my name. Other times, I would look up during the 8 a.m. communion service on Sunday morning and see him motioning to me from the church door. Dr. Hodd was an eminence on the coast because of his position as the only certified medical doctor, but he never once ordered me to make a flight. He simply said, "I need your help." That was quite enough. He cared about everyone and rose to the occasion for every emergency.

One winter morning, he told me that Gordon Anderson had a strangulated hernia and needed to be taken without delay to the hospital at St. Anthony in Newfoundland. Gordon's condition was too dire for the limited services at Harrington Harbour. I had not planned to fly that day because the temperature had fallen to 15 degrees below zero and the wind blew steadily from the northwest at 35 knots. But Gordon's life was at stake. Dr. Hodd, Henry Bobbitt, and Gordon's father, Reg Anderson, brought Gordon wrapped in blankets on a komatik down to the harbor ice and gently lifted him into the back of the Cessna. The airplane bucked and heaved in the turbulence. I was concerned about the comfort of my passengers but more worried about keeping control of the aircraft in the high winds. I climbed straight across the Strait of Belle Isle to be within gliding distance of a shoreline midpoint in the straits. Cloud bases kept us from getting up high enough in the ten-minute crossing so I looked for ice pans that would support the plane in the event the engine failed. As we adjusted our course to a southeasterly direction, the wind was on our tail. The harbor at St. Anthony soon came into view and the weather station on the hill showed the wind blowing at 45 knots. When we turned to land, the wind was so strong it felt as though we were being swept away offshore. In fact, we looked on open water as we made our approach to the frozen harbor. As we touched down, the plane barely seemed to move forward.

When the engine shut down, it took six men, three on each wing strut, to keep the plane from upsetting. Gordon was placed in another komatik and taken quickly to the hospital at St. Anthony. At that moment, Dr. Thomas was delivering a speech to high school students because it was Grenfell Day. He was interrupted in the middle of his speech and within twenty minutes of our landing, Gordon Anderson was in surgery. The operation was a success.

On another occasion, Dr. Hodd knocked on my door in the dead of night to say that Sam Ransom, 34 miles away in Wolf Bay, had contracted mumps and his fever had spiked to a very dangerous 104 degrees. Would it be possible to fly to him immediately? Although it was 3 a.m., a small army of men, dogs, and snowmobiles accompanied my crewman Gordon Kippen and me to the barachois, the coastal lagoon behind the island of Harrington, where my aircraft was tied down. Because it was early winter, the harbor ice was not thick enough to support the plane. The men carried lanterns, flashlights, torches, and snowmobile lights to provide the "runway lights." While in the air, we learned Sam had been taken to the Blais River, the local name for the Blais family homestead at Etamamiou. Flying over the river, we saw marker fires burning on the ice directing us to a landing spot. It is much easier to land on ice at night than on the water because the landing lights pick up snow and ice but water diffuses the light in night darkness. We landed and picked up Sam; just fifteen minutes later, he was being carried into the hospital at Harrington Harbour. Sam's condition was early evidence of a serious mumps outbreak that brought seal fishermen to the hospital from all directions. Because of the isolation of the region, families did not develop immunity to disease the same way families in an urban environment would. As a result, childhood diseases that were commonplace in more populous areas were rarer on the coast and held far more serious implications, particularly for adults.

On another winter afternoon, I was called to Wolf Bay to pick up Harold Jones, who had split his hand with an axe while cutting trees and was in danger of bleeding to death. As I landed, a light snow fell. The visibility was about two miles and the ceiling 1,000 feet. The storm had passed the day before headed for the northeast and then reversed course, a very unusual occurrence, and reduced ceilings and visibility to the east. I gave Harold and his family a choice. I could fly approximately 100 miles to a town in the west where there was a man who was not medically certified but acted as a doctor for those in the area. It would take me about 45 minutes to get to his door because the weather was good to the west. Or I could fly back thirty miles to the Grenfell Mission Hospital at Harrington Harbour, where Dr. Hodd waited, but the weather was so rough that it might force the plane down somewhere between Wolf Bay and Harrington. Harold took the gamble to get to Dr. Hodd. The forward visibility was so poor that we opened the windows and looked straight down. We picked our way back to Harrington following the telegraph lines, the shore line, and finally, a fairly uniform patch of stunted fir trees that extended from Cross River the last two miles to the snow landing area behind Harrington Island. I felt as though I had been holding my breath throughout the journey when I finally recognized a clump of trees about a quarter of a mile from my landing site. As I approached the snow strip, I was stricken to see more than a dozen dog teams racing home from a day of cutting stove wood directly across my path, completely blocking my landing area. With my head out the window, I made a skidding, uncoordinated turn to abort the landing. When I came in a second time, the dog teams were disappearing over the edge of the runway, leaving it clear for the plane.

There were moments of levity mixed with the pathos of accidents and illness. I remember one time Jim Ransom swallowed his dentures. This was not inconsequential. The foreign object stuck in his gullet threatened his life. My successor as the priest on the coast, Reverend

Jim Young, flew Jim Ransom to the hospital at St. Anthony. It was a windy day with heavy turbulence that rocked the small plane. Poor Jim Ransom became nauseated from the up and down movement. He no sooner stepped off the plane than he doubled over and vomited from airsickness onto the ice and snow, ejecting his teeth. Jim Ransom was a bit worse for wear, but his life was no longer at risk. The day Jim Ransom swallowed his dentures became part of coast lore.

One of the inevitable emergencies that came up on the coast involved childbirth. Although the women were extraordinarily resilient, complications did take place. The midwives of the coast were legendary in their competence, but I knew, as the de facto back-up ambulance pilot, that I would likely be faced with more than one coast baby unwilling to wait until I got his mother safely to a nursing station or hospital. I decided to get some training in obstetrics. I spoke to Dr. C. Lee Buxton, then the Director of Obstetrics and Gynecology at the Yale Medical School. Lee and I had met when we played ice hockey for the Yale graduate school team. He had delivered Sarah Bryan in 1956 and Sandy Bryan in 1961. We had become good friends.

I enrolled in a training course that included four hours of classroom instruction. I read a textbook on obstetrics and assisted in some deliveries to get some hands-on experience. I was completely unprepared for the reality of childbirth. It was terrifying. When the forceps and suction devices came out, I grew quite faint. The nurses sent me to sit in a corner on a stool with my head down. I recovered quickly enough to help with three deliveries and afterward felt better prepared to deal with an emergency.

I never needed to employ my limited skills singlehandedly but I did encounter more than one emergency birth without Dr. Hodd. In 1968, I was called from Harrington Harbour to St. Augustine. Londus Martin's wife was experiencing a difficult labor. I radioed Marie Carey, the nurse at Mutton Bay, who set off for the five-hour trip to St. Augustine in a small boat. It was only a 45-minute flight from Harrington Harbour to St. Augustine in a plane. I spotted her boat halfway between La Tabatiere and St. Augustine and landed in the open sea. With difficulty, we helped Marie move from the rolling, pitching eighteen-foot outboard motor boat into the floatplane and headed to St. Augustine posthaste.

We learned through radio communication that the situation had grown desperate. The resident nurse at St. Augustine was on holiday and there were no trained medical personnel to help with the delivery.

When we landed at St. Augustine, Londus Martin was waiting there with his pick-up truck. I sat downstairs with the relatives while Marie went to the mother. Within a very few minutes Marie safely delivered the baby, who had been in a breech position.

I was returning from St. Anthony one day during the winter of 1964 when I received a radio message from Dr. Hodd asking me to meet him at Aylmer Sound, where he was caring for Grace Bobbitt who was pregnant and very close to losing her baby. Dr. Hodd was afraid that Grace and her unborn child might die if not brought to a hospital. It only takes five minutes to fly from Aylmer Sound to Harrington, but it would have taken more than an hour to travel that distance by dogsled. I landed on Aylmer Sound just after a two-day blizzard had deposited two feet of new snow. At touchdown, the aircraft stopped after ten feet. I was stuck. The snow was so deep it was hard to open the cabin doors.

I informed Dr. Hodd that the plane could not take off again unless we could dig a path or a runway. Within minutes, thirty men were on the scene with shovels and snowshoes. In 20 minutes they dug a 400-foot runway, giving me plenty of room to take off on skis. Grace's baby was delivered at the hospital.

Dr. Hodd stood outside my window at daybreak one morning during the first week of January 1964 and called up to tell me about a terrible fire at Baie La Terre, 45 miles east of Harrington. He had received a telegraph that night telling him that Willie LaValle had mistakenly put boat gasoline in his woodstove to ignite the wood. There was a tremendous explosion in Willie's tiny house at Baie La Terre. People often used a small amount of kerosene to light a fire but the inadvertent use of gasoline had fearful consequences. Willie had been blown out the door by the explosion but his wife and six of his children suffocated and died immediately. Two other LaValle children had fortunately been away from home at the time of the explosion. As we circled Baie La Terre, I could see a black hole in the snow, the charred remains of Willie's house. We found Willie at a neighbor's house with severe burns on an arm, his face, and left shoulder. He was in shock and almost incoherent. We carried him to the plane and took off. I flew toward the bay to avoid flying over the village to spare Willie the sight of the remains of his home. Accidents were not infrequent. What never changed was the automatic response of the community. Time after time, the people of the North Shore pulled together to help a friend or neighbor.

The 400 or so souls of Harrington Harbour were vastly outnumbered by their sled dogs, who set up a hellish howl in the evenings and early morning, or when they were "set off" by a commotion. I had never heard such a sound. The dogs were then a crucial element of the coastal life. During the lengthy winter, they pulled the sleds, the komatiks, which were the only way to get into the bush to cut wood, haul water, and hunt game. The dogs were ferociously strong and indomitable. The snow and ice could not defeat them. While they were likely descendants of wolves and were far from domesticated household pets, they developed deep bonds with their human owners. The dogs had the uncanny ability to get a komatik and its human being home, even in a blinding snowstorm, or could provide the warmth needed to survive the night. They were the primary mode of transportation, and were kept outdoors and chained to metal stakes in the ground or left to roam as a pack on a nearby island. At Tabatiere where most dogs lived on an island, their keepers would row out each day to feed the dogs.

There are many tragic stories about the dogs going wild. I remember vividly the day I was called to take my plane and find Dr. Hodd, who was making calls to patients on *The Northern Messenger*, farther down the coast.

Nelson and Stella Shattler lived in a summerhouse on Fox Island during the summer fishing season. Nelson, in keeping with the custom, brought his dog team from their winter home in nearby Aylmer Sound and kept the dogs tied to a stake with light chains attached to the collars outside the house. The dogs were fed once a day with seal carcass, herring, or a mixture of chopped seal meat or herring and hot corn meal. This was the practice of hundreds of families from Natashquan to the Strait of Belle Isle. At times, a single dog might get off his chain. In Harrington Harbour, the residents called this "bursting" the chain. But a single dog off his chain was rarely vicious. The chained dogs in a pack could be extremely dangerous.

One day, Nelson and Stella's two-year-old daughter wandered out of her mother's sight as toddlers do and stumbled into the area where the dogs were chained. She died in an instant. Although the family lived less than a mile away from the main dock at Harrington and raced by outboard to bring the child into town, there was nothing that could be done. I took off immediately to find the doctor and spotted his boat from the air as it cruised away from Mutton Bay. I tied a message to a life jacket, dropped it from the plane to the boat, and it landed in the sea nearby. Henry Bobbitt was captain of the doctor's boat and also happened to be the grandfather of the child attacked by the dogs. In anguish, he brought the doctor over to my plane in a rowboat.

I will never forget the look on Dr. Hodd's face when I told him about the attack. His head tilted forward, his chin almost rested upon his chest, as he came aboard the Helio. His grief and sense of frustration was palpable. Dr. Hodd had known, loved, and cared for three generations of Shattlers and Bobbitts. He had seen everything over his years caring for the people of the North Shore and I could tell from the pain in his eyes that he knew there was nothing he could have done to save that little girl's life. There was no chance of survival. He could only make the official death pronouncement over that tiny torn and lifeless body. I tried to comfort the grief-stricken family. Providing some comfort to the grieving and trying to explain death are essential parts of any clergyman's portfolio, but those sorts of tragedies were always very difficult for everyone, including me. I had little girls of my own and Henry Bobbitt had become a dear friend. I mourned with them.

Just one year later, a young boy hitched his komatik to two dogs and directed his "team" in play down a snow-covered boardwalk at Harrington Harbour. Five-year-old Kimberly Cox was playing close by her father's fishing stage when the lead dog lunged off the boardwalk and grabbed her by the face. Kimberly's mother Clara came running when she heard the child's screams but, in a matter of seconds, the dog's teeth punctured Kimberly's cheek and forehead with deep painful gashes. Clara did not have time to find a stick to beat off the dog. Instead, she grabbed the jaws of the large dog and somehow pried them loose from little Kimberly's face. The strength of an impassioned mother can never be underestimated. She raced up the hill towards the Grenfell Mission

Hospital with the little girl in her arms. Fortunately, Kimberly did not lose her life or her eyesight, though it was a very close call. There were similar stories in every town. In some cases, parents were able to rescue a child just as chained dogs dragged the little one back into their shelter, usually an overturned boat cut in half and used as a doghouse. In other cases, the parents were too late. In Makkovik, a fishing town on the North Labrador Coast, the child of a Moravian minister wandered into the area where the dogs were chained. When the parents realized the child was missing, they searched and found only bits of shredded clothing.

The people of the North Shore embraced my family and made us feel at home. On November 23, 1963, I went to the mainland with Laurie Cox, who had the chore of vaccinating the sled dogs. We returned at night, a beautiful evening, and I noticed the hospital's Canadian flag at half-staff. We came ashore at Laurie's fishing dock (or stage, as they are called), and as I walked up the path, Dr. Hodd met me halfway. He motioned to a nearby rock and asked me to sit down. He put his hand on my shoulder and said, "Your President Kennedy has died. He was assassinated." I put my head down and cried. It was shocking news and I felt acutely lonely and very far from home at that moment. My wife and children and I had been in Canada for a five-month stretch, but at that moment I wanted nothing more than to be back in the United States with my parents and brothers and sisters. The next morning, Dr. Hodd insisted we ring the church bells. Then, every adult in the village came by the parsonage to express their sorrow to the Bryan family for the loss of our president. It was simply extraordinary.

Faith described our reaction in a letter to her family dated November 25, 1963. She wrote:

> Tonight, the night of Kennedy's burial, we still sit numb—hardly able to believe yet that the assassination ever could have taken place. It is amazing how rapidly the word spread. I'm afraid I didn't believe the first person who told me of Kennedy's death. I turned to our radio and found out the shattering truth. Since then, we have listened a great deal to our radio and our hearts have been warmed by the worldwide tribute being paid to Kennedy. How we

would love to see a newspaper and read a list of all the dignitaries who came to the funeral. . . . Everyone on the island was deeply concerned over the terrible murder.

Harrington Harbour is only a half mile or so from the mainland but it is still cut off and separate because there is no bridge. When the harbor water was in the process of freezing or melting, there was really no easy way to get off the island. It was too icy for a boat and the ice was not yet thick enough to hold a dog sled or pedestrian. For those times, between the coldest and warmest parts of the year, most residents were stuck in place. There were precious few outsiders or visitors in those early years so any newcomer was a welcome curiosity to break the monotony and bring in news of the outside world. It was part of my job description to visit parishioners, and with my plane, I planned to be conscientious and ply the entire coast and visit as many individuals and families as possible.

That is how I came to meet one of my favorite parishioners, my dear friend Aunt Lizzy. When I first met Aunt Lizzy Anderson, she was losing her sight. She had buried three husbands and was a woman of great character and inner strength. She lived on Shag Island in the summer. When I first worked on the Quebec North Shore, it was simply not possible to do house-to-house visiting during a brief six-week summer period. But in 1963, I had arranged to spend sixteen consecutive months in Harrington Harbour, my longest stay up until that time. My plan was well known, so Aunt Lizzy fully expected me to visit soon. I arrived in June for my long stretch and by mid-July, I had not yet had time to see her.

One afternoon in July at a wedding supper, Aunt Lizzy confronted me. She told me that I was not much of a minister because I had not yet visited her. She reminded me that she had been raised Roman Catholic and she made it emphatically clear that if she did not receive better care and concern from me as a representative of the Anglican Church, then she might just revert to the Roman Catholicism of her youth. I apologized but she was not mollified. So I tried to think of some way to win her friendship.

The Sunday after the wedding, a northeast storm hit Harrington Harbour with winds blowing thirty miles per hour. Even the small harbor waters were wild with turbulence. Nevertheless, I decided I was going to take a small flat with an eight-horse outboard and visit Aunt Lizzy on Shag Island. While it was not a life-threatening trip, it was certainly challenging with the wind and white caps. I was soaked by the time I reached the stage head and house on Shag Island where Aunt Lizzy lived during the warmer weather months with her daughter Jane and her son-in-law, Victor Cox. The grandchildren spotted my skiff and notified Aunt Lizzy that they thought the minister was making his way across the harbor. When I arrived, she gave me a hard time about visiting in such bad weather and taking such chances. But I could tell she was delighted I had made the effort.

We spoke at length and then prayed together. That day launched a friendship that lasted for seventeen years. Aunt Lizzy's vision continued to fail and within a few months of my first visit, she could only distinguish between light and dark. When I visited her, she would put out her hands, touch my face, forehead, and eyes, and say, "I know it is you."

I tried to visit Aunt Lizzy on Shag Island or Aylmer Sound as much as I could, at least once a month. The Bryan family called stormy weather "Aunt Lizzy" days because I made a special effort to see her in the worst weather. This tickled Aunt Lizzy, who would admonish me for coming out on "such a dirty day," which is how the local people described bad weather.

When I flew over Aunt Lizzy's house in Aylmer Sound on good days, I would often pass no more than twenty feet over the chimney. Just a few seconds before passing over the house, I turned up the propeller pitch to make a tremendous roar that, according to her family, would shake the small house and rattle dishes on their shelves. As far as Aunt Lizzy was concerned, the closer I flew, the better. She would proudly announce, "That's my minister!" to anyone within earshot. A flyby was as good as a visit to her.

It was a true blessing that I happened to be on my way to the Quebec North Shore at the time of her death and was able to conduct her funeral services. In the eulogy at the service, I said, "In her later years she lost her sight. But the light of her spirit never failed. If her friends stayed away too long, she scolded them when they came to her side. But then her hands reached out and she would slowly nod her head and in a gentle voice spoke of her life and the places she lived, of years gone by, of countless friends and relatives. Those who came to comfort Aunt Lizzie, went away strengthened by her."

It meant a great deal to me to do this for such a special friend. I enjoyed her honesty and directness. She was quick to give me a hard time if she thought I had been away too long but it was done in a fond and teasing tone that reflected our special friendship. She became cranky and quite helpless in her final years and it was doubtless trying for her daughter, but the family never complained and cared for her until the end, because that was the tradition on the coast.

When Uncle Sam Bobbitt retired to his rocking chair next to his stove, he, too, waited impatiently for a visit from his minister. He puffed endlessly on a pipe and expressed strong opinions. Uncle Sam had been churchwarden when he was younger and adhered strictly to the no work on the Sabbath rule. He delivered a stern lecture to me when he spotted me refueling the plane for a flight to Kegaska on a Sunday. It took a long time to convince him that running out of fuel and making a forced landing would be much worse than breaking the Sabbath rules.

Like Aunt Lizzy, Uncle Sam would be very upset if I did not come to see him as soon as I arrived back in town. "I thought you had forgotten me," he would bellow. "I almost had my eyes worn out looking for you." It was impossible to visit all the elderly residents of a village on the first day of a visit. This never got any easier because these dear old men and women paid close attention to the time and location of every single visit and noticed if I visited someone else before I reached them.

Every community on the coast opened its arms to strangers. When a stranger stepped onto the wharf in Harrington Harbour in 1960, and began to walk the 250 yards up the hill to the hospital, every single person he met would call out to him. If the stranger was talkative, it might take more than an hour to cover the 250 yards. That strong desire to engage with other people demonstrated to me more than any sociology book the importance of human interaction. Their lives in those years were relentlessly hard with few comforts. But they shared what little they had. There was not a single person in town that I could not count on to help me or any neighbor. Their profound faith, gratitude, and community spirit moved me deeply.

CHAPTER 5

The Great Outdoors

M Y BOYHOOD experiences at Tunk Lake nurtured my great love of the wilderness. At the end of each summer, I returned to my home on Long Island and attempted to replicate everything I loved about Tunk Lake in the nearby fields, woods, and tidal marshes. I constantly searched for new fishing holes, and I became enamored with hunting. In those simpler times, I would board the school bus with a 12-gauge shotgun and sit behind the bus driver. Schoolmates on the bus knew that I was going to spend the weekend with my best friend at Green Vale School, L. F. Boker Doyle. Boker shared my fascination with birds and reptiles. He was a classmate from first grade and by fifth grade he was also a budding ornithologist, entomologist, and zoologist.

Boker collected garter snakes, insects, and rodents. The snakes had to be fed, so we caught mice and tossed them into the snake tank. It was fairly gruesome but as young boys we found it fascinating. The garter snakes tended to multiply and get loose. A member of the Doyle family would turn on the tub water and out would slither a snake. Boker was a self-taught taxidermist, and became my taxidermy instructor. I was a willing but limited student. I even took a correspondence course in the craft of preserving animals. I spent hours mounting squirrels, crows, and other animals and birds, and I set up my own taxidermy workshop at home in an empty room. I called it my muskrat room. The most important part of the taxidermy process was curing the skin with arsenic paste. Back then no one said it was too dangerous for a boy to work with arsenic.

Boker and I earned money diving for lost golf balls at the local country club and used those dollars to buy glass eyes and the important, grimly named tools of the taxidermy trade: brain spoons, eye hooks, bone scrapers, and the hook and chain, a device nailed to the wall that held the animal while it was being skinned. We took the train into New York City to visit the gun and fishing floors at Abercrombie & Fitch and the fabled Schoeffer's Taxidermy on Seventh Avenue, a mother lode of marvelous devices. For my birthday, my eldest sister Hope went into Schoeffer's at my request to purchase the most arcane items with great aplomb.

My mother, father, and six siblings were largely bemused by my interest in what my sister Ruth called "stuffing birds." My big brother Jim, by then the Ordnance Officer on the aircraft carrier, the USS *Yorktown* (CV10), was a bit more concerned. He wrote home from the South Pacific beseeching my father to keep me out on the athletic fields and away from taxidermy. He need not have worried. Athletics always held precedence. As much as I enjoyed taxidermy, it never seriously challenged my love of hockey and other sports.

The proximity of the Bryan home to a freshwater pond called Beaver Dam, and the adjoining saltwater marsh, a natural muskrat habitat, helped hone my skills as a muskrat trapper. A causeway divided the two bodies of water. Muskrat trapping became a new obsession during seventh and eighth grade, and Boker worked with me on my trap line whenever he was with me on weekends. I was a relentless hunter of muskrat. I made daily trips to the marsh before school in the late fall. When I caught a muskrat, I would trudge up to the house and wave triumphantly to my father who was getting dressed to go into Manhattan to work. Many years later, he told me how delighted he was by that daily ritual. Muskrat pelts averaged $2.75 each on the fur market. My first shipment of twelve muskrats went to Sears Roebuck's fur operation in Philadelphia. My pelts were bought for an average $3.25 each and I received a check for $39 from Sears, a lot of money back then. I proudly used the payment to open my first checking account at the nearby Matinecock Bank of Locust Valley.

Both Boker and I were heavily influenced by his father, Luke Doyle, who served as an ambulance driver during World War I in Europe. We were mesmerized by his tales from the Western Front. He brought home many artifacts from the battlefield, including a German helmet that Boker and I used to dig pits to trap animals. We were inspired by scenes from movies showing pits utilized to capture wild African animals. Mr. Doyle also showed us a small pocket bible with a bullet hole straight through the middle that had belonged to a mortally wounded soldier. That bullet hole fired our imaginations. He told about traveling with an independent company to Crimea and Georgia during the Russian Civil War. He once saw Josef Stalin on a train.

We hung on every word. He told us that he and his fellow drivers were so exhausted by nightfall that they fell into a deep sleep in their tents and little could rouse them. Robbers took advantage of this. Boker's father had some jewelry, cufflinks and buttons that he valued, so he put a scorpion in the jewelry box. He told us one night his deep sleep was disturbed by a piercing scream. He raced out of his tent to find his jewelry case on the ground. The thief, stung by the scorpion, had raced off in a panic, leaving behind Mr. Doyle's possessions. Seventy years later, I still remember every vivid detail of each tale.

Our birthdays were typically marked by parties hosted by our parents. Mr. Doyle organized the best and most unusual birthday parties. Unlike the gatherings at our classmates' homes, there were no conventional games and activities. Instead, Mr. Doyle would organize us into pairs and hand each pair an inexpensive compass. Then he would blindfold us and drive us about ten miles from the Doyle house. The blindfolds would be removed and we then had to find our way through the fields and woods using only a compass as a guide. Boker and I always won these competitions. We would jog back, beating all our friends. It was great fun.

As Boker and I got a bit older, we graduated from BB guns to regular shotguns, and Mr. Doyle taught us about hunting and gun safety. He and his wife Rita, Boker's mother, chauffeured us around Long Island in pursuit of squirrels, pheasants, and other game animals and birds. The Doyles' patience and support seemed bottomless. We loved hunting for crows. With either Boker's mother or father at the wheel, we searched for crows with crow calls hanging around our necks in the late afternoons as the crows returned to their roosts.

When we were about twelve or thirteen years old, an elderly friend of the Doyle family hired Boker to rid her large barn of rats. Boker eagerly accepted the challenge and asked me to help. In preparation, we entered the barn one night and turned on the lights. When the light illuminated the cavernous barn, rats scurried for cover through at least twenty holes. The next day, we plugged all but three of the rat holes. We then prepared our .22 repeating rifles with small shot shells called "rat shot," lethal to rodents from up to 25 feet. We waited until it was dark and quietly entered the barn, flipped on the lights, and stood back to back in the center of the building, ready to fire. The sudden light caused the rodents to spring for the exits. They scurried to the holes and bounced back when they found the holes plugged. They raced around, tumbling over one another, scattering in every direction. It was utter mayhem.

I spotted a rat heading straight for Boker. The rodent grappled with Boker's trouser, ducked inside and scrambled up his pant leg. Boker was stricken with horror. He dropped his gun and reached down to grab the rat as it reached his thigh. He squeezed with both hands until his knuckles were white. A moment later, the rat fell dead at Boker's feet. The next day, we retired permanently from the rat extermination business.

These early experiences were great preparation for the Quebec North Shore, where the wildlife is one of the defining characteristics of the region. The ancient tribal people who crossed the ice bridge from Asia to the Americas so long ago would traverse the continent in pursuit of caribou, beaver, fox, marten, and mink. The first Basque fishermen in the sixteenth century were drawn by whales, seals, and cod. The writings of the early European adventurers and explorers show that they were astonished by the extraordinary richness of the fish and game.

When I arrived at the end of the 1950s, the region was still a paradise for hunters and fishermen. Though the cod fisheries were beginning to show strain from overfishing by the middle of the twentieth century, the sea still represented a decent living for those willing to work hard. Fishing was an intrinsic part of the history and way of life for most English- and French-speaking families on the coast.

Fishing for sport is very different. However, hunters and fishermen tend to be conservationists, recognizing the significance and importance of these wild environments, and can readily see how easily humans can destroy them forever. I served for many years on the board of directors for the Atlantic Salmon Federation, a non-profit organization dedicated to the conservation, protection and restoration of wild salmon and the ecosystems upon which they rely. My own interest in conservation took root in early hunting and fishing trips.

I hooked a three-pound landlocked salmon on Tunk Lake on the weekend of my nineteenth birthday in April 1950. My classmates Jack Pierce and Dick Fowler joined me for the weekend. We were seniors at Hebron Academy. I had enrolled at Hebron as a postgraduate student and been talking incessantly all winter about fishing for landlocks as soon as the ice broke. We rented a fourteen-foot wooden boat when we arrived at "Big Chief's," Harry Stanwood's outfitter camp on the lake, just days after the ice finally broke. The boat was not particularly sea-worthy, but it met our minimal needs. We attached a five-horsepower outboard and went from Big Chief's landing over to The Boulders, the Bryan family camp, across from Partridge Island.

On Saturday, we paddled out onto the smooth surface of the lake in my brother's Old Town canoe, and I soon hooked the salmon. It was the biggest freshwater fish I had ever had at the end of a line. I can still close my eyes and see the fish jumping out of the water behind the canoe and remember my exhilaration.

On Sunday, on our way back to Big Chief's Camp in the rented boat, we encountered rain squalls and a wind from the west/northwest gusting up to 25 knots. While we were about 300 feet offshore, and halfway to Big Chief's, a severe gust of wind hit us and the waves crested the gunwales. Water poured over Dick Fowler, who was sitting in the bow, and the boat filled with water in an instant. By now, we were about 150 feet from the shore. Jack Pierce carefully maneuvered the nearly flooded outboard motor as Dick and I grabbed a gunwale with one hand and a paddle with the other and kept the boat moving until close enough so our feet touched the rocks. By now the boat was completely submerged. The air was relatively warm but the icy water was shockingly cold, not helped by the fact that we were wearing light sweaters and blue jeans. When we reached the shore, we were all shaking uncontrollably from the effects of hypothermia and trauma. We righted the boat and headed back to The Boulders. We built a huge fire in the open fireplace and spent two hours warming ourselves and drying out our clothes. On our second attempt to return the boat to Big Chief's, we kept within fifty feet of the shoreline. This was an early and telling experience with ice-cold water and the sudden way in which weather can turn a happy-go-lucky fishing trip into a risky venture.

Many years later I flew Ernest Schwiebert, one of the world's most celebrated fly fishermen, who wrote extensively on the sport, up to the George River in northern Quebec. Joining us was my friend, Ted Rogowski, a photographer who flew with another great friend, the renowned angler and author Lee Wulff, on his salmon expeditions. In 1961 Ernie described that trip in great detail in his book *Remembrances of Rivers Past*. He wrote about racing over the rocks and ledges to play out the reel and allow the enormous Atlantic salmon, battling for its life, to become exhausted enough to pull in. We hooked three fish, each bigger than ten pounds, in the first fifteen minutes of the very first day. But the best was yet to come. We found a remarkable pool, which he described as being filled with "a flotilla of salmon, phalanx after phalanx, hovering in the current." We landed sixteen fish that afternoon, all between ten and eighteen pounds, and failed to land many others that managed to fight into the rapids and break off the lines. We created little "ponds" next to the river to store the fish, to be shared later with the Inuit guides. Although Ernie tended to embellish the details of his sporting adventures, he accurately conveyed the excitement and joy of fishing.

A similar story of extraordinary bounty was told in the October 7, 1963, issue of *Sports Illustrated* magazine. The writer Jack Olsen described deer hunting on Anticosti Island. The island is just over 3,000 square miles, a canoe-shaped outcropping of ancient rock near the opening of the St. Lawrence River in the Gulf of St. Lawrence. The plentiful white-tailed deer are not native to the island. Henri Menier, a wealthy French adventurer who inherited his family's chocolate business, bought Anticosti Island in 1895 from a British logging company. In a move reminiscent of a kind of nineteenth-century Noah, he imported 220 white-tailed deer and other wildlife to the island in pairs in hopes of generating a sufficient population for hunting. In 1963, Jack Olsen estimated the deer population at 55,000. Today the Canadian government owns and runs the island as a national park and estimates the white-tailed deer population at 166,000. The deer have no natural predator on Anticosti.

In his marvelous magazine story, Jack Olsen told how hunters so frequently brought down two deer with the same bullet that the locals shrugged off two-for-one shots as commonplace. He said that hunters typically spotted dozens of deer in a single day. By contrast, a deer hunter venturing into the woods of northern New England might not see more than one or two in as many days. The deer on Anticosti often wandered out of the forested area to the shoreline to feed on the scrub brush just beyond the beach and sometimes walked into the water to nibble at kelp. The photographer who accompanied Jack had an idea for the photograph: a hunter aiming his rifle at a big buck in his sights with the rising sun and St. Lawrence Gulf as a backdrop.

Despite the multitude of deer, the photographer's efforts to get the perfect picture were unsuccessful. The light was wrong or the deer moved too quickly. With their trip to the island drawing to a close, the *Sports Illustrated* team was getting a bit desperate. My friend Charlie McCormick was the fish and game manager for the Consolidated Paper Company, the owner of the island at the time. Charlie was a legendary character and agreed to act as their special guide on the island. He came up with the solution. A large buck with a magnificent rack of antlers had been shot earlier in the day, and was being stored at a walk-in freezer at the paper company. To help the photographer, Charlie carefully set up the freshly killed deer with ropes and straps attached to the ceiling so the deer would freeze into a noble standing position. The next morning, as the sun rose, the deer was moved from the freezer and put into place at the shoreline. A hunter assumed position and aimed his rifle at the frozen buck; the photographer stood behind him and captured the image. The ruse worked so well that *Sports Illustrated* used the photograph as the cover shot.

Anticosti is about 135 miles long and 35 miles wide, but the dirt roads at that time extended just 50 miles. The only way to get beyond the roads into the southeast part of the island was by boat or helicopter. It was possible to land a floatplane in the sea just off the island but conditions had to be right. There were two harbors: one at Port Menier, the only permanent settlement on the island, and the second at Fox Harbour at the southeast end. When I first visited the island, there was no human habitation between Port Menier and the southern tip of the island, more than 120 miles away. Charlie had walked around the island twice, a remarkable achievement given the wild conditions. There were a few summer cottages built on lakes near Port Menier by the paper company officials. On one of the lakes, Charlie had built a small camp, which my family occasionally used as an overnight stop between Harrington Harbour and Tabusintac, New Brunswick.

We arrived once to find bears had broken into the camp. Flour and broken jelly jars were strewn all over the floor of the cabin. Bear tracks were clearly visible in the remnants of a fifty-pound bag of flour that had been ripped open and spilled across the floor. We followed the smaller tracks of bear cubs into a bedroom, where the cubs left floury paw prints all over the top bunk mattresses when they evidently sprang joyfully from one bunk to another. Our daughters were so charmed by this that they wanted to spend the rest of the summer at Charlie's cabin in order to wait for the bear cubs' return.

I estimate that 75 percent of my flights along the Quebec North Shore, the Labrador coast, and Newfoundland's Northern Peninsula were flown at an altitude of 100 to 1,000 feet. At this relatively low altitude, I always felt in touch with the natural world below. The air was an illuminating spot to watch wolves tracking caribou and herds of caribou traveling through the wilderness. Caribou move faster than they appear to. What appears to be a slow walk is actually faster than a human can run on snowshoes. The caribou keep up the pace endlessly. A trotting caribou moves as fast as or faster than a dog team. At full gallop, a caribou is as fast as my 1964 Ski-Doo powered by an eight-horsepower Rotax engine.

Unless weather conditions compelled me to fly lower, I tried to stay at an altitude that would not force female eider ducks to lead their broods away from the safety of their nests to open water, where great black-backed gulls would prey on the baby ducks. On windy or stormy days, when I needed to fly lower, larger animals began to run when the plane passed overhead at 500 feet. Caribou seemed to tolerate more noise than moose and often paid no attention to aircraft at that level.

Black bears got restless even when a single-engine plane was above them at 1,500 feet.

Black bears try to avoid getting caught exposed in open spaces. Unless they were with cubs, black bears began to move as soon as they heard the first sound of an engine. When I spotted a bear, it was usually already galloping toward protective cover. Invariably the bear motion was what attracted my attention in hundreds of bear sightings over the years. Once, I almost came too close. Flying between Natashquan and Kegaska in 1963, I was passing over a dried pond a half mile in diameter when I noticed a bear in the middle. From an altitude of 1,000 feet, I made a turning descent to get a closer look and photograph him. After completing one turn, I was about fifty feet behind the bear, then near the low brush and alders at the end of the pond. The bear knew that whatever was behind him would reach him before he could reach cover. He stopped, wheeled, and stood on his hind feet, taking a swipe at the airplane as I passed overhead. I felt badly that I had frightened him in my eagerness to get a good photo. After that, I never flew a low pass at a bear.

In early October of 1963, my parents planned to travel from Long Island, New York, to visit us in Harrington Harbour. Their Air Canada flight was due into Sept-Iles at 7 p.m. I arranged for the Noorduyn Norseman, a single engine mail/passenger plane bigger than my Cessna and more comfortable for the two of them, to fly them to Harrington the next day.

I flew into Rapide Lake early in the morning on the day of their arrival in Sept-Iles. I asked Sarto Bastien, the game warden for the Sept-Iles region, if it would be alright for me to spend the day moose hunting. I planned to supplement our winter food supply for Harrington Harbour that year, and Sarto was glad to give me permission. I invited Peter Jennsen, a friend and unemployed bush pilot, to come along with me on the impromptu moose hunt, and at the last minute another friend, Jaques, a Sept-Iles native who was a bit of a loose cannon, asked to join the hunt.

Though I don't typically hunt big game, I was excited and proud to bag an enormous bull moose, sporting an impressive rack of antlers, not long into our hunt. Jaques had a large family, so I offered him the bulk of the meat, but I wanted the antlers for myself. Meanwhile, Jaques spotted two smaller moose in the vicinity of the first one and, before I could stop him, shot them in rapid succession. This presented a dilemma. I had permission to shoot one moose, not three. All I could think of was that Sarto Bastien and the government helicopter he used for patrolling his region might appear overhead at any moment. We had, however, a more pressing challenge. Three dead moose needed to be moved and butchered.

We needed a canoe to reach the moose, so we left Jaques with our gear and Peter and I flew ten miles upriver to borrow a canoe from a ranger camp. When we returned, Jaques had vanished. One hour later: still no Jaques, and we started to worry. We fired shots with Peter's rifle, and then, for greater effect, started the Cessna engine and allowed it to run for twenty minutes with the tail lashed to a tree. We hoped Jaques would hear the noise and walk toward it.

Finally, as darkness fell, Jaques appeared, clothes torn, covered with black fly bites, and carrying a broken gun stock. The saga of Jaques was not quite over, however. One month later a Wheeler Northland airplane arrived with one quarter of the moose meat and my antlers, along with a copy of the Sept-Iles newspaper, *L'Avenir*. I had to chuckle when I saw a front-page photograph of my antlers resting on top of a car, with a smiling Jaques standing alongside. In his arms, Jaques held the large Molson trophy, and six cases of Molson beer were stacked at his feet: the prize for bagging the third largest moose killed in 1963 in the entire province of Quebec and the largest in the Sept-Iles area.

Another time seventeen-year-old Eddie Rowsell caught a large lynx in a rabbit snare not far from his home four miles east of Alymer Sound. Eddie intended to sell it to the Hudson Bay Company for $75, but I persuaded him to sell it to me instead. I transported the frozen lynx across the U.S. border and took it directly to Ed Shaw, the taxidermist in Malden, Massachusetts. The result was a beautiful mount showing the lynx with his foot on a log baring his teeth in a snarl. It was my intent to take the lynx mount back to Harrington Harbour, where very few people had ever seen a lynx, known locally as a mountain cat. They are very shy and hard to spot. Upon my return in the Helio Courier to Fredericton, New Brunswick, to clear customs on my way back to the coast, I parked the Helio next to the terminal and reported to Inspector Newell, whom I had come to know during more than fifteen years of trips. The inspector asked to "take a look" in the aircraft. As I opened the large cargo door, he jumped on the amphibious floats and was greeted by a snarling lynx at the door. He yelled and jumped backward off the float, tumbling on the tarmac as far as the wingtip of the Helio. He was not amused. When we sorted out the story of how I obtained the lynx and had had it mounted and was bringing it back to Harrington Harbour, he relaxed. "Hold on," he said. We retreated to the Customs Office, where Inspector Newell poured through a mammoth manual and finally found a section titled "Taxidermy of Canadian birds and animals returned to Canada." I paid $125 duty and went on my way with Inspector Newell still dusting off his trousers.

Friends in Harrington often asked me to join them on hunting expeditions, particularly in the fall or, as the people of the coast say, "the fall of the year." Before leaving for Harrington for my first full winter in the north in 1963, I purchased a battery-operated, water-resistant, olive green phonograph, which could be used to play eight-inch discs of duck- and goose-call recordings. This was the latest thing to lure waterfowl within gun range. At the time it was considered a clever and very modern innovation but it was subsequently shown to put unusual stress upon birds in the wild and was soon outlawed.

I tried it a number of times but had little success because of technical glitches that caused the phonograph needle to stay in the same spot and play the half-honk of a goose over and over. The recordings included duck calls, squealing rabbits, the howl of wolves, cawing crows, and the sound of hawks. I am a long-time lover of pranks, as my family can attest, and I soon realized the recordings might be put to better use.

During the goose migration in Kegaska, my family and I hid the phonograph underneath the kitchen of a house where twenty or so men had assembled to tell stories of hunting and fishing exploits. As soon as they heard the honk of geese from the phonograph, the room emptied. The men dashed outside to see the geese fly overhead and were stunned and confused to see nothing.

One night in Harrington Harbour, we played the wolf record. Sam Waye and his wife Violet came out on the bridge in front of their house, just a few hundred feet below the Bryan house. We heard Sam say, "I think they're dogs." By this time, most of the resident sled dogs had left the island. Violet replied, "No, Sam, they are wolves."

We played the same ruse outside the canvas tents of the Inuit at George River and trappers at Cartwright Labrador and next to many homes on the Quebec North Shore. We always eventually fessed up as to the true source of the sounds and the trick never failed to trigger gales of laughter from everyone.

I pulled another stunt during the fall of 1963 while helping a group of Harrington Harbour fishermen pull small boats up on the shore. The strongest man on the coast was said to live in Middle Bay, 90 miles east of Harrington Harbour. This man could lift a 350-pound fuel drum as if it was a 75-pound bag of salt. As I helped pull the boat, I found myself on a rock ledge at the bow of the boat. The boat was pushed close enough to me that I could take advantage of the momentum, give a mighty heave, and yank it over the rock. I was by myself at that point and it appeared to spectators that I was single-handedly hauling a boat up the rocks. Word quickly spread of Mr. Bryan's exceptional strength. While this was far from true, I did not protest when children came up to me and said, "Mr. Bryan, you must be some strong!" I rather enjoyed the reputation even if undeserved.

Then one day, Barge Levy, a Choate School student who became a lifelong friend and was working as my aircraft crewman, helped me move dozens of drums of stove oil, the winter supply for the Anglican parsonage in Harrington Harbour, from the wharf to the side of the parsonage. Dr. Hodd loaned us the dilapidated hospital jeep to ferry the drums. We were trying to cut down on the number of trips so we piled too many drums onto the back of the jeep. As we labored toward the parsonage, a drum slid off the jeep and rolled away, lodging in the soft mud next to Roy Rowsell's house. After many hours hauling those drums from the wharf to the parsonage, at the end of the day it was difficult to summon the energy needed to retrieve the lost drum, so I left it for another day.

For the next month, Roy Rowsell asked me at least four times to move the 45-Imperial-gallon oil drum from the side of his house. I procrastinated but I knew I had to get it out of his yard at some point.

On the morning I retrieved the drum, which weighed more than 350 pounds full, I recruited five men to help pull it from the boggy area in front of Roy's house and move it to its place with the other drums stashed behind the parsonage. With the job complete, I remembered the strong man in Middle Bay and how he might have picked up the drum, placed it on his shoulder, and walked up the hill. It had taken five of the strongest men in Harrington Harbour to yank that one drum out of the muck. This struck me as an opportunity to have some fun.

I ran back to the parsonage and found an empty drum left over from the prior year. I carefully rolled it down the rock and placed it where the full drum had rolled next to Roy's house. When Roy returned home that night, he noticed the drum was still there. The next day, Roy was outdoors near the corner of his house building a coffin—Roy was the wharf agent for the Clarke Steamship Company and had a side business making simple pine coffins. I walked to Roy's house and went directly to the fuel drum. Roy acknowledged me with a brief wave and continued his work, but I could see he was watching me carefully out of the corner of his eye. I moved into position and grabbed both sides of the empty barrel. With a mighty heave and many grunts and groans, I yanked the drum out of the mud, raised it over my head, and walked back, placing it on the rock ledge.

As I passed, I noticed Roy's face frozen in amazement and incredulity. I could not look at him directly because I would have burst into laughter. Slowly, I rolled the drum back up the hill. That night, I enjoyed the reputation of being a parson with superhuman strength. It did not last long. I corralled Laurie Cox the following day and went to Roy's house to tell him the full story. We laughed long and hard over the prank and the notion that I might ever be capable of such a feat.

I could rarely pass up the chance to have some fun. I suspect this predilection dates back to my youth. When I spent that first long stint in Harrington Harbour in 1963 and 1964, I brought sufficient gear to spend ten winters in the North, including 12-gauge shotgun shells filled with emergency flares rather than shot.

Such things were utterly unknown in the North at that time, particularly among the Inuit who had lived successfully off the land without any modern gimmickry or conveniences for generations. Johnny

Ananack, an Inuit from Fort Chimo, worked at Bob May's fishing camp at Helen's Falls on the George River. I visited Bob often and was once stuck there for a few days due to bad weather. One night as we sat around the stove in a large, white canvas tent, we told stories of shooting ducks and geese on the wing. The Inuit told marvelous stories, interpreted by Bob, of their prowess in being able to hit anything flying.

I had some small weather balloons in my airplane that I had received from the personnel at the weather office of Sept-Iles. I challenged Johnny to hit an inflated balloon that I would launch outside the tent. Johnny was almost insulted by the ease of this challenge but he agreed to try. I told him he needed to wait until the balloon had risen up at least sixty yards before shooting. We all went outside the tent for the test.

I let the balloon go up into the uncharacteristically still air. This was the equivalent of shooting a sitting duck and Johnny was grinning ear to ear as he watched this easy target move slowly up into the sky. It was dusk, but the white balloon was clearly visible. I called out to him, "Now Johnny!" He raised the shotgun to his shoulder and fired. A bright red flare whooshed out of the barrel of the gun, burst the balloon, and continued far up into the sky. Johnny yelped, dropped the gun, and raced back to his tent as fast as he could. A month later, he was still insisting that the minister had brought the strangest shotgun he had ever seen or used on the George River.

Before the proliferation of snowmobiles, the dog team race was a major recreational event at winter carnivals on the North Shore. I did not have a dog team of my own but I enjoyed participating. I was usually able to borrow a team of dogs in any of the villages along the coast. My dog-driving skills were minimal and every family along the coast knew this. They found it funny that Mr. Bryan was so inept at such a basic life skill. I lagged far behind in most of the races I entered. While I never had a chance to race a fast dog team, I cannot use that as an excuse. In the four races in which I competed during the winter of 1963 and 1964, I finished dead last three times and second to last once.

Ches Jones loaned me his team of five dogs for the big race in Harrington Harbour in 1964. Within a minute of the start, I was already behind the 25 or so teams that began the race. Some of the experienced dog-team drivers carried whips, not to whip the dogs but to make a cracking sound that urged them to run faster. I did not know how to crack a whip or make the necessary vocal sounds dog-team drivers use to encourage their dogs aside from the "rata" for right and "ek" for left. However, on the day of the big race, I carried a .22-caliber pistol. When my dogs' pace slowed from a gallop to a canter, to a trot, and then to a walk, and things looked hopeless, I drew my pistol, aimed it in the air and fired. The startled dogs gave a tremendous leap forward. I promptly fell backward off the komatik into the snow and the dogs took off without me.

Fortunately, there was an extra dog trace of about sixty feet long trailing behind the komatik. It slipped under me as the dog team ran away. I made a desperate lunge, caught the trace and wrapped it around my arm. My dog team came to a halt and I was able to get back on the komatik and continue the race. A big and patient crowd had gathered on the "mesh," a peat bog that was the only flat part of the island, to watch the finish. They had to wait 45 minutes between the arrival of the second to last team and mine; when I appeared over the hill, they gave a great cheer. That night, Uncle Fred Cox, Laurie Cox's father, discussed the race by radio with Jim Foreman at Cape Whittle Light. The lighthouse keepers stayed at the lighthouses throughout the winters. It was lonely and solitary duty, particularly on carnival weekends when everyone in town gathered for the festivities. When Uncle Fred reported that I had finished last, Jim Foreman suggested that I probably did not know the right words to speak to the dogs. When frustrated with their dogs, local dog-team drivers used language that might be heard in a Marine Corps barracks. Many of my friends picked up on Jim's theory and joked many times that I would have done better if only I had used the right words. I tried to persuade them that I had unquestionably used "the right words" when I was off alone on the trail, but they never believed me.

CHAPTER 6

Bush Pilot

A S A BUSH PILOT, I was often called upon to carry odd loads from one place to another. It was not easy to transport large bulky items in the North. With no internal road system and months of stormy weather, deep snow, and sheets of ice, conveying large items such as lumber, canoes, rowboats, and outboard motors was a challenge. I discovered that I could airlift almost anything with a floatplane. It is just about impossible to attach any type of load to a wheel plane, but a floatplane has a built-in platform of floats and float struts capable of holding and hauling odd lots.

It is fair to say that I tested the limits of planes, particularly my Helio Courier, with the weight of the items I carried. When I had my first conversation with Bob Kimnach, the president of the Helio Corporation, he told me that the aircraft had gone through flight testing at the 4,400-pound weight, even though the plane's normal certified weight was 3,400 pounds. What I did not understand was that the aircraft, designed for agriculture crop dusting and spraying, was expected to dump about 1,000 pounds of disposable load within seconds.

Yet I flew that plane at more than 4,400 pounds and always felt confident the plane could handle it, even though it felt a bit heavy. The plane would lose some airspeed but a floatplane is already slower than a wheel plane because of the floats. The largest exterior load I carried on a Cessna 185 was a 14-foot, 300-pound clinker-built spruce rowboat. Ches Jones and I took the boat from Harrington Harbour to Lac Triquet. I felt a slight flutter in the left horizontal stabilizer because of the protruding load, but the plane's control was not impaired. We flew low at fifty feet to the Netagamu River and followed the river to the forks of the Netagamu and Mecatina Rivers. I then flew another six miles, hooked a left turn over a series of small lakes, and entered the north end of Lac Triquet. I took a photograph of it and later showed it to Dwayne Wallace, the president of Cessna Aircraft, who hung the photograph on his office wall to show the capability of his airplane.

Large outboard motors were relatively easy to attach to the floats. I carried 45-Imperial-gallon barrels, caribou carcasses, refrigerators and stoves, plywood, and even bedsprings once. Bedsprings pose a particular challenge because they vibrate in the air and create an uncomfortable shaking and shuddering sensation. I was so rattled by the effect that I aborted the flight immediately after takeoff.

The key to carrying large loads on a floatplane is to secure them properly. I usually tied three times as many lines to a canoe on an aircraft than I would have fixed to a car-top carrier. There are many reports of serious accidents from carelessly attached loads or from loads that disintegrate. In one fatal accident in Canada, an old canvas canoe came apart in the air and the debris carried away the horizontal stabilizer of a de Havilland DHC-2 Beaver.

I was carrying a bright red, thirteen-foot fiberglass canoe lashed to the floats of the Helio Courier across the Gulf of St. Lawrence to New Brunswick when I had a chance encounter with a Canadian Air Force F-111 fighter. The jet was likely on a military maneuver out of Chatham, New Brunswick. The pilot passed on my left side no more than 200 feet away. He had partial flaps and landing gear down in order to get slow enough for a better look, though he still whizzed by at a high rate of speed. I remember he wore a gold helmet and he shook his head in disbelief when he saw the canoe attached to the single-engine floatplane flying 6,500 feet over the Gulf of St. Lawrence.

I had been in Harrington Harbor for about two weeks in the summer of 1960 when neighbors asked me to fly to Wolf Bay to pick up ten lobsters. Friends in New England had transported lobsters in their float compartments, but I soon discovered that confined lobsters made a real mess. To avoid the need to clean and air out the float compartments after a lobster trip, it seemed easier to put them in a carton and stow them in the cabin.

I was not yet familiar with the direct route between Wolf Bay and Harrington Harbour; on my way back, I reached behind my seat for a chart. My hand missed the seat pocket and went into the carton of lobsters. A two-and-a-half-pounder grabbed my right index finger with its claw. I howled with pain and instinctively yanked away my hand. The lobster that was latched onto my finger came out of the box with two other lobsters clinging to him. The only way to free my hand was to put the tangle of three lobsters between my knees, let go of the yoke with my left hand, and try to pry myself free. I freed my hand, but for the next fifteen minutes three lobsters cavorted around the rudder pedals. I tried to keep my ankles clear and managed to get my heels up on top of the toe brakes for the duration of the flight.

Years later, I made another lobster flight. I received a last-minute request from friends planning a big lobster shindig in Sept-Iles. They asked me to bring fifty lobsters from Harrington Harbour on my way down that way. The weather did not cooperate and it took me two days and five stops to make the trip. At each stop, I moved fifty lobsters from cartons into makeshift lobster cars at each harbor in between Kegaska and Sept-Iles. In a tribute to the hardiness of these crustaceans, only two lobsters died. My friends were delighted to take possession of the 48 survivors. Needless to say, I was delighted to hand them over.

During the long icy winters in the early 1960s, supplies invariably became exhausted before the ice melted and ships could once again ply the coastline and replenish the stores. In March 1963, I was asked to bring in a new supply of communion wine for the Anglican and Roman Catholic clergy who had run out. I tucked eight gallons of St. George's wine at $4.90 per gallon behind the seat of the Cessna 185 when I left Sept-Iles to return to the coast. Gordon Kippen was with me when we took off on a cold dull morning. Light snow soon reduced visibility to one to two miles. There were few visible landmarks to guide us so we followed the telegraph line cut along a straight right-of-way, parallel to the coast and less than half a mile inland. I thought about what might happen if forced to land in the trees. Dead or alive, Gordon and I would likely be found doused with eight gallons of St. George's wine.

I remember one particularly arduous trip from the George River to Harrington Harbour via Goose Bay. Bob Schmon Jr. sat in the right seat of the Helio and Laurie Cox sat behind on top of the survival gear. The wind, heavy rain, fog, low scud, and severe turbulence forced us to make a number of stops to wait for showers to pass. We went hours without any food and finally Laurie decided it was time to eat. As I peered ahead into heavy rain straining to see my way, I suddenly thought the airplane was on fire. To my horror, Laurie had lit the Coleman stove in the back of the plane and was warming up soup to prepare a meal for us. "I'm cook aboard the aircraft," he said with a twinkle. Had there been ignitable fumes, the plane would have exploded. We decided peanut butter and jelly sandwiches would suffice in the future.

Airdrops were another task that I undertook as a bush pilot. This was a useful way to deliver items "on the fly." The Federal Aviation Administration in the United States has firm regulations prohibiting tossing anything out of an airplane. Canada is not quite so strict. My first airdrop took place when Douglas Rowsell, the postmaster at Harrington Harbour, asked me to deliver some mail to Bishop Brown aboard the Anglican mission boat *Glad Tidings,* then en route to Kegaska. I found the boat about twenty miles west of Harrington near Yankee Harbour. I circled and indicated I would make a drop. I put the mail in a tobacco can and my passenger, Wiley Reynolds III, one of the first Quebec Labrador Foundation volunteers in 1961, prepared to make the drop. When I came back up into the wind over the boat, I told Wiley I would give him the drop signal. Wiley opened the right-side window and I slowed the aircraft to eighty miles per hour. We were about 150 feet above the *Glad Tidings.* My plan was to have the mail drop in front of the boat and I began to explain this to Wiley, "Now, Wiley . . ." As soon as he heard the word "now," he let the tobacco can go with a flick of his hand. I made a steep turn and watched the can arc down toward the boat. The balding, seventy-year-old bishop was standing near the transom and the can moved closer and closer to the *Glad Tidings*. Through good fortune, the can missed Bishop Brown by three feet and splashed into the water about six inches from the boat. The impact of the can on the water drenched the bishop and Father Burke, but they waved thanks as their boatman Ches Yarn turned the boat around to retrieve the mail.

The tobacco can with the mail inside was heavy enough to have killed the bishop and I apologized to him when he returned to Harrington. He insisted it was a perfect shot. An object dropped from an airplane is traveling at the same speed as the plane. A projectile moving at eighty miles per hour can do a lot of damage. I generally tried to wait until I was directly over a target before making a drop.

Ella Bell of Forteau, in southern Labrador, once asked me to bring her a hymnal. I found a traditional hymnal I knew she would like. Ella did not care for the new hymnals coming out in the late 1970s. On a very windy day, I flew the Helio Courier over Forteau and weather conditions made it advisable to drop the hymnal rather than land the plane on the lake and walk to Ella's house. As I circled, I spotted Ella gardening near her house. Her lettuce patch was laid out in neat rows and she was pulling weeds. As I came down low, I was focused on avoiding the cliff just to the left of her house. I opened the window. The hymnal was wrapped in a plastic bag with a fifteen-foot-long cloth streamer to make it easier to find. Instead of waiting until I was over Ella, I let it go too soon. The next thing I saw was a ten-foot furrow in Ella's lettuce garden. The hymnal lay at her feet. She reached down, picked it up and gave me a hearty wave, not knowing that her well-meaning minister could have unwittingly knocked her unconscious with a hymnal.

At Christmas of 1963, I was asked to bring Christmas mail to Lionel McKinnon, the Flat Island lighthouse keeper, and his staff who were not able to leave the lighthouse to return to their hometown of La Tabatiere. Gordon Kippen was working as my pilot's helper. The families of the lighthouse staff gave us a mail sack that weighed ten to fifteen pounds. They also gave us two snowshoe hares that had been snared earlier in the month and would be a delicacy and treat for Christmas, some Christmas gifts, and a box of peanut brittle. It was a cold and overcast day and the air was moist. I knew I might have problems with carburetor ice and was reluctant to pull back the throttle. But to make the drop, I had to reduce power. Lionel and the others at the light station were outside and waiting. As I buzzed the lighthouse, I realized that it would be impossible to make an emergency landing on the small rock island if I had a problem. A plane moving at 65 to 90 knots would go right off the cliff and into the sea. Likewise, a ditching in the choppy water at the base of the cliff would be extremely dangerous in the skiplane.

I slowed down the airplane on the second turn, put the mail in my left hand and opened the window. I focused on the lighthouse. Lionel stood waiting with his arms outstretched. I missed him but the mail hit a coal bin next to the lighthouse. The mailbag burst open and letters and packages went in all directions. There was not much wind that day and I saw children running to pick up the scattered mail. It was now time to drop the rabbits, which were frozen solid, the snares still around their feet. I had closed the window after the first drop; it was very cold. As I came back for another approach, I opened the window again. The slip stream caused the rabbits to bounce around and the toenails of their frozen feet scratched my left wrist. As I came in for the drop, the snare wire tangled around my wrist and I was unable to release the rabbits. It was now snowing and I was once again descending toward the wintery sea. There was a raft of eider ducks just to the left of the lighthouse and as I passed over them, I remember thinking that even the ducks looked cold. I applied power and felt reassured when the engine responded. On the next turn, I was able to drop the rabbits. They hit the base of the light.

On the third and final turn, I let the peanut brittle go. The box arced down toward Flat Island, hit the side of the cliff and burst open. Eager children rushed out and tried to retrieve what was left of the package. I was happy to turn and fly back over water to the safety of the ice between Gros Mecantina and La Tabatiere.

After the Flat Island drop, word got around that I could drop just about anything out of the airplane, and I received so many requests from the lighthouse keepers along the coast that I made frequent drops during the winters of 1963 and '64. The day after President Richard Nixon resigned in August of 1974, a group of salmon fishermen from New York came to the Grande Romaine Club. They had a copy of the

New York Daily News with them. I stopped by Romaine that morning and later that afternoon traveled to Robertson Lake. The Robertson Lake crew was out on a camping trip in a narrow area where I could not land the plane. I took the newspaper, wrapped it in a plastic bag, and dropped it to them. They were able to read that day's newspaper from New York City in a remote Quebec lake some 1,000 miles away.

Not every drop was planned. It is illegal to bring citrus fruit across the Canadian border. On one of our many trips between New Brunswick and Ipswich, Massachusetts, we found ourselves at 5,000 feet with a cache of oranges that had to be pitched out the window into a remote forest from a mile high. It is also easy to overlook an errant piece of equipment in a rush to take off. I once forgot a sixteen-millimeter movie film canister on top of the float. The canister broke open and the reel rolled along the Beverly Airport runway spilling 1,600 feet of film from one end to the other, much to the exasperation of the control tower operator. In order to salvage the film, I jogged down the runway, twirling the reel on a pencil to reel it back in.

I became acutely sensitive to weather. The least shift in wind speed or temperature could make an enormous difference between a quick safe flight and a dangerous one. And the environment often made the simplest tasks, such as eating or refueling the plane, more difficult if not impossible. Many times, an uneventful trip became a memorable one because of the constant threats posed by adverse weather.

I landed at Happy Fraser's fishing camp on the Etamamiou River on a windy morning in July 1963. A cold front had come through the area the night before and northwest winds increased during the morning. At about 10 a.m., Happy asked me to fly him 35 miles west to the village of Romaine. I was willing but told him we needed to leave immediately because the wind, then gusting to 35 knots, might become stronger by mid-day. It was so turbulent I had trouble controlling the airplane after takeoff. Rather than fly a direct course to Romaine over rough ground where it would be difficult to land in an emergency, I decided to take a longer route via Wolf Bay and the offshore islands where a water landing would be easier.

Two miles west of Wolf Bay, the surface wind blew even stronger than the winds we encountered at takeoff. The Cessna 185 bucked and bounced around. I had rarely experienced turbulence so severe. The sea turned white with foam and sheets of spray exploded over rocks and small islands. I told Happy that we might have some problems getting into Romaine and suggested we land straight ahead in the sheltered cove of a nearby island where the water was relatively smooth. We taxied ashore and pulled the plane up onto a small beach.

I rummaged through my survival gear for the raisins, vacuum-packed chocolate bars, freeze-dried noodles, Lipton cup-o-soup, and waterproof matches. Happy was delighted to find a stout, silvery package marked "meat and vegetable stew." I filled an aluminum pot with water at the water's edge per the package instructions, mixed in the dehydrated stew and fired up the Coleman stove. Happy was impressed that I was so well-prepared. We were hungry and looking forward to digging into the simmering stew. I dished out the stew and Happy took a big bite. A look passed across his face. He gagged and spit out the food and exclaimed, "This is the worst stuff I have ever tasted." I took a small bite and realized I had made a fundamental error. The directions called for mixing the package contents with water, freshwater, not sea water. We could find no potable freshwater on the island so it was a long hungry wait through the afternoon and into the evening. At 8:45 pm, the wind dropped back down to about 25 knots. Two weary and very hungry men got back into the airplane and headed to Romaine.

I had another unfortunate episode with food while flying over Anticosti Island. I had left Ipswich for the Beverly Airport on a trip back to Harrington Harbour. I stopped at the local market and filled a Styrofoam container with fresh meat to supplement our regular diet of local fish. I noticed fresh crabmeat salad sitting in a cool bin while walking to the checkout and could not resist buying a one-pound carton. Although I stored it on top of the cold but unfrozen meat in the Styrofoam box, forty hours passed before Tim Nadeau and I stuffed the crabmeat into sandwiches. This, it transpired, was too much time for the crab. Not long after we'd polished off the sandwiches, my stomach began to churn. As Tim and I continued to insist unconvincingly to each other that we felt fine, we hit fog in the Gulf and I realized it would be impossible to land safely on the water. We pushed on grimly on to Harrington Harbour, and by the time we arrived, I had decided, yet again, that the trusty peanut butter and jelly would be the safer bet when flying over water and hours from human habitation.

While I was the first minister to use a floatplane to reach my parishioners, I was not the last. The Reverend Jim Young took over after working for the Quebec diocese as the minister for the Magdalen Islands, a small archipelago in the Gulf of St. Lawrence. The family of a young friend, George Baker III, donated a Cessna 180 to the Quebec Labrador Foundation for Jim's use. He upgraded a few years later with a two-seater Piper Super Cub 150, one of the greatest planes ever made. Reverend Young was followed by Reverend John Blick from England and Reverend John Neal from New Zealand.

I had the distinct honor of flying five bishops around the Quebec North Shore. Archbishop Philip Carrington was the first bishop to fly with me in 1959. We met at Lac St. Augustine not far from the Ancienne Lorette Airport in Quebec. He told me had never flown in a floatplane. I talked him through all the preliminary details before the takeoff. When we were in the air, I made the gentlest turns imaginable and flew over the Cathedral of the Holy Trinity before returning to Lac St. Augustine to land. Archbishop Carrington thanked me and said, "I enjoyed that, Bob, but I am more comfortable in boats." My first flight with Bishop Russel Brown was during his visits to the coast beginning in the summer of 1961. The bishop had some pilot training in the 1930s so he was a relaxed passenger. Bishop Timothy Matthews loved flying in the QLF aircraft. He would remain glued to the side window identifying all the villages and outposts along the way. I remember him pointing out the home of his son Tom and daughter-in-law Barbara as we passed over Mutton Bay. Bishop Alan Goodings was always eager to take part in the aircraft operations. When we landed after a flight on the coast, he would quickly become a part of the ground crew. M. E. Reisner's *History of the Anglican Diocese of Quebec 1793 to 1995 Strangers and Pilgrims* included some words I had written about Bishop Goodings as part of a tribute at his memorial service in January 1993. "When we landed the airplane at a village in the evening, friends would appear at the cockpit door and call out 'Come right up, Bishop. We have boiled the kettle and we will have a cup of tea.'

"He would reply, 'Thank you, I will be there in a minute. I must help button up the plane.' Then lying on his back in the snow underneath the engine, he would button up the engine tent and standing on a fuel drum, help secure the wing covers without mittens in minus 25 degree centigrade cold. In the morning he would appear at the plane driving a borrowed snowmobile and say, 'Now then, Bob, what can I do?'"

Bishop Bruce Stavert was the fifth bishop of the Diocese of Quebec to fly in N369E. Bruce was familiar with aircraft operations because he had made several flights with me during his years as a priest serving St. Paul's River and later with the Innu in Schefferville. Bruce sat next to me in the cockpit. During tense moments of low visibility and fog, he never flinched and was always helpful as we navigated through adverse weather. Bishop Denis Drainville never had a chance to fly in Cessna N369E, but during the winter of 2005 he became the first Quebec Diocesan bishop to travel the entire coast by snowmobile.

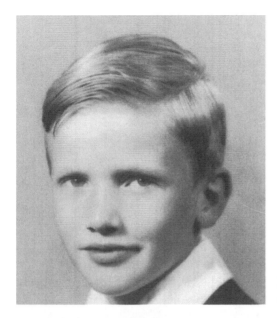

Robert Bryan as a young boy.

With my parents at my ordination to the Episcopal diaconate, June 1957. St. John's Church of Lattingtown, New York.

Me with my *Bert and I* partner in crime Marshall Dodge (right) and the illustrator of the *Bert and I* book, Mark Andres (left).

Our camp at Lac Triquet in 1964. L–R: Me, Kerry, Sarah, and Faith.

Conducting a church service among the Inuit, north of Labrador in 1964.

No, not a "shotgun wedding"—just the traditional ceremony in 1960. La Tabatiere, Quebec North Shore.

Cruising down a rock slope at Snuff Box Inlet, Mutton Bay in 1968.

Our daughters, Sandy, Kerry, and Sarah, with a nice catch of trout at Lac Triquet near Harrington Harbour.

The great Kegaska dog-team race, March 1964. Prior to the advent of the snow-mobile in the 1960s, the dog team and komatik were the primary means of winter travel. I'm in the white snow suit, slightly right of center in the mid-ground. I never had a dog team and my attempts on the komatik were always a source of great amusement to the coasters.

Our arrival at Harrington Harbour, 1962.

Bob walking on tundra.

With Kerry by the Grumman Widgeon, 1975.

Sharing a laugh with "Uncle" George Ransom in 1975.

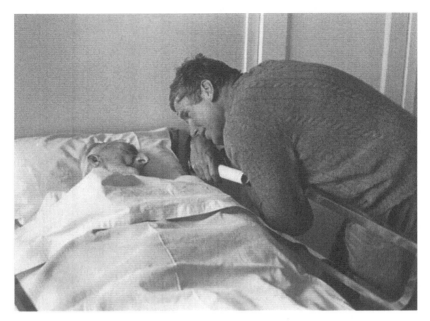

Reminiscing with "Uncle" Norm Jones over some of our adventures two days before his death at Harrington Harbour Hospital in 1977.

Introducing hockey legend Bobby Orr to the children of Harrington Harbour in 1981.

With my ace mechanic, Enis Cribb, in front of Cessna "69Easy."

This is the photo the president of Cessna Aircraft hung on his office wall to show the load-carrying capabilities of the Cessna 185.

The Stubbert family and their lobster-fishing camp at Coacachou in 1972. The little girl standing in front of her father is Gladys Stubbert. Now an Anglican priest, she serves as chaplain of Kegaska.

Dick Rockefeller refereeing a kid's soccer match at Mutton Bay.

Me and Trish in 2003 sitting on the left float of N369E.

Bob and his sister Joy outside their stick fort at Harrington Harbour (Ed Miller).

Tom Nadeau covering a fuselage at Hotchkiss QLF.

Summer volunteer Doug Eisenhart with children at Harrington Harbour.

Transporting a skiff on the floats.

Covered up for the night.

Kirby Bobbitt and Barge Levy help launch a boat at Harrington.

Bob gases the plane.

Faith and girls weigh a trout.

Bob (left) pretends to take a nap while octogenarian Uncle Walt takes the controls.

Sarah, Kerry, and Sandy display Christmas-present bounty.

The Helio Courier on skis.

Bob shaking hands with a young boy before taking off (Cotton Coulson).

A child sits on a thawing caribou.

Laurie Cox shooting on hockey legend Bobby Orr in Harrington Harbour.

Bob (right) and Bobby Orr with a nice catch at Lac Triquet.

Bob photographed this 360-foot high ice berg in St. Paul's River from the cockpit in July 2001.

Campers at Tabusintac.

Wolf Bay seen from the air.

Securing the plane during a storm.

CHAPTER 7

In the Blink of an Eye

M Y ROLE as a bush pilot on the coast brought me in close touch with many tragedies. Life was precarious in the North. In the blink of an eye, a life could be lost. There were no police or fire departments and limited emergency services. As a result, the people of the coast had an acute awareness of their own mortality, a deep and abiding faith, and a reliance on neighbors.

The safety net that existed in those years lay in community. The ongoing battle to survive in a hostile climate fostered a sense of communal responsibility. On any day an individual and his family might need help from the entire village. No one held back. While these people did not view themselves as "poor" in a conventional sense, they had little extra in terms of material goods. The culture, however, set the high bar of hospitality. These were people who would give you the last piece of bread and the shirt off their back without hesitation. At the same time, self-reliance was prized. There was an expectation that individuals would work hard to support themselves and their families. There was wood to cut, wood and water to haul by dog sled, food to trap and hunt. They were and remain a hardy people.

Split-second decisions made at sea and on the ice fields are crucial to survival along Quebec's North Shore. Men set off in small boats in weather and sea conditions that would scare the wits out of a Coast Guard Auxiliary training officer. The instincts of the local people were honed by generations of experience. While people of the coast respect the outsiders who come in to teach, practice medicine, or serve their Church, they recognize the limitations of people who, unlike them, were not born with the sea in their blood. They are watchful, protective, and humorously condescending in a most inoffensive way of those of us who come to stay with them. Dozens of times, a friend would pull up beside me on a snowmobile and apologetically say, "I think I'll go along with you if you don't mind." An outsider in a small boat, even on a well-traveled route, was a source of worry until he arrived at his destination. It was the practice to make a radio call to report a safe arrival. There was legitimate reason for this concern. In 1969, a school teacher from the southeastern United States was teaching in the village of Old Fort Bay, Quebec. He received a new pair of snowshoes as a gift from a friend. The first day out, he headed about a mile from the village to a series of small ponds he knew well. Snow began to fall during his walk and visibility was reduced to a few feet. He became hopelessly disoriented and wandered all night. He died fourteen hours after the storm struck. In reconstructing his route, it was estimated that he walked nearly twenty miles in vain to find his way one mile back to the village.

Someone born and raised on the coast would have dug a hole with a snowshoe—locally called a racquet from the French word, *raquette,* for snowshoe—and crawled in to wait out the storm. In the winter of 1964, Seldon Harding of Harrington Harbour became lost while driving his dogs in a severe blizzard just a few miles north of the town. He stopped, dug a hole with his raquets, pulled the dogs inside, and, as temperatures fell to twenty below, he not only survived but also stayed warm thanks to his dogs. His biggest problem was digging himself out in the morning and getting to shelter quickly before his damp clothes froze on his body.

There were many near misses. Billy Bobbitt and his brother Don were returning from Derby (pronounced "Darby"), between Etamamiou and Cross River/Chevery, to Harrington Harbour one day in the mid-1960s in their 26-foot open boat, loaded down with logs bound for the sawmill. The strength of the northwest wind made it difficult to hold their course, and the boat experienced engine trouble. Morley Rowsell, returning from Derby in his boat, came upon them and offered them a towline. For hours, Morley struggled to make progress, but as conditions grew worse, Morley feared he might also be stranded. Billy and Don suggested he give up the tow and said they would continue work on their engine and perhaps toss an anchor. Morley continued on his way to get help. However, Billy and Don could not start the engine and their anchor line was not long enough to hold them in place.

Their boat was carried farther and farther into the gulf, as the wind grew stronger and the seas rougher. That night their parents, Uncle Sam and Aunt Maud, desperately worried. Billy and Don drifted through the night. Billy suggested they dump their cargo overboard to lighten the boat but Don would not hear of it. The next morning, search parties fanned out to look for them and the Coast Guard and Air Search Rescue were notified.

The lightkeeper's wife, Florence Anderson, at St. Mary's light kept a constant vigil of the sea. As she scanned the horizon that day, she spotted something white in the distance and thought it might be Billy and Don. She called her husband Sam and they both looked through their binoculars. Sam jumped into his light-station boat and headed out. When he reached the drifting boat there was no sign of life and Sam feared the brothers had been lost at sea. Then he heard music coming from the cuddy. Sam called out but received no answer. He brought his boat alongside and peered down into the cuddy. Billy and Don were lying on their bunks, listening to a windup Victrola, not the least bit upset and oblivious to the flurry of concern their absence had generated.

On another occasion, Billy was on his boat off the islands near Harrington Harbour when his engine quit. He was alone. Night came and Billy calmly lay down in the bottom of the boat and went to sleep. He could have drifted all the way out into the center of the gulf or as far as the west coast of Newfoundland. Instead, he tied his boat to a fisherman's buoy and waited for rescue. Fortunately, it came the next day.

Not every emergency ended happily. In March 1974, Morley Rowsell and his uncle, Nelson Rowsell, left Harrington on their snowmobiles to procure a meal of eider ducks for their families. When they reached the tip of Mecatina, four miles east of Harrington Harbour, they discovered a small iceberg a few hundred feet off shore. They launched a small double-ended row boat into the calm water and pulled it up after them onto the iceberg. However, the slick ice turned the canoe into a toboggan and Morley could not hold onto the bow line. It slipped through his cold hands and the boat shot out into the water. Within seconds, it was thirty or forty feet away from them and they were stranded on an iceberg.

Morley was agitated and became more panicked as time passed. When the iceberg started to move with the rising tide, Morley took off his coat, ran across the ice and, despite his uncle's protestations, dove into the water to try to swim to shore. Morley was not much of a swimmer and after thrashing about in the paralyzing cold water, he raised his arms and slipped beneath the surface. Nelson was grief-stricken; he could do nothing to help his nephew. The tide rose and he drifted out to sea. He broke the stock of his gun and used the wood from the stock and a small gun case to build a tiny fire to warm his hands. He huddled for hours on the iceberg shivering with cold. He occasionally spotted the lights of the village of Whale Head (Tête a la Baleine) to the north as he drifted southeast into the gulf. He was unsure of his position and dozed off from time to time. Suddenly, he felt a bump and nudge and woke to find the iceberg had grounded on the shore of Mecatina.

The iceberg carrying Nelson had gone out with the tide and returned with the tide at almost the exact spot where Nelson and Morley had first climbed on top of it. Nelson jumped onto his snowmobile and returned to Harrington to report the tragic news of Morley's death to his wife and three children.

The first trained pilot from Harrington Harbour was Gordon Waye. He had just finished high school and was back in town working on the town wharf in the summer of 1963. He was excited and eager to become a pilot and fly mail and passengers along the coast. He died in May 1965 while a passenger in a Beechcraft 18 on floats heading to Goose Bay to pick up an airplane for Wheeler Northland Airways, his employer. At the time of departure, the pilot was unaware that there was severe icing with turbulence ahead. The aircraft was destroyed when it hit the top of a mountain about 75 miles north of Sept-Iles.

One of the hardest days of my life was accompanying Gordon's casket home to Harrington Harbour. I came ashore in the cove near

Gordon's house where his parents waited for their son's body with friends and relatives. Gordon was an only son, the first pilot from Harrington Harbour, and a source of pride for the entire coast. I felt in some way responsible because I had encouraged him to be a pilot. His father Sam Waye's first words to me were: "Thank you for helping Gordon do what he always wanted to do." I was humbled by the depth of his kindness. After the funeral service, Sam and Violet, Gordon's mother, followed me to the floatplane ramp and handed me a gift of a bag of fresh scallops. Their generosity of spirit and their perspective was characteristic of the coastal people.

On January 5, 1964, I landed on the frozen lake at La Tabatiere to pick up Myra Morency and her one-year-old son Donald to fly them to hospital in St. Anthony, Newfoundland, where her husband Hiram was dying of cancer. Seven-year-old Gilbert Morency wept on the ice as we took off. He wanted to see his father, too, but the plane was already at gross weight, so he could not join us.

Gordon Kippen, my crewman, was with me. We strained to find ice pans large enough to land the plane in the event of emergency as we flew along the coast to Blanc Sablon and then cut across from Greenly Island to the Newfoundland coast. As we reached Greenly Island, it began to snow and we picked our way across the straits looking down at ice slabs from 300 feet. About 25 minutes after passing Greenly Island, we reached Newfoundland and encountered moderate to heavy snow. It was obvious that it would be too dangerous to continue to St. Anthony. I spotted a lake that bordered the new two-lane gravel "highway" on the coastal route to St. Anthony. We circled Blue Cove, the closest village to the road, and landed on the lake. As I taxied to shore, the forward section of the tail ski hooked onto a small crevice and pulled the tail bar out of the tail bulkhead, causing it to collapse and drag behind in the snow. Families from Blue Cove had seen the circling plane and immediately driven snowmobiles out to the lake. We were quickly rescued and transferred to a pick-up truck driven by two Royal Canadian Mounted Police (RCMP) officers on their way to St. Anthony. Gordon Kippen and I huddled under a bearskin for the three-hour drive in the uncovered truck bed. When we arrived at St. Anthony, Myra was escorted to Hiram's hospital room and I followed close behind. Hiram was alert and questioned me closely about the seal fishery at La Tabatière. I went to sleep in the nursing residence and was awakened at 2 a.m. by Dr. John Gray, who informed me that Hiram had died. Myra had made it to St. Anthony five hours before Hiram's death.

For the next three days, I traveled by road to Blue Cove to meet with Gander Aviation Company employees, who agreed to repair the damage to the tail bar and interior bulkheads. While the plane was fixed, I spent time visiting patients in hospital. One of the patients was Gladys Flynn from the Northeast Lighthouse on Belle Isle. I had a long talk and celebrated Holy Communion with her. She left St. Anthony by the weekly mail plane on January 9 to return to Belle Isle.

On the morning of January 10, I returned to Blue Cove with Gordon Kippen to prepare the Cessna to fly back across the straits to Blanc Sablon. The wind was picking up from the north and frost remained on the wings despite vigorous roping of the wings. The frost caused a loss of lift and noticeable instability in flight. Carefully avoiding turns, we slowly climbed straight ahead and ten minutes later the frost sublimated (a process that causes a solid to change to a gaseous state without becoming a liquid) allowing us to make a turn on course to Blanc Sablon. By the time we reached the Blanc Sablon airport, the wind was blowing thirty knots at sixty degrees across the runway. I crabbed the aircraft to try to stay straight but I was drifting when I touched down. The cable that is hooked to the ski trailing wheel parted with a loud bang, but I was able to slow down and taxi across the snow-covered tarmac and meet Northern Wings Limited agent Antoine Jones. Because of an approaching blizzard, Antoine had called the hospital in Blanc Sablon and arranged for the members of the Oblate Brothers to come out to the airport in a B12 Bombardier snow bus and drive Gordon and me, Antoine, and two airport workers back to the village. During the four-mile run to town, the front ski broke off the Bombardier. We were rescued again by a half dozen Ski-Doos.

When we arrived at Blanc Sablon, we learned of the worst snowmobile accident in Canada up until that time. Four people and their Autoboggan snowmobile had plunged over a 600-foot cliff on the north side of Belle Isle. The Autoboggan was carrying Gladys Flynn returning from hospital. Gladys was tucked into a coach box on a komatik and was accompanied by snowmobile driver Cecil Wellman and assistant light keepers Frank Roberts and Fred Slade. Frank Roberts was standing on the rear of the komatik holding onto the coach box. Four untethered sled dogs followed the Autoboggan. Cecil had brought them along from the Northeast Lighthouse for an exercise run to the southwest end of the island earlier in the day.

Cecil knew the twelve-mile trail well but it was clear that at some point along the route he got off course. Tracks in the snow on small ponds along the way indicated there was confusion. They veered to the north side of the island traveling through stunted fir and rocks. Their course took them to the edge of the cliff. After three hours of waiting past the estimated time of arrival of the four to the Northeast Light, Gladys's husband, Clarus Flynn, began a search in the darkness. His concern had been confirmed when the dogs arrived home unaccompanied. Clarus and Gladys's brother, Henry Fowler, had to wait until dawn to scour the entire island with a team of dogs. It did not take them long to discover tracks to the cliff. The only mark apart from the track of the rig going off the cliff was the impression of dug-in boots, probably made by Frank from the rear of the komatik and coach box. Heartbroken, Henry and Clarus returned to the Northeast lighthouse to plan the recovery and to contact the RCMP. The southeast wind had drawn ice off the north side shore so they maneuvered a twelve-foot flat-bottomed outboard three miles along the shore to avoid ballycaters, or sharp, protruding fragments of ice. They reached the frozen bodies but could not get them safely into the skiff. A Labrador Airways de Havilland Otter carrying a doctor and two Mounties flew overhead and landed in Batteau Pond, two miles from the northeast point. They arrived in a second small boat and joined Henry and Clarus in the recovery effort. As the snow increased and the visibility dropped at times to zero, five men were now at serious risk. Through careful seamanship, Henry and Clarus brought the boats along the shore back to the landing dock, and the bodies were carried to the boat shed.

The Reverend Carl Major, an Anglican Minister from Mary's Harbor, flew eighteen miles over the water in his Super Cub on skis to reach Belle Isle before that day's snowstorm to console the bereaved families at Northeast Light. Sixty miles to the east in Blanc Sablon, I was locked in a fierce snowstorm at Antoine Jones's house listening to the heartbreaking radio messages from the light stations at Belle Isle to the Lightkeeper Ches Thomas at Greenly Island. The following day, the Otter was able to take off for St. Anthony with the four bodies, along with Clarus Flynn; Mabel Wellman, the widow of one of the victims; and her two young children. What haunts me to this day is the description of the agitated and nervous dogs who refused to go a step further toward the edge of the cliff when Henry and Clarus were about to make their terrible discovery. Sled dogs are known for their uncanny ability to safely guide a komatik and driver home. Henry Fowler, now 78 years old, said to me recently, "They'd all be alive today if dogs had been leading the way."

Another agonizing event took place when Eric Osborne's boat capsized at the mouth of the harbor one half mile from Kegaska only hours after I had dipped my wings to them in greeting as they chugged homeward from a day of fishing. My daughter Kerry and I had flown from Kegaska to the Romaine Club, a fishing camp east of Kegaska, and had seen the young men whom I knew well: Eric Osborne and his brother Brian, Andy Mansbridge, and Randall Jones. We had admired their big catch as we'd looked down at the four men in their rubber overalls, waving up at us. It was a perfect day, sunny and calm with a light swell, a scene that elicited the sense that all is right with the world.

At Romaine, I was arranging to have a 45-Imperial-gallon drum of fuel delivered to the dock at Kegaska to refuel there and fly back to New Brunswick. I was speaking on the phone with Jimmy Butt, the Anglican Church lay reader and friend from Kegaska who would be helping with the refueling, when Jimmy suddenly cried out, "Eric's boat has turned over!" He didn't know if the fishermen were wearing life vests or float coats. I raced down the steep hill, slipped the lines, and leapt aboard the plane, backfiring the engine in my rush to take off.

Within sixteen minutes I was west of the village and spotted a man pulling himself onto a rock from the water as an outboard motorboat approached him. I turned out toward the sea to see if I could locate the others. The only things visible in the water were fish from the boat. Because of their high natural oil content, the dead fish floated just below the surface and drifted with the current in a northwest direction. I followed the current back and on my first turn noticed the shadow of the bow of the 55-foot boat 15 feet below the surface. The stern was resting on the bottom. I circled a number of times and on one pass saw one of the victims about ten feet below the surface.

A fleet of outboard motorboats arrived on the scene from all directions hoping to find survivors. By CB radio, I gave directions to Gordon Kippen to mark the spot with a buoy where I had seen the body. For the next thirty minutes, I flew overhead and spoke via HF radio to a contact "ashore" in Kegaska who in turn spoke to the searchers in the outboards. That is when I learned that Brian Osborne had made it safely to the ledge but his brother Eric, Andy Mansbridge, and Randall Jones had been lost. Eventually I returned to Harrington Harbour to refuel and prepare for a long difficult day. Rescue planes were on the way from the Canadian Mounted Police and Coast Guard.

When I spoke with Brian later that day, he told me that he heard the sound of my airplane as he neared the shore, and that his first thought as he pulled himself onto the rock was of my niece, Beth Bacon, a QLF summer volunteer who taught him how to swim. Brian reported that he and his shipmates had first climbed onto the turtled hull and yelled for help. When the boat sank beneath them, they desperately grabbed the fish floating on the surface and tried to maintain buoyancy by holding the fish close to their bodies. The boat, called *Eric's Pride,* was recovered and brought back to the harbor. The pain of the loss for such a small community was great. Everyone in town knew or was related to the victims. Roderick Jones, father of Randall, surmised that the dry upper planks of the boat had been porous, and with the bigger load—their biggest catch of the season—took on more water, which caused the boat to capsize. For Roderick and his wife, it was a particularly painful loss. Randall's twin brother had died of appendicitis several years earlier.

I wanted to do something to comfort the community and commemorate the lives of the three lost fishermen, so I arranged for a bas-relief sculpture of their profiles to be placed on a rock beside the little church on the harbor. It meant a great deal to the people of Kegaska to honor the men in this way.

As I have noted before, I was extremely conscious of safety and always took precautions. For long flights, Laurie Cox of Harrington Harbour was my trusted crewman and companion. I always knew that if forced down with Laurie, we would survive indefinitely: three months, six months, a year, it would make no difference. Laurie knew how to keep a fire going, build a shelter, and find food. He was not only a lifelong friend; he acted as my very own personal survival insurance policy. He had some hair-raising adventures of his own. Laurie went seal hunting one day in 1960 in a thirty-foot boat with a two-cylinder ten-horsepower motor. He and two fellow fishermen and their crews collected between 45 and 50 seals. As the day ended, he met up with friends in two longliner boats: Gilb Bobbitt in *Polyanne the First* and Chester Jones in the *Cape Whittle*. Ches Jones's boat engine died and the fishermen decided to stay out all night together on the sea. But the next day the weather grew worse and they found themselves jammed in the ice. Stranded in a blizzard, on an ice floe, the fishermen lost all three boats along with thousands of dollars of seals. They walked across the floating ice, dragging their flats, or rowboats, behind them, at times jumping from ice floe to ice floe. In the early morning of the third day, the sea was calm and they could see the distant pencil line of the shore. Distributing themselves between the flats, they crossed the open water to shore. Reaching land near Romaine, they walked up over the hill into the village where they were able to send a telegram to Harrington Harbour, letting their families know they were alive. After four days at sea, all fifteen men survived and, as Laurie related afterward, the men never got their feet wet.

There were so many examples of talent and skill in the North. I often speak about the boat builder, Roderick Jones from Wolf Bay. He was an unusually gifted student and everyone in the four family lobster fishing community marveled at his intelligence. Roderick read every word of the Encyclopedia Britannica at the age of twelve.

Roderick took to boatbuilding as a child and soon he was considered among the most skilled boatbuilders on the Quebec North Shore. In 1962 Roderick built the new Anglican Mission Boat, *The Hollis Corey*, to replace the decommissioned *Glad Tidings*, which had served the Anglican Church for forty years. Roderick singlehandedly built the 36-foot boat in Wolf Bay. He used no power tools, only hand tools. He used the tide to haul the half-completed hull onto makeshift ways.

The Quebec Labrador Foundation raised a substantial amount of the funds for the building of *The Hollis Corey* and solicited funds for the purchase of needed accessories, including navigational instruments, ship's bell, foghorn, running lights, and a search light. After completion and commissioning in June 1962, *The MV Hollis Corey* was turned over to its new captain, Ches Yarn of Mutton Bay.

Roderick became a close friend and flew with me to the United States on a trip that included a visit to the Smithsonian Institution in Washington, D.C. In 1967 Bus Mosbacher, the two-time America's Cup winning yachtsman, introduced Roderick to Robert E. Derecktor, the famed builder of the twelve-meter yacht, *Intrepid,* built that year, and owner of Derecktor Shipyards. Bob Derecktor questioned Roderick closely about how he designed and built boats. Roderick asked for a two-foot piece of wood and a spokeshave, a knife-type tool used in woodworking. Within forty minutes he produced a model of a Quebec North Shore fishing boat. He said, "You pick off the lines from the model. And you are ready to build a boat." Derecktor invited Roderick to move to Long Island to work at his famous Mamaroneck shipyard. Roderick declined because he would not leave the Quebec coast.

One summer evening I was sitting with Roderick outside his Wolf Bay house when we noticed a large passenger liner westbound, presumably headed for Montreal. The ship was hull down on the horizon, so we could only see the white super structure. It was at least 20 miles away. I suggested we go out and take a closer look. We boarded the Helio and 25 minutes later we were alongside the huge ship. The ship was moving at 20 knots into a 25-knot wind. We slowed to 60 knots and were keeping station with the ship. It must have been cocktail time. The men on deck wore tuxedos and women evening gowns, and they had drinks in hand. They vigorously waved at us from the deck as we turned back to Wolf Bay. Roderick was silent for five minutes. Then he turned to me and said, "If I had the time, I think I could build one of those." I did not doubt it.

CHAPTER

8

Flying in the North

I T WOULD BE impossible to overstate the impact of fog on the Quebec North Shore. The Grand Banks off the coast of Newfoundland, where the chilly Labrador Current meets the much warmer Gulf Stream, is reputed to be one the foggiest places in the world. We experienced much of the spillover from that climatic reality on the coast for much of the year, particularly in the summer.

I do remember one time in July 1968 when fog grounded three floatplanes and a helicopter in St. Augustine, Quebec. A Bermuda High pumped warm, moist air over the Gulf of St. Lawrence, effectively locking the 200-mile coastline and its villages from Natashquan to the Strait of Belle Isle in a dungeon of fog. Visibility shrunk to a few hundred yards and the ceiling to fifty feet. However, just three or four miles inland, the curtain of fog lifted as dramatically as the front curtain of a theater to reveal beautifully clear conditions with warm sun and visibility of thirty miles or more.

I was flying from Labrador to St. Augustine when I saw that a fog bank had formed on the Quebec North Shore. I decided to fly south, follow the St. Augustine River to the line of fog, and land in a lake to wait for conditions to clear. It was a beautiful, sunny, and clear trip, flying at low level at 100 knots from the Grenfell Hospital site in North West

River, Labrador, over the snowy peaks of the Mealy Mountains to the headwaters of the St. Augustine River, through the extraordinary river valley, and finally to the Laurentian Plateau, where there were no survey or power lines, fishing camps, or any other sign of human habitation. It is a breathtaking and primeval sight that looks much as it did at the end of the Ice Age.

Twenty miles north of St. Augustine, I discovered that the fog bank ended very close to the village. The top of the fog bank was 1,500 feet, so I climbed over it and continued to fly south until I was sure I was over St. Augustine. I had spotted telegraph poles about four miles north of the village just in front of the bank of fog. People below could hear my aircraft engine overhead. Although I was flying above the fog where it was clear, it appeared to those on the ground that I was flying through the fog. I returned north to the telegraph line, landed on the river, and slowly taxied downstream. The fog was so thick that I could barely see more than 200 feet ahead of the nose, but I kept my left wingtip near the riverbank and knew from past trips that there were no shoals, rocks, or rapids there. I kept on going until I reached the floatplane dock at St. Augustine.

I was greeted by a crowd of amazed and incredulous villagers that included the pilots of the grounded floatplanes and helicopter. The latter thought I had committed a fearfully reckless act in flying through the impenetrable fog. I quickly explained how I'd gotten into town, but some remained unconvinced.

Just then, a local nurse pushed through the group of men on the dock and told me she had patients who needed to be evacuated to the hospital at Blanc Sablon. There were nine patients waiting in a row, including an Innu baby and a boy who had a two-inch spoon fish lure taped to the side of his face. A spoon lure looks like the inside of a tablespoon and has three very sharp hooks dangling from the bottom. Two of those hooks had pierced the side of his ear, so his mother taped the fishing lure right to the side of his head. I told the nurse that I would probably not be able to land on the lake at Blanc Sablon because of the fog but could likely find an opening on the St. Paul's River. The patients could then be transported from the river by boat to Blanc Sablon. I also explained that I could only take three people at a time in the floatplane so I would have to make three separate trips.

Then the most remarkable thing happened. The patients and their families talked among themselves. They did not draw straws or leave the selection to chance or even ask the nurse to decide the order of evacuation. They effectively engaged in their own form of triage and agreed to send the sickest and youngest first. So the Innu baby and his mother and the teenager with the spoon lure came first. I was so impressed by their selflessness and consideration of the most vulnerable. They were all in need of medical care.

With the first trip, I taxied back upriver to the telegraph line just beyond the fog where flying conditions were perfect. I was able to land visually at the north end of the lake at Blanc Sablon and the patients were loaded aboard the plane. I made three trips between Blanc Sablon and St. Augustine that day and each time I arrived for the next three patients, everyone at the dock, from the villagers to the downed pilots, became more bewildered. The fog at the dock was so thick that it seemed impossible to the pilots that taxiing a few miles upriver was all that was needed to break into the clear. People believe what they want to believe and many chose to believe that Mr. Bryan could see through the fog. Not so.

I rarely flew through fog in all my years of flying, but have done so when I could climb clear of the fog by flying straight up through it on instruments. On the warmer days of summer, when fog hugs the coastline and the sky is clear overhead, the stratus layer is from ground level to 2,000 feet. To climb successfully through fog, it is obviously essential to avoid any obstructions, such as hills or towers. Whenever I inadvertently flew into fog, I would carefully climb straight out without turning or making any other maneuvers. The most dangerous move a pilot can attempt in fog is to make a 180-degree turn at low altitude. It is possible to lose altitude without realizing it and the flight can end in disaster if a wingtip touches the water and the aircraft cartwheels and disintegrates. There have been many tragic accidents in many parts of the world when a pilot miscalculated the distance to the water.

People of the north had different reactions to flying in an airplane. One day I received a radio call from Nain in Labrador from Father Frans Peters, the Flemish Oblate priest who started the first school in Davis Inlet, one of two Innu communities in Labrador. An Innu named Francois had shot himself accidently in the hand with a .22 rifle. The puncture wound had sealed and become infected and his lower arm was turning black with gangrene. Francois needed to be taken to the IGA (Grenfell) hospital at North West River, 250 miles south.

I picked up Francois, who seemed very nervous. During the two-and-a-half-hour flight, he never took his eyes off the ground. He seemed to be studying the landscape. Two days after we arrived, I visited him at the hospital. Dr. Anthony "Tony" Paddon, the skilled surgeon and son of the founder of the hospital, the legendary Dr. Harry L. Paddon, had operated on Francois and saved his arm. I mentioned to another visiting Innu that Francois had seemed to be watching the ground for the entire airplane trip south. He asked Francois why he did that, and Francois explained in Innu-aimun (the Innu language) that he was simply paying attention to every mile of muskeg forest, rock, and tundra so that, in the event of bad weather or engine failure, he would be able to walk out. These members of the Innu Nation bands thought nothing of walking hundreds of miles, even while suffering from a grievous wound.

That sort of practicality was endemic on the coast among everyone, not just the Innu and Inuit. I met a remarkable nurse in Nain, Labrador—Dorothy Maud Jupp, whom everyone called Miss Jupp. She worked for many years at the IGA nursing station in Nain and after retirement wrote a book about her experiences called *A Journey of Wonder & Other Writings*. Miss Jupp was a woman of impeccable training, strength, and courage. She was also tough enough to survive the rigors of life in Nain, including the care of local people suffering from massive starvation after World War II.

Whenever I visited, she was hospitable and gracious, but it was very clear that she was in charge. She was a veritable encyclopedia on Nain and its history. I not only admired her strength of character but often found her intimidating. One day Bob Schmon Jr., Laurie Cox, and I arrived in Nain at 11:30 a.m., just in time for lunch, after a 150-mile flight from the George River. It was raining and the wind blew at twenty knots out of the northeast. There was little shelter in the lee of the wharf. We tied up the plane behind a fishing boat and a local fisherman rowed us ashore.

We were hungry and cold, and happily anticipated a home-cooked hot meal at the Nain nursing station. When dinner was served, my plate held a boiled potato in questionable condition, tough-looking carrot sticks, a rather sad turnip, and an ugly piece of bear meat the color of a hockey puck. Bear meat has a well-deserved reputation for being next to inedible, though some hunters say a bear that feeds on vegetation tastes much better than one that feeds on fish. Presented with a hunk of tough bear meat, I nearly gagged.

But Miss Jupp was watching me, so I politely tried to get some of it down. Laurie Cox was much more accustomed to boiled game than I was but he was also struggling to eat it. Bobby Schmon took tiny bites and pushed the rest of his food into a single pile, apparently to make it less conspicuous. When Miss Jupp looked away, I stuck my bear meat into my pocket, a deft maneuver I had practiced and mastered in my grade school lunch room when presented with liver, which I loathed. Miss Jupp noticed my plate was nearly clean and said, "Now, my son, you will have some more bear meat," to which I quickly replied, "Oh, one portion is sufficient for me, Miss Jupp, but I believe that Laurie Cox would like more!" If Laurie had had a baseball bat in hand at that moment, he would have clubbed me. Miss Jupp promptly shoveled another piece of bear meat onto Laurie's plate.

When we returned to the plane, the wind had picked up to twenty knots and the rain had reduced visibility to a mile. I remember pulling crackers and marmalade from the survival kit before taking off. After a two-and-a-half-hour flight, we headed toward Goose Bay, where the weather had improved. We landed on a lake, unpacked our dehydrated food, lit a fire, and prepared one of the best-tasting meals I can ever remember.

In the fall of 1963, I tried to fly every day except when grounded by fog or high wind. But keeping my 1962 Cessna 185 filled with 100-octane fuel was difficult. The fuel used by most of the mail and passenger float-planes, the Cessna 100s, the de Havilland Beavers, and the Otters, was 80-octane. I had 100-octane fuel shipped by the freight boat that made weekly rounds of the villages on the Lower North Shore. When I could not find sealed drums of 100-octane, I bought empty drums in Sept-Iles and filled them with fuel for shipment to the coast.

The old barrels were often contaminated with water, dirt, and rust. I used a rigid system of filtering fuel through chamois and felt filters and drained fuel from the bottom of the tanks regularly, but some contamination often ended up in the Cessna 185 wing tanks.

I took off from Harrington Harbour on November 6, 1963, for a quick trip to Kegaska with my wife, Faith, my six-year-old daughter Kerry, and fisheries officer Reuben Evans. It was a beautiful day at the start of the eighty-mile trip. But suddenly, at 900 feet over Washicoutai Point, 20 miles east of Kegaska, the engine quit without warning. The southwest wind ruled against landing on the sea on the windward side of the point, so I turned back to the leeward side and landed without power near Little Gull Island, a landmass of less than two acres that is little more than a mound of smooth rock and moss.

I climbed out onto the floats and paddled the plane into the tiny cove, then radioed Kegaska to inform Les Foreman of our predicament. It was an hour before sundown, too late for anyone to come to our rescue that night. I told Les we would pitch a tent and stay there for the night, but the next day, we would need 15 gallons of 100-octane fuel. Meanwhile, I drained the tanks, the sumps, and the sediment bowls to eliminate the water and dirt in the system.

Alphonse Jennis at nearby Musquaro had heard my mayday signal and directly summoned his nephew Armond and set off for Little Gull Island by boat. They arrived after dark. By that time, we had pitched the tent, pulled out the survival gear from the plane, and built a drift-wood fire. Little Kerry thought it was a great adventure. When the plane engine quit, she displayed no concern. Reuben Evans reacted to the dead engine with an alarmed "Uh-oh, Uh-oh!" Kerry was completely calm and asked, "Are you all right, Mr. Evans? Do you need a sick bag?"

Alphonse was triumphant upon his arrival. He was the first person to the rescue, well ahead of parishioners from Kegaska. He did not know that I had told them not to attempt a rescue at night because we were happy and safe with our survival gear on Little Gull Island. Alphonse wanted us to all get into his small outboard-motor boat and return to his home at Musquaro, six miles west of Washicoutai Point. The wind had picked up and I knew a small boat heavy with six people would be at risk, so I persuaded Alphonse and Armond to spend the night with us and wait until morning to decide our next move.

That evening around the camp fire, Alphonse entertained us with spine-chilling stories of hunting and trapping in the old days. It snowed during the night but we were snug in our sleeping bags in our tent. The next day, friends arrived with the fresh fuel and we continued on our way to Kegaska.

Alphonse was a special, much loved character with a generosity of spirit and resilience so typical of people on the coast. I was grateful to Alphonse and told him I wanted to repay him for the trouble he went through in trying to rescue us, but he would have none of that. I persisted and finally he agreed to let me fly him and Armond back to their trapper's camp, forty miles north of Musquaro. I made four round trips with his winter gear ten days later, just before the winter freeze-up. His camp was a classic trapper's camp: a small one-room cabin with moss chinked between the seams of the logs for insulation. It had two small windows and a tiny door, about three-feet high and just wide enough for Alphonse and Armond to squeeze through. Bears often tried to raid the camp in their absence and they were too big to get through that small door.

Alphonse played the accordion and was one of the premier musicians on the Quebec North Shore. About eight years after my Little Gull Island incident, I officiated at a wedding in Kegaska. Alphonse was invited as a special guest with his accordion. I flew up to a fishing camp five miles up the Musquaro River where Alphonse worked as a summer guardian and camp manager to give him a ride to the wedding. When we landed in Kegaska, Alphonse stepped out the door of the aircraft, sat on the step across the float struts, and played his accordion. We taxied to the crowded floatplane dock where friends and wedding guests awaited our arrival. It was a special moment of festive joy.

The Reverend John Burke was another memorable North Shore character. I was assigned to serve St. Clement's West, the portion of the Quebec North Shore east of La Tabatiere, from Kegaska to Lac Sale. St. Clement's East stretched from St. Augustine east to Bradore and was the domain of Father Burke. I was always called Mr. Bryan; Father Burke was old school and preferred to be addressed as Father in the tradition followed by Anglo-Catholics and Roman Catholic priests. He was a staunch Anglo-Catholic of great discipline with a no-nonsense approach to doctrine and worship. For example, altar candles were not used in Mutton Bay, a choice he viewed as a sacrilege. Whenever he visited Mutton Bay to cover for the resident priest, he would promptly light candles on the altar. This created great consternation in the village but he would not be deterred from following practices he believed right and proper.

One day in the summer of 1963, while visiting Father Burke, I anchored the Cessna 185 a few hundred feet offshore in front of the village. There was no wharf at St. Paul's River at that time. Within an hour of my arrival, the wind picked up from the southwest. I glanced out at the plane and the anchor seemed to be holding. Father Burke wanted to show me some church repairs so I accompanied him into the church. He was wearing his cassock, his usual attire even for walking around the village. He also favored a traditional black biretta. Just as the heavy church doors closed behind us, someone banged hard on the door. A young lad about thirteen years old burst in. Breathless, he tried to deliver a message but Father Burke stopped him and ordered him to first remove his hat in church.

The boy obeyed and removed his cap but he was so agitated, he could not speak. He stammered and struggled and could not convey the message to us. Father Burke snapped, "Has the cat got your tongue?" which only made the boy more self-conscious and distressed. At this point, the boy turned and pointed through the door. I instinctively thought of the airplane and broke into a run. Father Burke was right behind me but he paused on the church steps to light a cigarette.

The Cessna was dragging anchor in a thirty-knot wind and was just about to come ashore. I raced to the rocks, plunged into the water, and grabbed the spreader bars between the plane's floats just before they made contact with the rocks. I was in water up to my chest and realized right away that I would not be able to hold the floatplane against the wind. Then, suddenly, Father Burke was beside me. His cigarette stuck out at a jaunty angle from his mouth as his cassock floated around him like the petals of a flower. Together, we saved the aircraft.

John Burke had a well-earned reputation for being tough and physically strong. He never shrank from a physical challenge. He was also creative and developed an airboat with an airplane engine and propeller to get around during the ice breakup. It did not work as well as he hoped but it was a good try. Father Burke was a chain smoker. His addiction to nicotine led to a special rescue mission in the spring of 1964.

At the end of April 1964, I had been on the Quebec North Shore for the longest stretch of time since I first came north. It was time for a family vacation and my Cessna 185 was due to go in for its annual inspection. I did not return to Quebec until the third week in May with my brother-in-law Lawton Lamb, who was going to help me reinstall the floats on the plane. I enticed Lawton on a trip to Rapide Lake with the promise of great fishing.

The "spring" warm up can be teasing and misleading in the North. The temperature at night dropped 20 degrees, so any melting that took place during the gradually warmer days quickly refroze overnight. It was almost too cold to fly on floats. At every water takeoff, freezing spray dulled the control surfaces. The northern ice began to move into the Strait of Belle Isle by mid-May, so massive icebergs and ice pans jammed every square foot of water from St. Augustine sixty miles across to Ferolle Point, Newfoundland.

Father Burke had left two weeks earlier for a visit to Greenly Island, a rocky island in the Strait of Belle Isle that held a lighthouse. Greenly Island became famous when the first plane to cross the Atlantic from east to west, *The Bremen*, landed there on April 13, 1928, in the most publicized flight in history. It was a tremendous achievement at the time because a number of pilots had tried and failed—many lost their lives attempting to fly across the Atlantic Ocean from the east. Ice conditions can change rapidly in the springtime and Father Burke got stuck on the island, and he ran out of cigarettes. He was desperate to get off the island and when he heard I had returned from vacation, he radioed for a rescue in order to return to St. Paul's River. He asked me to bring along two cartons of cigarettes and assured me there was plenty of open water to land and take off.

My brother-in-law and I flew over the pack ice at 500 feet on May 23. Lawton had piloted planes for years but told me it was the most frightening hour he had ever spent in an airplane. We saw nothing but jagged broken ice the entire trip. A forced landing would have been life threatening. Ice pans were jumbled together, tilted on their sides in ragged forbidding chunks. There were very few level spots on the ice longer than fifty feet. Had there been an emergency, we never would have been able to land safely.

We finally approached Greenly Island and it was chock-a-block completely iced in. The short space of open water of the day before had disappeared, and there was not enough clear water to make a cup of tea. There was no way we could land. We radioed to the lighthouse keeper, my friend, Ches Thomas, and told him we would not be picking up Father Burke. Father Burke was sorry not to be rescued, but he wanted his cigarettes. He stood next to the lighthouse in his cassock with his arms outstretched waiting for the drop. Lawton questioned the sanity of such a "rescue" mission. He shook his head in disbelief, knowing we had to fly back over the ice-choked Strait of Belle Isle and was nonplussed when darkness descended about forty miles and twenty minutes short of Harrington Harbour. Fortunately, the water at Harrington was clear of ice. We used the lights from oil lamps in the houses on the harbor to guide us safely to a landing.

I had another risky mission when asked to pick up a young man suffering from what was described to me as a mental collapse at Shekatika, a settlement east of St. Augustine. The young bachelor had been courting a woman and she had spurned him. He was devastated and threatened to kill himself and others. A shotgun and box of shells went missing from his house.

Only about 25 people lived in the settlement at that time and they feared for their lives. Dr. Marcoux in Blanc Sablon asked me to pick up the unhappy man and bring him back to the hospital there. When I first circled over the settlement, I saw the six houses and the green roof of a schoolhouse. There was not a person in sight. Gordon Kippen was with me and we landed and taxied up to a large rock jutting from the shore. As we came alongside, a man appeared. I had a feeling he was the disturbed patient.

I could see faces peering from behind curtains, someone crouched behind scrub bushes and others partially hidden around the corners of the houses. I asked him, "Is everything all right around here?" He replied that everyone was fine and asked what he could do for me. I introduced myself and said his name. While he appeared distraught, he insisted that there was nothing to worry about and he appeared to calm down when I spoke gently with him.

Then I left Gordon with the young man and made the rounds of the houses to gather information. While no one wanted any harm to come to the young man, the residents were apprehensive and fearful. When I asked him if he would accompany me to Blanc Sablon, he became indignant. I realized that it would take some time to persuade him to come with us so I decided Gordon and I would spend the night at the settlement.

A resident promised to keep an eye on the man and tell us if he headed to the area where he had hidden his shotgun and shells. Gordon and I had no supper and spent a restless night sleeping under the desks at the schoolhouse. I hardly slept a wink. The next morning, we were very hungry and walked to the house of the young woman so admired by the disturbed gentleman. An elderly woman graciously offered us a breakfast of gull eggs.

After breakfast, I spoke again to the young man who was very determined to stay put. I told him that Doctor Marcoux was worried about him, cared about him, and wanted to help him. This seemed to get through and he finally agreed to come with us.

There was a heartrending and emotional departure from the settlement as his family and neighbors came to bid him farewell. We put him in the back seat and took off. He pointed out trails on the ground where he set his rabbit snares or shot ducks. By the time we arrived on the lake at Blanc Sablon 45 minutes later, he seemed relaxed. Doctor Marcoux met us. He put his hands on the young man's shoulders and greeted him by name. I was touched by the doctor's gentle and caring manner.

That afternoon, Gordon and I flew to Lac Rapide at Sept-Iles, following the medical plane that was carrying the patient. I was horrified when two RCMP officers hauled the young man off the medical plane and put him in a straitjacket just moments after we landed on Lac Rapide. My protestations were in vain. I will never forget that sad boy looking at me, beseeching my help, while a nearby official politely reminded me that if I interfered, I would be arrested. We did not learn until later that government officials intended to take the young to a mental health hospital in Montreal against Dr. Marcoux's wishes. The report of his threat with the shotgun had led the RCMP from Sept-Iles to assume that the patient was dangerous and violent. Fortunately, the young man was able to return home a few years later and carried on with his life with the help of his family and friends. The coast way was to take care of their elderly, their sick, and their own, regardless of the difficulty.

I often flew north of the Quebec North Shore to Labrador, where I met many of the Inuit people who displayed a hardiness and pioneering spirit I found worthy of emulation. One of those admirable people was Johnny May.

I met Johnny May in 1961. He had been born with a congenitally short left arm but this did not slow him down in any way. His parents were Bob and Jean. Bob May grew up in Colorado and came to Fort Chimo in Ungava Bay during World War II, where he met Jean, the daughter of an Inuit. After the war, Bob and his family helped develop a salmon fishing camp called Arctic Anglers on the George River, the first Atlantic salmon sport fishing camp in the far north.

Johnny grew up to become a skilled naturalist and pilot; his air service in Kuujjuaq (known then as Fort Chimo) became the most successful bush pilot operation in the area. He had extraordinary adventures that time and again showed how quickly a routine flight can become dangerous. He once flew into Port Burwell, Northwest Territories, north of the northern tip of Labrador, with the Christmas mail for the Inuit settlement on Christmas Eve. After landing on the saltwater ice, he decided to stay for the night rather than risk flying in the dark. The local Inuit directed him to a cove to tie down the ski plane for the night. They did not realize the ice was not strong enough to support the Noorduyn Norseman, a Canadian single-engine ski plane that could carry seven people. As Johnny taxied his plane into the cove, the ice gave way and the aircraft collapsed into the water. The wings on top of the ice kept the plane from sinking to the bottom of the harbor but the fuselage was under water and Johnny was trapped. As the cabin flooded with water, he left the cockpit, grabbed an ax from the cabin and fought to break out, but the water forced him back into the cockpit. He made a valiant final effort to exit through the pilot window on the left side of the cockpit. Johnny is thin and he was able to wedge himself through the small window. The top of his fur parka emerged through the broken ice. The Inuit on the scene spotted the parka, grabbed it by the fur ruff, and yanked him through the hole in the ice. They took him by snowmobile to Sam Ransom and his wife, Agnes, the local Department of Northern Affairs (DNA) workers. Johnny arrived frozen stiff in a sitting position. The Ransoms cut his iced clothing off his body, and a few hours later, Johnny was enjoying Christmas Eve dinner with the Ransoms.

There was another close call in September 1972. I flew back from the George River to Kuujjuaq with Johnny, Peggy and David Rockefeller, their daughter Eileen, and my wife, Faith, after a salmon fishing trip on the George River. Their son Richard, who was a legendary volunteer for four straight summers in the 1960s and early '70s in Harrington Harbour, flew back to Harrington with Rick Bullock in the Helio. We took off from the Mays' camp in Pyramid Hills in a twin-engine Beechcraft 18 on floats. Johnny was flying the plane and I sat in the right seat. We carried five passengers, luggage and a load of salmon and caribou. We were at "gross weight" at takeoff, but the twin Beechcraft left the water effortlessly and we climbed to 1,000 feet for the 100-mile journey.

At least five times during the one-hour flight the left engine started running rough. Each time Johnny put the nose down and started a gentle left descending turn toward a lake or river. After a few seconds, the engine ran smoothly and we returned to course. There was no way that twin engine plane on floats would have been able to maintain altitude if one engine quit, but I felt confident Johnny would be able to make a safe landing. When we arrived at Kuujjuaq at the floating dock on Lake Stewart, I was relieved.

I made a huge mistake with my friend Gordon Kippen in the winter of 1972. Gordon, who had been my able and loyal pilot's helper in 1963 and 1964, asked me to fly him north of his home in Kegaska one day to shoot caribou. He had heard that a number of caribou were in the area and he was allowed to shoot two for his family for the year. We spotted fifteen caribou from the air on a small pond about a mile from a lake where I was able to land on the snow. We put on snowshoes and made a lengthy trek through the bush and up and over some hills to get to where they were foraging.

Without delay, Gordon shot the two caribou he was allowed. He was pleased to have finally been successful after a few trips into the bush that winter on which he had come up empty-handed. With an ax and knife he began to butcher the animals to prepare the meat for transport back to Kegaska. I realized that the small pond next to the caribou was big enough for me to land safely. To avoid two or three treks back to the plane over a mile of difficult terrain with a heavy load of caribou meat, I proposed to fly the plane directly to the pond where we could load it up. He asked me to first fly back to Kegaska to pick up Fred Mansbridge as a helper and a tarpaulin to protect the floor of the plane from the caribou quarters.

It took me about thirty minutes to walk back to the aircraft and another twenty minutes to fly to Kegaska. It took another hour to find Fred and get the gear. I had been very careful to mark the spot where I took off and flew over Gordon on the way out to pinpoint his exact location. But I did not anticipate the snow squalls that developed in the two hours since I left him there.

The squalls reduced visibility to a mile, and in some places, a half a mile. As I proceeded north, land forms blurred and I knew it would be difficult to relocate Gordon. I was deeply worried thinking of having left a friend stranded in the bush with no survival gear. Gordon had a knife, an ax, a cigarette lighter, and some cigarettes. He may have been able to build a fire, but the weather forecast for later that evening called for three days of bad weather. I could not recognize anything on the ground but I held to my compass course and Fred and I peered out the side windows of the Helio looking for any sign of Gordon.

Suddenly, I thought I saw some dark objects on the snow below out of the corner of my eye. I made a turn and there was Gordon. He did not wave his hands because he assumed I knew my position and knew exactly where he was standing. He was completely unaware of the desperate situation that was developing. I was grateful to be able to land next to him and pack the meat on the plane and take off quickly for Kegaska with Gordon and Fred on board.

I learned an important lesson that day. As the pilot it was my responsibility to bring Gordon safely back home. It was a terrible mistake to leave him alone in the bush without proper survival equipment. It is easy to get casual about the fickle and ferocious nature of weather in the wilderness after years of living and working in the North. But that day, I understood that I had to always assume a defensive position and never take for granted the unpredictable sub-Arctic climate. There were certain immutable things about life in the region. The dangers posed by nature in its pristine state were part of life in the North.

When I still felt very much like a rookie bush pilot, I had the distinct honor of meeting a British military legend. Charles Frederick Algernon Portal, also known as First Viscount Portal of Hungerford or Lord Portal, was a genuine war hero. He was a pilot and then a flight and squadron commander in World War I, flying light bombers over the Western Front, and during World War II he was the commander in chief of the Bomber Command. He was the principal advocate of bombing German strategic targets. He was a critically important figure during World War II. In many of the photographs of key Allied summits during the war, he was standing with Churchill and Roosevelt and other dignitaries. A bronze statue of Air Marshall Portal stands next to those of Churchill and famed Royal Air Force Commander Hugh Dowding on the banks of the Thames near Parliament in London. I met him because he loved to fish for Atlantic salmon and he had become a great friend of T. B. "Happy" Fraser, the president and general manager of the Atlantic Salmon Association of Canada, and other men who fished for Atlantic salmon at the Etamamiou River near Harrington Harbour.

In July 1962, Happy, a friend whom I could never deny, summoned me from Harrington Harbour and told me that Lord Portal needed my help. He lectured me on Portal's place in history and how he was one of the great patriots who helped save England from Nazi tyranny. The esteemed guest needed a lift from the Quebec North Shore across the wilderness of Labrador to Cartwright. In those years it was difficult to get connecting flights and without a floatplane, it might take as long as a week for Lord Portal to get to his fishing spot.

When I met him, he was 69 years old. I was 31 and still had a great deal to learn about the region. But I felt honored to do a favor for such a great hero. At the time, my pilot's helper was Martin Love, a sixteen-year-old from Greensboro, North Carolina, who had not flown more than twenty miles inland from the Gulf of St. Lawrence. The three of us took off from Etamamiou in the direction of Goose Bay on a familiar route. I followed the Mecatina River upstream 130 miles to Minipi Lake, then set a compass course directly toward Cartwright. This course would allow me to intercept the Eagle River, which I would follow east-northeast for another ninety minutes to Lord Portal's destination at the mouth of the river, near Cartwright. However, on this second leg of the trip, we saw nothing but thousands of small muskeg lakes that bore little resemblance to anything on my chart.

At one point, I calculated I had two hours and fifteen minutes of fuel aboard. I started to worry and then spotted a tiny stream and a rapid that appeared to be flowing northeast. Within a few miles, the stream got bigger and a number of tributaries entered the main stream. I realized it was likely the headwaters of the Eagle River and felt relieved. Just then I felt a tap on my shoulder. I turned and Lord Portal's penetrating eyes fixed squarely on mine.

"Do you know where you are, lad?" he asked. With great relief and joy, I banked the plane forty degrees to the left, pointed down and said, "There is the Eagle River. We will be landing in one hour and twenty minutes." The very idea of getting lost in the wild with Lord Portal aboard horrified me. Lord Portal sat back and relaxed.

We landed a few miles below the falls where the Canadian Air Force Camp at the Eagle River was located. There were three houses in a clearing by the edge of the river where I tied up the plane next to some cod fishing boats. I went to the first house to see if I could get some refreshments for my special guest. The woman who answered the door saw my clerical collar and assumed I was a preacher intent upon proselytizing her and her family. I explained that I was an Anglican clergyman from the North Shore of the Gulf of St. Lawrence and had a distinguished man and war hero, Lord Portal, on my plane. He would enjoy some tea. She grudgingly said, "I guess he's no better than the rest of us." Without another word, she filled an empty forty-ounce gin bottle with coffee that had the unappetizing look of Mississippi River flood waters. She mixed in sugar and cream and handed it to me with half of a "bun of bread."

I carried the coffee and bread back to the plane. Lord Portal took one look at the gin bottle and said he was not thirsty after all. Before too long, the Royal Canadian Air Force outboard arrived to take him on his way to the salmon fishing camp.

Martin and I refueled at nearby Cartwright and then headed back to Harrington Harbour. I pitched the coffee concoction and bread out the window somewhere over the wild. I aimed for a big boulder with the gin bottle and the payload did not come close to the target. I was relieved that my distinguished guest who had played such a strategic role in wartime bombing was not around to witness my miss.

CHAPTER

9

Birth of the Quebec
Labrador Foundation

WHEN I first began to work on the Quebec Lower North Shore, I still had a full-time job as chaplain at the Choate School. Choate had been preparing young men for college since the end of the nineteenth century; another decade would pass before it merged with its sister school, Rosemary Hall, to become co-ed in 1971. The school had many distinguished alumnae, including John F. Kennedy, class of 1935, then the newly elected president of the United States. Choate was considered one of the most prestigious boarding schools in the world. The contrast between the lives of boys on the bucolic campus of Choate in Wallingford, Connecticut, and those of the boys of the North was as vast as the geographic distance between them.

The children of the North Shore received a rudimentary education in one- or two-room schoolhouses led by dedicated teachers whose own educations were often quite limited. Most of the teachers were born and raised in the communities where they taught. The teachers held certificates but many had never received more than an eighth-grade education. Disciplinary practices at my daughter Sarah's small school in Harrington Harbour harkened back to the "old days" and involved a rap on the knuckles with a ruler or a yank on the ear, though Sarah was spared this discipline given her status as the daughter of the minister. These non-university trained teachers did a remarkable job despite limited resources because they were thorough and conscientious, and they truly cared about the children. Boys and girls learned the basics: reading, writing, and arithmetic, and perhaps a bit of Canadian history. There was only so much a single teacher could do, however, to meet the needs of a group of children of varying ages and abilities in the same classroom. Schooling essentially ended by the age of thirteen for these children. Indeed, most of the one-room schoolhouses only went to the fifth or sixth grade. There was not a single secondary school in the entire region. While the outside world and economy were changing in a way that put a premium on higher education and specialized training, there was still not much need for extensive book learning in the North. There were few jobs available outside of cod fishing and trapping. Most boys would follow their fathers into the fishing business. Their sisters followed the example of their mothers, who helped process the fish, kept home and hearth together, and raised the children. The days had a natural rhythm that stayed the same year after year beginning with wash day on Monday and ending with the Saturday night baths and Sunday, the day for church and rest. Women baked bread on Tuesday and did other chores weekly on specific days. Their houses were immaculately clean at all times. The few formally educated people in the region—medical doctors, boat captains, ministers, airplane pilots, and government officials—generally came from the outside. Many of the doctors and ministers hailed from other parts of the British Commonwealth, such as England, New Zealand, or Australia. But just as there were children of pioneers in the Wild West of the United States who read voraciously by candlelight and yearned to learn more about the outside world, this basic human impulse existed here as well.

By contrast, the expectations and opportunities for the boys at Choate were unlimited. Most came from upper middle class families who assumed, accurately, that their sons would grow up to become executives on Wall Street, leaders of government, and administrators of the nation's top medical and educational institutions. It was well known at

Choate that John F. Kennedy had been a very bright but erratic student when enrolled there. He was known for being a prankster rather than a scholar and founded a club called the "Mucker's Club" for himself and his like-minded antic friends. But Choate had a powerful influence on Kennedy. JFK's headmaster at Choate, the Reverend George C. St. John, often said to his students, it's "not what Choate does for you, but what you can do for Choate." This is believed to have inspired one of the most legendary quotes from John Kennedy's Inaugural Address: "Ask not what your country can do for you, ask what you can do for your country."

I was awed by the vibrancy and resourcefulness of the children of the Quebec North Shore, and struck that they had so few options for schooling and the extra-curricular activities I so enjoyed as a boy. I would fly to Quebec from Wallingford, Connecticut, where boys thrived in a stimulating and enlivening environment, both academic and athletic, and arrive on the coast to see boys and girls who were the same age, often with the same intrinsic talents and intellects, but none of the same opportunities. Even in the summer, their outdoor activities were restricted by tradition and the environment. None of them, for example, ever learned to swim. The water temperature of the sea was simply too cold. They might play around at low tide in the coves where their fathers kept the boats but there was nothing systemic or organized. There were no Boys and Girls Clubs, YMCAs or community recreation centers, no organized sports, hockey rinks, or baseball fields. The children invented their own games, as children always do. They played traditional games like gun-balls, a game similar to jacks using actual lead shot, and rounders, played with a sponge rubber ball and a stick. I remembered the fun I had during my own childhood summers at the local swimming club on Long Island and at day camps with organized sports and arts and crafts. I longed to share some of what I had been given as a young person.

Inspired to do something for the children, I brought my first three teenaged volunteers up north for the summer in 1961: Wiley Reynolds, Godfrey Kaufmann, and Sandy Jones. I could only bring one at a time with me on the floatplane so the other two stayed behind at Rapide Lake while the designated rider took turns flying up and down the coast with me. Each time we stopped, the boys invariably organized some sort of a game with the local children. I hoped to turn these impromptu games into a real program. We called our interns "the volunteers" and the people of the coast called them "the students." By the following summer, 1962, I had twelve volunteers and set about finding a way to provide some organized fun for the children of the North Shore. Faith's cousin, Clare Tweedy McMorris, was the first female volunteer.

The idea of using volunteers was not original. My model was the International Grenfell Association (IGA), still called the Grenfell Mission by locals. The IGA had been relying upon volunteers to supplement its staff for decades. These volunteers built and rebuilt wharfs and replaced the roofs at the nursing stations and hospitals. They also supported the crew on the IGA's supply boat, *The Nellie Cluett,* and later *The Lady Grenfell.* Volunteerism was coming back in popularity. In the United States on March 1, 1961, President Kennedy issued an executive order creating the Peace Corps, a force of American volunteers who went overseas to educate and bring potable water and new agricultural techniques to some of the poorest people on the planet. I hoped to do something similar on a more modest scale, drawing upon high school and college students in the United States whom I knew would seize the opportunity to travel to this faraway spot and, I was certain, would learn and grow from the experience as they provided a vital service to these children.

I found a key ally in Dr. Gordon Waddell Thomas, a surgeon and the longtime superintendent of the International Grenfell Association. I first met him in the summer of 1962 when I carried a patient from Harrington Harbour to St. Anthony in my floatplane. Our friendship clicked right away and continued until his death in 1996. Born in Ottawa and educated at McGill University, Dr. Thomas came to St. Anthony in 1946 to work as the medical officer and surgeon for the International Grenfell Association. He was appointed executive director and surgeon-in-chief in 1960 and held that position until 1977, when he became honorary chairman of the board for the last twenty years of his life. He not only understood my vision for the children of the Quebec North Shore but also agreed that it was important and offered the assistance of the IGA.

We drew upon the existing IGA infrastructure in the region and he provided some essential funding as the volunteer program got underway and then expanded over the next few years.

Gordon Thomas was a devout Christian and his life embodied the Christian spirit. Our friendship was bolstered by a shared love of trout and salmon fishing, ice hockey, and aviation. Gordon was interested in the Quebec Labrador Foundation's approach to summer volunteer services, youth programs, and day camps. In May 1967, I was appointed special assistant to the superintendent. The QLF summer program continued under the Grenfell umbrella until 1971, when the QLF was able to run the programs on its own.

I made many medical evacuation trips from the Quebec North Shore to St. Anthony, Newfoundland, in the 1960s and 1970s. Gordon and his wife, Pat, welcomed me into their home whenever a trip to St. Anthony required an overnight stay. During the winter I wore sealskin boots. They provide effective protection against the wet and cold of a Canadian winter but get stiff and need to be soaked in water to loosen up. On one trip, I used the sink in the Thomases' second-floor bathroom to soak my dry boots. While we were enjoying breakfast with Pat and Gordon in their dining room, Pat exclaimed, "What's that noise?" It was the unmistakable sound of running water. I froze, instantly realizing I had forgotten to turn off the tap in the upstairs bathroom. Water was pouring from the sink and down the carpet of the front stairs to the first floor. I was mortified, but Pat and Gordon comforted me in my anguish; the mistake somehow endeared me to them. The Thomases often regaled their guests with stories of "the waterfall." It became one of their favorite stories.

Gordon and I often discussed the aircraft needs of the IGA. They needed a twin-engine plane for long hauls, often in instrument conditions. It was a major and costly purchase and it took a long time to find a suitable new aircraft. Finally, there was a breakthrough. Lundrigan Equipment, a well-known construction and heavy equipment operator in Newfoundland, put its Rockwell Grand Commander up for sale. Aviation buffs in the International Grenfell Association and I gave the aircraft the once over. In his book, *Sled to Satellite*, Gordon wrote: "I asked for a special meeting of the IGA Board to seek their approval for the purchase, knowing I had to put up a strong case. I brought along Reverend Bob Bryan, 'the flying parson' of the Quebec Labrador Mission who was working with me in setting up a student volunteer program. His own flying experience, his eloquence, enthusiasm about the role of aircraft in the North, and his Yale background helped secure their reluctant approval."

To help close the deal, we flew the Rockwell Grand Commander to Teterboro, New Jersey, the most convenient airport to Manhattan where the IGA board was scheduled to meet. Dr. Thomas and I agreed that the support of Admiral Frank L. Houghton, a retired flag officer of the Royal Canadian Navy who worked as business manager for the International Grenfell Association after his retirement from the military, was crucial to a "yes" vote for acquisition of the Grand Commander. We invited the admiral to come along for the two-hour ride, and he agreed.

The plane was scrupulously prepared for the journey. Beyond the routine mechanical check, the cabin received a special cleaning and a vase of flowers was even placed at the bulkhead. We departed for Teterboro, flying at 9,000 feet. The outside air temperature was ten below zero, but the cabin heater kept the interior at a comfortable 75 degrees. However, 45 minutes into the flight a warning light in the cockpit announced the cabin heater had failed. There was an immediate scramble. We suggested Admiral Houghton lie down on the coach underneath the cabin's two blankets. Dr. Thomas shed his goose-down jacket and the rest of us followed suit, piling our coats on Admiral Houghton, who was then in his late sixties, an older man by the standard of the times. We wanted to do everything we could to make certain the trip was comfortable and enjoyable for him, and we also wanted the Rockwell Grand Commander! Keeping an eye on the admiral's morale, someone jested that it was too bad we did not have access to the in-flight bar to offer Admiral Houghton a brandy or tot of rum to keep him warm. The Lundrigans were known to enjoy a cocktail, and had routinely carried booze in their very elaborate on-plane bar. But Gordon Thomas was a teetotaler and disapproved of drinking. Feeling that the board members of the IGA might be put off by the presence of alcohol on the plane, he had the bar removed before the flight to New Jersey. Despite the lack of fortifying alcohol, the blankets and good cheer did the trick, and when Admiral Houghton arrived at the Union Club he was full of stories about his exciting plane ride and enthusiastically endorsed the Grand Commander purchase. QLF pilot Rick Bullock and his cousin Gus later helped the IGA find a Piper Navaho and then a ten-passenger Piper Chieftain to continue the important twin engine program for the non-profit organization.

The volunteer program was a success for both the people of the North Shore and for the volunteers. At first most of the volunteers were preparatory school students I knew at Choate or came to know through my own contacts at Hotchkiss, Hebron, and other New England preparatory schools. In those years before the expansion of scholarship programs and awareness of the value of diversity in a student body, private school students were mostly the children of the upper economic classes. Most of those young people had little, if any, exposure to a simpler way of life and certainly not to the geographic isolation of the coast.

I felt strongly that the volunteers would benefit from this type of exposure. Seeing children who survived and adjusted in the wild of the North without all of the support and material comfort they enjoyed could only nurture compassion, understanding, and a level of maturity. It might help them appreciate the advantages so many of them took for granted. The program worked better than I could have imagined. Those young students became compassionate leaders in their own time. They never forgot what they learned during those summer internships.

Eventually, the volunteers were drawn from schools and universities all over the United States, Canada, and even England. They were bright, highly motivated and adventurous. They found themselves plunked down in isolated villages and lived with local families whom we supported with a small stipend for room and board. They drew upon their own skills and resourcefulness to run day camps for the children of their village or outpost.

I received a letter in September 1966 from one summer volunteer, Arcy Gilbert, just after he returned to school at Washington College in Chestertown, Maryland. Arcy wrote the letter in long hand on school stationery. He wrote:

Never have I spent a more meaningful summer and made so many wonderful friends. There are times here at college when I sit in my room and the books are two feet high and radios, record players, televisions and guitars are all blaring full blast; and the beer and cigarettes are being passed around and guys dancing and raising Cain, when I stop and wish I were in Canada by a stream talking to a lake trout or in Riney's kitchen or wrestling with the children or taking care of Fred's dogs ... I feel very fortunate and flattered that I perhaps gave the people some knowledge in comparison with the great amount that I learned from them.

It was so gratifying to read that letter. I received many other comments and letters like his over the years.

As for the children of the North, they had great fun with the volunteers, or as they called them "the students." Moreover, the "students" opened for them a window to the outside and through that window the children of the Quebec North Shore saw glimmers of possibilities for themselves. Thus, the recreation program expanded the horizon of their personal ambitions.

In the summer of 1962, we began to sponsor organized sports for the children in each village. We started with a swimming program. The bitterly cold water of the Gulf of St. Lawrence was a hindrance to swimming, but various small ponds were employed for the purpose. In the 1970s, my friend and fellow Hebron board member, Mike Grossman, the owner of Grossman's Lumber, a family business based in New England, suggested we should use aboveground swimming pools. Thanks to Mike's generosity, we purchased several of the pools. Mike was a graduate of Hebron Academy and known for his charitable giving and love of the outdoors.

There was a real need for water safety skills in a region where most of the adult men made a living fishing from the sea. Often when a boat capsized, a fisherman lacked the basic swimming skills needed to save himself. Sadly, this happened far too often, and many friends and young men I knew drowned. Two of Aunt Lizzie's three husbands died by drowning. This problem is not limited to the North. I have been told about children who grew up in South Boston and Dorchester, two neighborhoods right on Boston Harbor, who never learned to swim either. These children did not have the experiences and opportunities available to children from more affluent homes.

The children took to swimming like ducks to water. They learned different swimming strokes, basic lifesaving and survival tactics, and how to dive properly. Those who completed the swimming courses received certificates. We also set up sports teams. The volunteers set up playing fields and taught the rules and regulations of each game. I managed to wrangle some used sports equipment from schools, friends, and relatives. Harrington Harbour kids wore Hotchkiss, Hebron, and Holderness jerseys with the big "H" on the front with great pride. We pulled together baseballs and bats and soccer balls. The children of the North Shore had never used a real soccer ball or baseball bat. The interns set up playing fields and taught the rules and regulations of each game. A handwritten tally of sports equipment for Harrington Harbour dated August of 1966 reads: 49 baseballs, 5 soccer balls, 2 footballs, 5 softballs, 1 basketball, 36 field hockey sticks, 9 baseball bats (2 new), 2 badminton rackets, 9 baseball mitts, 4 pair of hockey shin guards, and 24 mosquito nets.

It did not take too long before we were sponsoring North Shore "Olympic" Summer Games between villages. I became heavily involved in the track and field competition, which included sprints, long jump, cross country running, high jump, and shot put. A love of track and field goes back generations in my family and I had spent a great deal of time on the track at Hotchkiss. During the summer, the parents of the Quebec North Shore children were intently focused on fishing and let their children play independently. The season was short so some families would move onto one of the small islands for the season to be closer to the inshore cod fishery to maximize the seasonal haul. There was great pressure to pull as much cod as possible from the sea during those precious weeks of warmer weather. The family's survival literally depended upon the income from the summer fishing season. But the parents were open to recreational programs. Some parents accepted these organized activities because they carried the imprimatur of the Church. My position as an Anglican priest helped them accept this deviation from the norm. They also enjoyed watching their children competing with others and having so much fun, as any parent would. Furthermore, our modest "Olympic Games" were a wonderful opportunity for entire families to socialize with friends and relatives from different villages and provided a welcome break from the hard work of fishing and salting cod.

I had always loved to sail as a boy and wanted the children of the North Shore to enjoy the same experience. The local fishing boats of an earlier generation had made way under sail. Some still had a mast and sail, but sail or no sail, the handmade wooden boats in the area were working boats, not intended for recreational sailing. I called upon friends and acquaintances, many of them prominent yachtsmen, to donate a number of the classic fiberglass nine-foot Dyer Dhow sailing dinghies in order to set up a junior maritime training program on the coast. Donations came from Emil "Bus" Mosbacher, Jr., a Choate School graduate who was a two-time America's Cup winner as well as the chief of protocol during the Nixon administration, and Frederick E. "Ted" Hood, a world class sailor and sail maker from Marblehead, Massachusetts. The Hovey family donated several boats as well. Chandler "Bus" Hovey was a gifted yachtsman who had a lifelong involvement with America's Cup racing despite contracting multiple sclerosis at the age of thirty. His daughter Nancy worked as a summer intern for QLF. We cobbled together a small fleet and, under the leadership of Henry Miller, a Choate student and avid sailor, the summer interns taught sailing, racing skills, and water survival tactics up and down the coast. We sponsored popular regattas in Harrington Harbour at the end of each summer. A few years later, I managed to secure the donation of a 42-foot sailing sloop. I asked Henry Harding, a Hebron Academy graduate and longtime summer intern and sailing instructor, to sail it up from the Chesapeake Bay to York Harbor, Maine. Another crew, led by my friend Andre Sigourney, a deep-water sailor of some note, sailed it from Maine around Nova Scotia, and into Harrington Harbour. We taught navigation, piloting, and seamanship skills from that boat. The children not only had a fabulous time but acquired skills that would serve them well as adult fishermen.

Hockey is to Canada as baseball is to the United States. It is the official national winter sport and the people of the Quebec North Shore were well aware of professional hockey, though very few ever saw a game. The closest National Hockey League team was 850 miles away in Quebec City. The fishing families had very little extra money for things like ice skates or hockey sticks. The boys would take turns using the few pair of worn moldy skates available in each community, impatiently waiting on the shore for their time on the ice. Some children fashioned hockey sticks from the crooked root of a juniper tree. Despite the lack of equipment, the youngsters headed out in late October as soon as the ice could bear their weight and before the late winter wind and cold and mounds of snow made it challenging to play outside. There was no heavy equipment available to move several feet of snow from the ice to clear space for a hockey rink.

I managed to scrounge the needed hockey equipment from Choate and other schools. Crates of skates arrived from New Haven, Cambridge, Lakeville, Wallingford, and Waterville, Connecticut. Most of the skates were second-hand. There was a motley collection of racing skates with long blades and hard and soft toes, old-fashioned shoes with skate blades that looked like the hull of Admiral Dewey's warship, a pair of skates with curled-up toes like something from the *Arabian Nights* fairy tales, and another gigantic pair of hockey skates that might have been discarded by an Ice Follies clown. The young boys of the North did not mind a bit. They were thrilled to have their own skates.

Our enthusiastic volunteers set up a hockey clinic in the summer and taught the boys how to shoot a puck off a sheet of plywood. Later in the fall, we built the first ice skating rink on the North Shore in Harrington Harbour. The first challenge was getting wood to frame the rink. Uncle Dan Bobbitt, the premier builder in town and owner of a sawmill, offered his services. Uncle Dan and his son Kirby and I took off with a chain saw in Uncle Dan's 26-foot boat powered by a one-cylinder Acadia engine. We motored over to the mouth of the Mecantina River, about six miles east of Harrington. There was a huge waterfall at the mouth of the river. Kirby and I climbed up over the falls with the chain saw and walked up river about half a mile to a stand of spruce trees that were large enough to fell and make the boards. We cut the trees as close as we could to the river and then pushed the logs into the river. They went over the falls and Uncle Dan, waiting down below, hooked a line onto them. Once we got about eight or ten logs, we returned to the boat and towed them to the sawmill. We went through the same routine over and over until we had enough logs to make the walls of a 160- by 70-foot rink. We used a two-horsepower engine to pump water to flood the pond. The sub-freezing temperatures kept the ice solid throughout the winter. We often had to move snow from the rink and build a man-made passage-way, a snow tunnel, just to get to the rink through huge piles of snow.

I loved hockey and played at Yale for four years, but was an undis-tinguished journeyman. In Harrington Harbour, I was a hockey star. I taught the boys how to stick handle and shoot a puck, carve a rink turn, slice down the rink dodging phantom defenders, and slap the puck past an imaginary goaltender. As the season wore on, my players thought I was slowing down but in fact the boys just got better and better. The boys, true Canadians, were hockey naturals and quickly surpassed their coach.

Nearly twenty years later, I had the distinct honor of bringing a true hockey star to the North Shore. Bobby Orr, a native of Parry Sound on Lake Huron's Georgian Bay in Ontario, is one of the greatest ice hockey players of all time. In 1981, he was 43 and had been retired for 13 years. He retired at the age of thirty after twelve memorable seasons, ten playing for the Boston Bruins, because a series of knee injuries had destroyed his left knee. His jersey, number 4, was retired with his decision to leave pro-fessional playing. I met Bobby Orr through Roger Baikie, QLF Canadian director and floatplane pilot who brought Bobby to the Quebec North Shore for his first visit. Bobby is as good a human being as he was a hockey defenseman. For decades, he has been reaching out to those in need, par-ticularly children. His quiet charitable acts are rarely publicized. He agreed to come to the North Shore to run hockey clinics for the children. Bobby was also an avid fisherman and went cod fishing with Laurie Cox and Alfred Bobbitt and trout fishing at Lac Triquet with me. For his first win-ter visit, I picked up Bobby in the Cessna 185 at the airport at Sept-Iles. He was laden with sports equipment and memorabilia he brought along to give to the children. His knee was sore, so I put him in the rear seat to stretch out his leg. This knocked off the plane's weight and balance, factors I had carefully calculated in advance. The weight and placement of passengers and cargo directly affects the operation of the plane. The flight from Sept-Iles to Harrington Harbour was a difficult one because of the extra weight in in the back.

A few days later, when I landed the plane on the river ice at St. Augustine for a day trip, it seemed as though the entire village of 1,000 people was surging toward the aircraft to see the legendary hockey star. I appealed to my friend, a legend in the village, the powerfully built Jack Bursey, to keep the crowd from pressing against the airplane and possibly damaging it. A roar from Jack was enough to push the crowd back a few precious inches.

The scene reminded me of another moment when a jubilant crowd surged toward a hero. Back in 1928, my father had taken my older brothers, Jim, then ten years old, and Bill, then seven, to Roosevelt Field in Garden City, Long Island, not far from the Bryan family home, to watch Charles Lindbergh take off for his historic solo flight across the Atlantic. I had not yet been born. My father received as a gift a copy of the film taken by his friend Clarence Chamberlin, another pioneer aviator, which included newsreel footage of Lindbergh's arrival in Paris. When Lucky Lindy touched down after his incredible feat, thousands of people surged toward *The Spirit of St. Louis,* crashing through a wire fence at Le Bourget Airport in an exuberant throng. I watched that film a thousand times and that thrilling scene was burned into my memory.

When Bobby Orr stepped out of the airplane, the crowd went wild. Snowmobiles roared over the ice toward us. Grown men clamored toward the plane for a glimpse of the sports legend. Young boys literally leapt into the air with excitement. The scene brought back that newsreel memory of Lindbergh. It was remarkably similar. For the next four hours, Bobby Orr responded with patience and kindness to every single person who approached him. He autographed hockey sticks, photographs, arm casts, and even Canadian currency. He skated with the young men in the village and they competed to show off their hockey skills. He demonstrated some of his legendary moves. By the time the sun was setting, Bobby Orr held the heart of St. Augustine.

Bobby Orr came back to the coast several times in both the summer and early winter in the early 1980s to hold hockey clinics for the children. Those children, now grown, still talk about learning hockey moves and tricks from one of the greatest ice defensemen of all time. Each time he came back, he greeted those he had met on earlier visits like old friends with warm embraces and questions about their health, children, and businesses. He took to my friend Laurie Cox on his first visit and when he returned, he traveled miles by snowmobile to see a memorial cross the Cox family had erected for their son Donald, who had died a year earlier when he mistakenly drove his snowmobile off the trail and into the gulf and drowned at the age of sixteen. Donald had died the day before Orr's visit the previous year. Donald was my aircraft ramp chief and had waited in vain when a snowstorm struck Harrington Harbour the evening I was supposed to arrive with Bobby Orr. The next day, Bobby had accompanied me to the Cox's home, where the family was in deep mourning over the loss of their boy. Clara, Donald's mother, had taken to her bed in grief. Bobby Orr gently held her hand and spoke quietly to her.

With the early success of the recreation programs, I began to think about nurturing the leaders of tomorrow and opening up other opportunities for the promising young boys and girls. Local leadership would go a long way toward helping the people of the region preserve their unique culture and determine their own destinies. I was intimately familiar with the practice of sending students away from home to be educated. And while I may have been a bit biased because of my personal experiences, I valued the boarding school education and wanted my young charges on the North Shore to have the same chance as the children of the more economically privileged.

I decided to begin with one boy, Philip Nadeau. Philip was the son of a fisherman from St. Paul's River. He was the oldest of ten children. He had six brothers and three sisters. Phil was a wonderful young man: bright, kind, and ambitious.

I spoke to the headmaster at Choate and he agreed to let Philip take the admissions test required of all potential students to assess their ability and knowledge. Not surprisingly, Philip did not do very well in the test. His intellect, skills, and solid values could not be measured by a traditional academic exercise, but I was sure Philip could one day become a significant leader on the North Shore. I remember picking him up at his family's fishing wharf to take him out to Choate while he was plucking an eider duck for the family dinner. I suspect there was not another boy at Choate who could dress waterfowl with his easy familiarity and skill. On the way off the coast, I took Philip deer hunting on Anticosti Island. Philip shot a deer and his first thought was his family and whether he could get the deer meat to them to supplement their winter food supply. I wrote to Charlie McCormick, the Anticosti game manager, when we returned to Choate and asked him if it would be possible to send a box of deer meat to Philip's family.

Philip enrolled as a first-year student at Choate in September of 1964. In a letter to a friend in La Tabatiere that fall, I wrote, "Philip is off to a good start and although he will have to work very, very hard, I am sure that he will make the grade. He sits in the same pew in Chapel that the late President John Kennedy sat in when he was a boy at Choate School 25 years ago. Now we have to find a boy from La Tabatiere, as well as other communities on the coast, to take this opportunity to continue their education."

Philip did indeed make the grade. He graduated from Choate and earned his college degree at Bowdoin, the renowned liberal arts college in Maine. He grew from a marvelous boy into an impressive man. He returned to his home in St. Paul's River, where he taught school and eventually won election as mayor. He later held a key administrative post in the pulp and paper industry at Kruger Paper Company. He maintained his connection to the Quebec Labrador Foundation and eventually became chairman of the QLF Canadian Board. Philip's younger siblings followed him to boarding school. His younger brothers, Murray, Mel, and Kirby, all attended Hebron along with their cousin Tim. Philip and his siblings set up the QLF Gerald and Hazel Nadeau Scholarship Award in honor of their parents and in gratitude for the start the QLF and its donors gave to them. Philip, our very first scholarship student, fulfilled our fondest dream of cultivating local youngsters who would one day become leaders in their communities.

I founded the Quebec Labrador Foundation in 1960 in order to operate the summer volunteer program, but it later became the vehicle for raising charitable dollars to finance the secondary and trade school educations of the children on the coast. For the first few years, all of the donors came from the United States. My friends and relatives and acquaintances responded to my importuning with grace and generosity. My father-in-law, Dana Storrs Lamb, dedicated the royalties from his nine books on fishing and the outdoors to the fund. Then Canadians joined in. Over the next 50 years, the foundation awarded more than 1,200 scholarships. Our remarkable young men and women became nurses, teachers, businessmen and -women and, as I always hoped, leaders in their communities. We helped train more than thirty pilots. Some did not return permanently to the North Shore. That is to be expected. You cannot offer opportunity to young people and not expect them to follow their own paths. But every single one retained a loyalty and love of the region. Those who eventually moved "outside" returned frequently to visit family and remained engaged and interested in the place that in their hearts will always be "home."

There is a risk for those who come to remote insulated regions to presume that they know best and their way is better. I never felt that way and believed those who are convinced that their personal values and experiences are better than those of others and attempt to foist their way onto others are destined to fail. They also run the risk of destroying a precious and unique culture. From the beginning, I had deep admiration and respect for the people of the North Shore and Labrador, for their stoicism, their strength, and their independence. I did not want to change them in any way and did not think it necessary that they change. Yet it was undeniable that they were limited by the extraordinary isolation of the region and vulnerable to manipulation by outsiders. My goals were to further self-government and self-determination and to somehow make their everyday lives easier and safer. The people of the North Shore knew better than I or any other outsider what was best for them.

By the late 1960s, the government of Quebec introduced a program to send children from the North Shore to other parts of the province for secondary education. The students boarded with families who received a subsidy from the province. The program had mixed results. Some students did very well. Others dropped out because of the lack of support so far away from home and, for many, their lack of adequate academic preparation for high school. The Reverend Jim Young, who had a senior position on the North Shore school board, did a superb job of coordinating the logistics of the program. A remarkable Eastern Townships woman, Mrs. Joan Thomson, took on the job of housing the students and watched their progress with great care.

At QLF, we maintained very close contact with our scholars and made certain they had mentors and support every step of the way. When Philip Nadeau first enrolled at Choate in 1964, I felt as though I was enrolling my own son in the school. I brought him back and forth to campus in my airplane and our home was always open to him and the others who followed. For years, we had students from the North boarding with us in Massachusetts. Faith welcomed them with the words, "Make yourself at home. You are part of the family." Despite increased access to further schooling for coasters in the years that followed, we maintained the scholarship program because so many of our young people yearned for specialized training in various trades and crafts or needed help going on to college or graduate school.

In those years the *Bert and I* album sales were thriving, so I used a share of my royalties to supplement the scholarship fund. When L.L. Bean, the legendary Freeport, Maine, outdoors store, agreed to sell *Bert and I* albums as part of their winter catalogue, a marvelous marketing opportunity for us, 75 cents of each record went into the scholarship fund for coasters coming to Hebron. I recognized the importance of outside financial support for my work from the very beginning. I borrowed my father's 16-mm movie camera, state-of-the-art equipment for amateur filmmakers back then, and recorded as much of life and wildlife on the coast as I could, sometimes from the air. I took a number of still photographs as well, and put together a slide presentation that I could use before schools, churches, and civic organizations in the United States to tell the story of the Quebec North Shore and to raise some money to support the work of the summer volunteer and youth scholarship programs. Over the years, the finest images came from the cameras of Candace Cochrane, Ed Miller, Henry Harding, Greg Granna, and Beth Alling.

In a letter to Bishop Russel F. Brown in October 1961, I told him that I had taken more than 1,000 photographs the previous summer and brought the 100 best slides to Dr. Paul Vieth, head of the Department of

Audio Visual Education at Yale Divinity School. Dr. Vieth was a former professor of mine and he agreed to help me produce a filmstrip telling the story of life on the Quebec North Shore and the enduring mission of the Anglican Church. The photos included pictures of seals, icebergs, fiords, airplanes, dogs, boats, cod fishing, Inuit people from Labrador, and people of the North Shore. It also included pictures of Bishop Brown traveling on the *Glad Tidings*, the mission boat on the coast. In the filmstrip, I made sure to mention he was a prominent player.

I worked closely with the International Grenfell Association because of my role as an ad hoc air ambulance driver. Starting in the early 1900s, the IGA managed medical care through the nursing stations and hospitals they established along the Labrador Coast, the Quebec North Shore, and the northern peninsula of Newfoundland. The Grenfell Handicraft shops, selling hand embroidered clothing and hooked rugs, provided a livelihood for many women.

As time passed, the small non-profit organization evolved and adjusted. To remain solvent, IGA turned over all its responsibilities to the provincial government in 1981. It still operates today under government auspices as the Grenfell Regional Health Services in coastal Labrador and northern Newfoundland.

When I launched the summer internship programs, the IGA viewed the work as compatible with its mission and the organization hired me as a director of summer volunteer programs. Their support helped finance the program. My annual reports to the association included detailed descriptions of the cost of fuel for the airplane. The floatplanes were an enormous asset in the North but it cost quite a bit of money to keep them in operation. My wife Faith's letters to her parents from that era often describe me as being out of town to deal with some maintenance issue or other for the plane I operated at the time.

As much as I enjoyed working at Choate, I always knew I would never be a "lifer" on the staff. The pull of the North was too great. From the very first summer on the coast, I was trying to figure out a way to make the Quebec North Shore more than just a summer gig. The demands of my work on the Quebec North Shore outstripped the time I had in the summer, so I resigned from Choate in 1967 to devote all my time to what became the Quebec Labrador Foundation, and to the

International Grenfell Association. The IGA offered me a job as assistant to the superintendent. One of my jobs was recruiting for the office, so I worked out of the New England Grenfell Association office. The volunteer program I started was originally called the Quebec Labrador Mission Foundation, but we removed the word "mission" to distinguish it as a non-denominational organization. We moved QLF into a 200-year-old gristmill near my new home in Ipswich, a lovely seaside town on the North Shore of Massachusetts. I could fly to Harrington Harbour in my floatplane in just over nine hours from Massachusetts with one refueling stop in Tabusintac, New Brunswick. I felt that I was well positioned for what became my life's work.

By 1970, the IGA board cut back on the summer programs as part of a shift in policy. The end of the eight-year relationship with IGA forced me to take the Quebec Labrador Foundation to a new level.

CHAPTER 10

The Ski-Doo and Other Modern Marvels

THERE ARE certain technological innovations and inventions that utterly change the status quo. Young people today, for example, doubtless view the time before the smartphone or the personal computer as akin to the Dark Ages. These devices transformed the way people work and communicate and were so quickly adopted that it is hard to remember what it was like before nearly everyone carried a cell phone. The snowmobile had a similar impact upon life on the Quebec North Shore. It fundamentally changed everyday life in the most remote and inaccessible parts of Canada.

The earliest mechanized sleds on the Quebec North Shore were called Russian toboggans. During World War II, the Russians, familiar with long, cold winters, developed a motorized sled that incorporated a tractor device. Most were half-tracks with forward skis, a chain sealed track, and attached brackets and steel cleats. The modern snowmobile was created by an inventor from Quebec—Joseph-Armand Bombardier— and the first versions were intended for tourism or large industries, such as mining companies. At first, Bombardier sold a large enclosed snowmobile, the B12, which carried up to twelve people. It was expensive and intended for commercial or institutional use. Grenfell used one as an ambulance at the hospital in St. Anthony. In larger communities B12s were used as school buses or taxis. Each came with a hatch on the roof for ready escape in the event the transport fell through the ice.

For decades, Bombardier dreamed of inventing a small, one- or two-person vehicle to traverse the snow, but it was not until gasoline engines became smaller, lighter, and more efficient at the end of the 1950s that he was able to produce a commercially viable personal snowmobile. In his biography of Bombardier, Leonard S. Reich recounts a story in which the inventor boarded a bush plane in April 1959 to visit a good friend, Maurice Ouimet, an Oblate priest who ministered to the Ojibwa people of northern Ontario. Father Ouimet yearned for an efficient, speedy way to travel to his parishioners. Just as I relied upon my plane, he hoped to find a way to more quickly and efficiently cover miles of snowy terrain. On that significant trip, Bombardier brought with him a prototype of a snowmobile that he called the Ski-Dog because it was intended to replace the dogsled. According to the company official story, his printer made a typographical error on the first sales brochure, and the Ski-Doo was born.

The first personal snowmobile was a 350-pound machine with wooden skis that retailed for about $900. It was powered by a 4-stroke Kohler engine that enabled it to go up to 24 miles per hour. After three days of successful testing in the wilds of Ontario, Mr. Bombardier presented the prototype as a gift to Father Ouimet and returned to his home in Valcourt to launch production of the first recreational snowmobile that autumn. The Ski-Doo was a huge commercial success. While competitors eventually developed their own versions of the snowmobile, the machines are still universally called Ski-Doos in the North after those first popular, widely available snowmobiles. Mr. Bombardier entered the Canadian history books as one of the most influential businessmen and inventors of his time.

Before Mr. Bombardier's ingenious invention, travel on the North Shore was difficult and practically impossible for much of the winter, except by dog team and komatik. Traveling on a dog sled was not exactly luxurious. It was cold, often dangerous, and definitely not for amateurs. The dogs fared better than their owners in the worst conditions. The dogs seemed to have a sixth sense that guided them home through the most horrific storms, and they had an extraordinary sense for ice. They instinctively knew if it was unsafe. There were many tales of sleds arriving back in a village after days of snowfall without the human owner who had gotten lost in the bush. The dogsleds were a time-honored tradition in the wilderness and some people were disappointed at the speed with which so many discarded their dogs and sleds for the newfangled machine.

But the convenience of the snowmobile was undeniable. To this day, people use the snowmobile to pull komatiks, often with the traditional "coach box" that allows riders to bundle up in blankets and travel in relative comfort through the cold. Although those early snowmobiles were noisy and could be very cranky, they were simpler to keep than dogs. They did not require feeding or health care, of course, and the snowmobile started with a single pull and boasted a bright headlight to allow fast, safe travel at night. Those early snowmobiles were put to extraordinary tests. They were driven at maximum speed over extremely tough terrain. For example, a snowmobile leaving Harrington Harbour for La Tabatiere some 32 miles away might start the journey on a wooden boardwalk, climb a steep hill, cross bare rock, bog down in saltwater slop, and bounce along over 30 miles of rough ice before arriving at the destination. Traveling between those villages in the winter was the equivalent of participating in the grueling off-road Baja 500 desert race in Mexico every single day. But it was an undeniable improvement over the past.

The snowmobile had a transformative effect upon the quality of life for many residents of the coast. Before the Ski-Doo, the wife of a fisherman in a remote village likely remained at home for the entire winter, except for an occasional Sunday afternoon trip by dog team to visit relatives in a nearby village. With the snowmobile, 2 sisters in Harrington Harbour thought nothing of jumping on a snowmobile at 1 p.m. and riding to Aylmer Sound, 11 miles east, to visit their mother before traveling back home in time to begin preparing supper at 4:30 p.m. That ease of travel relieved much of the isolation and loneliness of the long winters. The snowmobiles also fed the winter carnival craze. Half the residents of an entire village could and did travel ten to fifty miles to a host village for a carnival nearly every weekend with speed and ease unknown in the dog sled era.

The risk of getting lost in blizzard conditions, however, was higher with a snowmobile than with a dog team. Dogs know how to get home again. Before GPS devices and other innovations, men carried basic survival gear with them and often traveled in pairs or larger groups for safety. They were also careful to avoid getting caught in a storm. In the North, accidents were and still are endemic because of the harshness of the weather and climate. Donald Cox's untimely death certainly reminded us all of the risks of taking a wrong turn.

A 26-foot trap boat with a one- or two-cylinder Acadia or Imperial engine would take about 4½ hours to get from Harrington Harbour to Mutton Bay, a distance of 27.5 miles, traveling at a speed of 7 knots. A snowmobile could make that trip in less than an hour. Although the families had limited funds, most of them managed to buy snowmobiles, which then cost about $1,000 each and had an average life expectancy of three years because of the hard use. Within a matter of a few years, the snowmobile had become an indispensable piece of equipment, as important to coast families as an automobile or two is to a suburban family in the United States. By 1966, most of the dog teams were gone. A few dogs remained as house pets but the hardy packs that made legendary trips through the winters for decades were obsolete within five years of the introduction of snowmobiles to the area.

Given my love of flying and machines, it is probably no surprise that I was also an early user of the snowmobile. In the autumn of 1963, I was among the first in Harrington Harbour to buy a Ski-Doo. Much like Father Ouimet, I quickly recognized the value of this new tool to my ministry. My first snowmobile was a Bombardier Ski-Doo with a six-horsepower Rotax engine. The machine was sent to me from Baie Comeau through a friend of Happy Fraser. I paid $560 for it. It arrived in Harrington Harbour by coastal steamer in late November 1963. The ice bridge had not yet formed between Harrington and the mainland so the Ski-Doo was carried by small boat to the mainland, where I was able to use it traveling from Cross River to the west, and from Barachoix and east to Whale Head. I believe there were about three snowmobiles in Harrington Harbour in 1962. There were about 25 the following year and 65 the year after that.

By the end of 1963, a more powerful eight-horsepower Bombardier Ski-Doo became available. I had no difficulty selling my six-horsepower and acquiring the faster and more powerful eight-horsepower Ski-Doo. I used it throughout the winter of 1964, and kept it for decades in mint condition. It is now on display in the museum at Harrington Harbour. Within a remarkably short period of time, the Ski-Doo became ubiquitous and nearly every family came to rely upon the new machine. In fact, many families ended up with two machines: one for work and one for everyday transportation.

The Ski-Doo did, however, require some adjustment. Operators quickly learned that snowmobiles lost traction on ice and could be hazardous on a steep slope. The eight-horsepower machines were powerful enough to tow a komatik with a 350-pound 45-Imperial-gallon fuel drum lashed to it. Going downhill in slippery conditions, however, was dangerous. The snowmobile would begin to slide, the komatik would jackknife, and a wild crash might result. Fortunately, soft snowdrifts often absorbed the impact and injuries were infrequent when an operator lost control of a Ski-Doo with a heavy load aboard a komatik.

There were many hazards, some quite humorous, in this transition. During the winter of 1963-64, I estimate that fewer than 10 percent of families owned snowmobiles on the North Shore. Dog-team travel continued to be the way most people traveled that winter. Snowmobiles followed the tracks, trails, and runs established by dog teams. This carried a certain risk. Dogs on the go, having left home in the early morning after gorging on seal meat the night before, relieved themselves as they pulled on their traces, leaving behind a splattering of seal-based excrement on the path shared by the dog teams and the fleet of new snow machines. When a snowmobile ran along the trail, the rubber tracks picked up the fresh excrement and flung it back behind the Ski-Doo. Anyone riding on a komatik behind the Ski-Doo would be plastered. This hazard became the greatest concern of those who rode in the komatiks behind a snowmobile that winter.

The earliest Ski-Doos had a simple wire throttle that could be operated by the use of a finger or thumb of the driver holding onto standard bicycle handlebars. The simple system was prone to malfunction, particularly when the machine was left outside at night and freezing drizzle or rain collected on moving parts.

One morning in January 1964, Faith left the parsonage with Sarah, then seven years old, Kerry, then five, and Sandy, a toddler who would turn three the following month. The parsonage was built upon solid rock. After a freezing rain, the face of the rock became extremely slippery. Roy and Betty Rowsell lived just 200 feet down the rock from the parsonage. Faith climbed aboard the snowmobile, put the children behind her and started the machine. The engine caught, but unbeknownst to Faith, the throttle was frozen wide open. The machine shot down the rock toward the Rowsell house. Faith jumped off the out-of-control speeding sled, pulling the girls with her. But little Sandy clung to the back of the Ski-Doo and did not get swept off with the other two. Faith screamed, "Get off! Get off!" and at the last moment, Sandy jumped, just seconds before the machine flew off the face of the rock like a rocket and crashed into the side of the Rowsells' house, driving a hole into their kitchen wall. Sandy, fortunately, was too young to understand the peril she faced. For months afterward when asked about the incident, she would reply, "Mummy said, 'Git-tof, git-tof!'" It all made sense to her.

Although a metal floor covered the rubber track of the snowmobile, it was very easy to tangle loose clothing or a rope in the treads and bogey wheels. One day Father Gabriel Dionne was traveling from the Presbytery in Tête-a-la-Balene to Harrington. He wore a cassock that flowed in the breeze. As he drove, his cassock snagged into the track and bogey wheels and Father Dionne found himself rolling over in his snowmobile with his cassock jammed into the track. When the machine stopped, Father Dionne could not move because his cassock had pulled him tight alongside the snowmobile. Fortunately for him, some men on snowmobiles came by shortly and found him, incapacitated by his cassock but laughing at the absurdity of his plight, and rescued him.

I had my own experiences with clothing woes aboard a snowmobile. I left Mutton Bay one day in January 1964 as a passenger aboard Ron Shattler's snowmobile. Ron owned a Bosax, which used a track wheel behind the machine resembling the paddle wheel of a Mississippi River boat. As we headed uphill, the tilt caused us both to lean back and my scarf caught in the stern wheel of the Bosax, yanking me backward and upending the machine. Fortunately neither of us were hurt. After untangling the scarf, we were on our way.

From the beginning of my time in the North, I tried to capture images of the amazing spectacle of this wild land. I knew I had the opportunity to take photographs of a life that had never been recorded. I often trained my father's 16-mm movie camera and my 35-mm Zeiss Contaflex still camera on wildlife I spotted from above, including the caribou herds or bears wandering over the muskeg. I wanted others to see what I saw from my plane. I could not really know it at the time but I was also recording a way of life and an environment that was in the midst of major change.

One day in February 1964, I left Harrington Harbour by snowmobile for Aylmer Sound. It was a cold but calm and beautiful afternoon when Faith and I set off pulling a komatik loaded with a movie projector, a duffle bag full of films, and a 3,000-watt, gasoline-powered generator. At the time, there was no electric power in Aylmer Sound. I was delivering on a promise to provide two hours of entertainment, including my homemade films of caribou herds moving along the coast. Everyone in the village wanted to see the caribou pictures. Television would not arrive in Aylmer Sound for another ten years. A few people on the coast owned movie projectors and managed to find some old Hollywood westerns for rent in Montreal. They would ride a circuit traveling from community to community to put on shows that were very popular, if infrequent. To show local films was unusual and caused a great stir of interest.

Faith and I set up the projector in a village schoolroom packed with every man, woman, and child from the village, except for most members of the Chislett family. Uncle Bill Chislett was disabled and confined to his easy chair at his house. His six unmarried sons and their mother rarely ventured from the home. On this night, however, his son Giff Chislett came out to see the films. When I was packing up to go home, Giff pleaded with me to bring the entire rig over to his house so his father could see the films. His father had never seen a movie in his life. It would make for a very late night if we did this impromptu stop, but the weather was good, which meant the trip home should be uneventful. I agreed.

Giff's mother, father, and brothers had all gone to bed. But he roused them within minutes and lit the oil lamps. The entire family gathered in the kitchen. I set up the movie projector screen and left the generator outside. Then I realized we did not have an extension cord long enough to reach from the projector to the generator outside the kitchen door. I very sadly announced that it would be impossible to show the films.

Giff jumped to his feet. He moved the movie projector closer to the kitchen wall and moved the komatik with the generator closer to the side of the house. Then, without a second of hesitation, he grabbed a brace, found a large drill bit, and drilled a two-inch hole into the wall of the kitchen, right through the side of the house, creating an opening big enough to push through the electrical plug so the cord from the projector reached the repositioned generator. We fired up the projector within minutes and Uncle Bill and the entire family happily watched the caribou films. It was the first moving picture that Uncle Bill had ever seen.

By the time we left for Harrington Harbour, it was nearly midnight. The weather remained good and it was a clear and calm night. The snowmobile and dog-team tracks could be seen clearly in the headlight of my Ski-Doo. After 35 or 45 minutes, we came out onto the saltwater ice, a clear stretch of 3 miles that would take us directly to the back of the island, up over the hill at Harrington, and home. I pushed the throttle at full tilt in my eagerness to get home after a very long day. Faith rode on the komatik with the generator and movie projector. As I closed in on the back of the island, I slowed the speed slightly and glanced back to make sure Faith was ready to hang on as we started up the final hill. I nearly fell off the snowmobile in shock. Faith was gone! Evidently, when I added power as I approached the three-mile stretch of ice, the jolt of sudden speed caused her to fall over backwards and off the sled. She called out but I did not hear her over the sound of the Ski-Doo engine.

With my heart in my throat, I turned around and raced back to Aylmer Sound on the Ski-Doo tracks. After about fifteen minutes, which seemed like hours, I spotted Faith in her sealskin parka trudging along the trail. She knew I might not realize she was gone until I arrived home. So with the quarter moon and stars lighting her way, she had decided to simply walk home on the tracks.

The snowmobile was not the only invention that brought change in the 1960s. The Quebec North Shore became one of the last rural sections of Canada to get electricity. When it came, it had a profound effect upon the quality of life and even the culture of the coast. Hydro-Quebec, the government-owned utility company, was created in 1944 by the government of Quebec in response to corruption in the exclusively private electric power industry that occurred during the Great Depression. One of the purposes of nationalization was to speed up rural electrification, but the daunting task of bringing electricity to the most remote sections of the province did not take place until the government nationalized the remaining eleven private electric companies in 1962 and constructed the massive Daniel-Johnson Dam on the Manicouagan River. The dam was completed in 1968, clearing the way for the distribution of hydropower to that part of Quebec, although many of the villages of the North Shore still relied upon generators.

I remember the year-long process of planting hundreds of electric light poles and stringing electrical cables. Much of the region was on top of solid rock, so the process involved a lot of dynamiting. I remember being in Mutton Bay one day while the crews were preparing to explode dynamite to install a pole. The crew put a steel mat over the blasting hole to dampen the blast. The explosion sent the 200-pound mat flying into the air. It crashed through the roof of Mrs. Roger's house and wound up in her kitchen. Fortunately, she was not in the kitchen at the time. The power station in Harrington Harbour was about 150 feet from our house. It was essentially a big generator. Similar power stations were built along the North Shore and soon everyone had electricity.

The introduction of electric power was transformative. Before electricity, everyday household tasks, such as laundry, were cumbersome and laborious. We all pumped water by hand, cooked on wood stoves, and relied upon wood to heat our homes. Faith described the elaborate process of getting enough hot water to wash clothing in a letter to her family written on November 25, 1963. We had a gasoline-powered washing machine. Most families did their laundry completely by hand. She wrote:

Wash day today. It was so cold last night that we left our oil heater going in the living room. I filled a huge wash tub full of water before I went to bed and put it on the heater. It was a treat to have hot water when I woke this morning. I was able to start our gasoline engine washing machine early (Incidentally, it sounds like an outboard motor, has a choke, spouts flame and smoke, gets stuck, but WORKS.) I hung the clothes out and my hands practically froze and I know it's going to be colder on future wash days. Tonight we have our laundry hanging on lines above our wood stove in the kitchen. The clothes were all frozen when I brought them in with Edna at three o'clock.

As soon as electric power became available, the residents of the Lower North Shore became avid consumers of the household appliances that had already revolutionized households in more populated areas. They purchased electric stoves for cooking in the kitchen, electric lights for every room in the house, electric washing machines, and all the other electronic fixtures and gadgets that make life more automated and much easier. Pegging clothing and bed sheets on the line for the sun- and wind-dried freshness is still the preferred method of drying clothes, however, and Monday wash day features strings of colorful laundry. Many families still keep their battery-powered radios, because they are more reliable, particularly during storms that might knock out electricity for hours or days on end. Of course, the television had the same hypnotic effect upon the coasters as it did on people who lived elsewhere.

The Lower North Shore availed itself of the television stations in Newfoundland, just across the Gulf of St. Lawrence. This part of Quebec is far closer to Newfoundland than it is to Quebec City. Many women from the fishing families became rapt fans of the dramatic daily soap operas. Visits and visiting had long been an important part of the culture. I spent an enormous amount of my time going from house to house. The ritual was the same in each house. I would be plied with tea and treats; we would exchange news and tell stories; I would lead a prayer and then say farewell. Invariably, my hosts would insist, "You've got lots of time, Mr. Bryan." They insisted I had time whether I stayed for three minutes or three hours. In fact, I did not have all the time in the world, but their yearning for human interaction and the importance they placed on a visit from the minister made it very difficult to tear myself away. It was the knowledge that the next family was impatiently waiting for their visit with the minister that got me on my way. I was frequently greeted with: "Mr. Bryan, you are a stranger!" At first I was taken aback because I tried so hard to be available and sensitive to each person and family, but I quickly realized that they said that to anyone they liked to see often and it was not a reflection on my attentiveness or diligence.

After the initial introduction of television, I found that the television set was on when I arrived and my hosts often kept it on. They might lower the volume but they were transfixed by the flicker and thrum of the images on those snowy black-and-white sets. The women in particular, who spent most of their lives in one village, and spent most of their day working at home, were entranced by the characters in the over-the-top soap operas with their daily love affairs, betrayals, murders, and other deceptions. The lives portrayed on the soap operas were radically different from anything they had ever seen.

The people of the North were very house-proud. They kept their small homes immaculately clean. The women scrubbed every inch on a regular basis, including the ceilings. Their hand-built, brightly painted homes were kept fresh and trim. Of course, the trash went into the sea. But they did not let unused gear pile up messily in their yards. Cash was a limited commodity, and there was no opportunity to "grow" savings. In the early 1960s there was not a single bank on the Quebec North Shore. I knew of fishermen who kept thousands of dollars under their mattresses for years, and one fisherman who had more than $200,000 sealed up in cans stashed away in his home. I convinced friends at the Canadian Imperial Bank of Commerce in Toronto that the coast represented an opportunity for a novel and enterprising bank, a floating bank aboard the *Jean Brilliant*, the 165-foot coastal steamer that cruised the 460-mile coastline of 15 villages from May through October. They agreed to a bank in a small 8- by 10-foot room aboard the ship with a securely locked safe to hold the cash. The bank paid interest on both checking and savings accounts. Banking is a fundamental block in building a viable integrated economy. The bank gave families the ability to write checks, borrow money, and later obtain credit and debit cards.

The *Wall Street Journal* covered the story with an article titled "Out of Way Villages in Canada are Served by a Bank on a Boat: Clients in St. Lawrence Area Rise at 3 a.m. to Greet it; Dealing in Furs on the Side."

I also witnessed a dramatic change in the cod fishing industry. When we first arrived, fishing was a family business. The men got up at 2 a.m. and went out to fish, returning 6 hours later, surrounded by gulls, their boats so loaded down with cod that they sunk deep into the water. They forked the fish out onto their fishing stages, where the women joined them to gut and fillet the cod. They tossed the entrails of the fish into the water, where the gulls dived and feasted. The cod would be placed on drying racks built from the wood of inland trees. The fish would then be salted and stored in barrels. Laurie Cox always recommended that the barrels be filled to the very top because buyers would check a random barrel and pay according to the amount of fish in that barrel. During the summer of 1962, I flew from Harrington Harbour to Blanc Sablon and looked down upon hundreds of cod traps filled with fish. Little did we appreciate that those scenes signaled the end of an era and way of life.

There are many reasons for the collapse of the cod fishery. The fish stocks were severely depressed from overfishing by factory trawlers from as far away as Russia and Portugal, and by the widespread use of the monofilament gill net that became very popular in the 1970s. The government at this time was subsidizing fishermen to improve efficiency, but these monofilament nets were too efficient. They reached deep into the sea and even affected spawning fish. The old cod traps and jigging, or hand lining with a series of baited hooks on a line, may have been less efficient, but those methods did not deplete the stocks. Furthermore, when a monofilament net is lost in a storm, which happens often, it continues to fish forever in a wasteful and endless cycle. As more fish are taken in the untended net, the loaded net sinks, and when the fish rot, the net floats up again, repeating the cycle. Another problem was that the capelin, a small smelt-like fish that the cod fed upon, were destroyed by the bottom-fishing commercial trawlers from Newfoundland and the Gaspé. Increased numbers of seals, who prey on fish, may also have been a contributing factor.

It is now clear that the cod fishery was mismanaged for decades. The fishermen of Gloucester and New Bedford in Massachusetts, for example, suffered as much as the fishermen of the Quebec North Shore. The treaties and laws approved after the fishing stocks collapsed amounted to too little too late. Debate continues to this day over the causes of the collapse of the cod fishery. When the foreign trawlers and draggers were banned, Canadian trawlers and draggers took their place. Climate change and a warming trend in the sea also put strain on the stocks.

There was another cultural change that took place in the 1960s that came from the outside. For the first six years of the Quebec Labrador Foundation volunteer program, a majority of the volunteers came from preparatory schools, high schools, colleges, and universities in the United States. About 90 percent of the interns were citizens of the United States, 8 percent were Canadians, and 2 percent came from the United Kingdom and France. At that time we were sending about 150 volunteers to coastal villages on the northern peninsula of Newfoundland, the Quebec North Shore, northeastern New Brunswick; as far north as Nain, Labrador; and as far south as Washington and Aroostook Counties in Maine. At the height of the volunteer program, we held a formal orientation program in late June at the Airport Hilton in Montreal. At the final banquet concluding the orientation, the boys wore sports coats, button-down collar shirts, and neckties. Their hair was tidy and trimmed above the ears and each was clean-shaven. The girls wore dresses or kilts and sweaters. Had we all been beckoned to the grand ballroom to meet the Queen of England, not one of the 100 to 140 young men and women would have been the least bit out of place.

In 1968, everything changed. I arrived at the Montreal Airport Hilton to meet the summer interns and was greeted by a group of youngsters who looked as though they had survived an explosion in a mattress factory. The boys sported shoulder-length hair and ragged sweatshirts, and went barefoot or wore torn sneakers or moccasins. The girls wore torn jeans or long, loose skirts with floppy t-shirts. Their hair was long, flowing, and tangled. I thought I was greeting a pack of sheepdogs. You could barely tell the boys from the girls. Long hair covered eyes and facial features. There was not a single suitcase in evidence. They carried their gear in duffle bags or knapsacks and backpacks. The musical *Hair* had opened that April on Broadway. It was as if the entire cast had shown up for the orientation.

I was deeply apprehensive about the reaction these disheveled young people might receive on the coast from families who adhered to a conservative, old-fashioned lifestyle and had not yet heard a whisper of the cultural change then underway in the United States. The Age of Aquarius had not yet arrived on the North Shore. During orientation lectures, I tried to impress upon the volunteers that they were guests in communities where the lifestyle had not changed a bit in 150 years. I tried to explain that families would be aghast if their own children came to the dinner table looking as though they had been keel hauled. I'm not sure they really appreciated what I was saying and I held my breath as we dispatched the volunteers to the northern outposts.

The immediate and vociferous reaction from some of the people of the North was as I expected. I received radio messages, telegrams, and telephone calls from village mayors, clergy, and the heads of families who were acting as hosts for the volunteers. They simply did not know what to make of these ragtag teenagers. I thought the jig was up. The cultural dissonance between youth culture then cresting in the United States and the traditional lifestyle of the Quebec North Shore seemed too great. I began to think of how to orchestrate a mid-summer evacuation of the student volunteers. I felt terrible to have caused such distress for these people whom I had befriended, people who had confidence in my judgment and who had warmly accepted the young men and women in earlier years with the expectation these teenagers would act as role models and counselors for their isolated children. The emergency evacuation proved to be unnecessary. After three weeks, the irate messages, telephone calls, and telegrams fell to a trickle and then stopped. I was amazed, but I realized that the basic values, goodwill, and spirit of the volunteers, and their interest and care for the children in the day camps, completely overwhelmed any concerns caused by appearance and dress. By the end of the summer, not a single family voiced indignation over the length of hair or bare feet. As their teenagers began to leave the coast for secondary and specialized education in other parts of Canada and in the United States, they saw their own children returning home for vacations in the casual "hippie" style that became prevalent. The people of the Quebec North Shore did not have a lot of exposure to different styles and cultures, but they recognized quality and character even underneath all that hair.

CHAPTER

11

Environmental Change
in the North

THE PRESENCE of sea ice and icebergs in the Gulf of St. Lawrence is a routine occurrence every spring. As winter ends and the spring warm-up begins, chunks of ice break off the glaciers or ice shelves of Greenland, just below the Arctic Circle, and drift south. Yet in the summer of 1991, multi-year sea ice and icebergs appeared in the Gulf during July. Ice is still customary in the Strait of Belle Isle between northern Newfoundland and Labrador in July but by mid-month, there are rarely more than five to ten icebergs in a five-square-mile area. However, during the summer of '91 the ice appeared along the Labrador coast and the east coast of Newfoundland and then came through the Strait of Belle Isle into the Gulf of St. Lawrence. On July 11, ice covered 70 percent of the Strait of Belle Isle. At its narrowest point, the Strait is sixteen miles wide.

The oldest residents of the Quebec North Shore could not recall seeing icebergs or that much sea ice during the month of July. At mid-month, there were stretches of drift ice extending for sixty miles just off Harrington Harbour. On July 12, an iceberg at St. Paul's River measured 210 feet above the surface. The Coast Guard estimated the iceberg went 450 feet below the surface, where it grounded out. Individual large icebergs and some pans grounded along the shore and in some bays. I measured one iceberg through the radar altimeter on the plane on June 8 at 260 feet above sea level. This represents just one tenth of the total size. About 90 percent of an iceberg is under water. The Coast Guard estimated one ice pan along the southern Labrador Coast to be more than eight miles wide. None of the longtime residents of that part of Labrador had ever seen one so large at that time of year.

Icebergs are composed of pure freshwater. There was no industry or human activity to pollute the water and air in the far north when it was formed. Because oxygen is captured in the ice, there is a distinctive pop and sizzle sound as it melts. It is created under such pressure that glacier ice lasts twice as long as ice created in a refrigerator. The glaciers build up over thousands of years so some of the ice in the bergs is estimated to be more than 15,000 years old. I wanted to chip off a chunk of this ancient glacial ice. There was one small berg near Harrington Harbour that I kept eyeing. I thought I might be able to safely taxi up next to it in the airplane, cut off a piece, and store it in the freezer.

My aircraft crew members that day were Tim Nadeau and Duke Barnett. We spotted a small iceberg about five miles east of the Etamamiou River. Icebergs are notoriously dangerous and difficult to judge. Because most of the ice is invisible under the water, it is never certain when it might suddenly crack, break up, roll over or move suddenly. This one was in a shallow cove and firmly grounded so it did not appear to be a risky prospect. I could see that the lip of the iceberg stretched about twenty feet under the water. We taxied over the lip and up to a small crown of ice that looked easy to knock off and load aboard the plane. There was less clearance than I expected so the left float momentarily grounded on the ice, but we were able to push back with a paddle. I thought it would be easy to crack off a small section jutting from a separate piece about the size of a bathtub. From the floats, we poked at the ice with our boots and a paddle to no avail. Finally, Tim Nadeau pulled out our emergency survival saw and worked away to saw off a piece about one-and-a-half by two feet in size. It was surprisingly heavy; it felt as though it weighed at least sixty pounds. I lifted it into the plane's cabin and we flew back to Harrington Harbour with the primeval ice formed thousands of years earlier. I brought about thirty pounds of the iceberg back to Ipswich with me and melted off a small piece from time to time to use the water for baptisms. I would say the water was 5,000 years old, older than Christianity and the river Jordan where John the Baptist baptized his cousin Jesus.

Any change in water temperature, up or down, has an effect upon wildlife. When the icebergs came that July, the temperature of the water off Newfoundland measured far below freezing down to 656 feet. When salt water freezes, codfish and other fish become inert. That summer the Atlantic salmon migrating into the Gulf managed to get around Newfoundland through the Cabot Strait up into the Gulf into the Gaspé area and farther up along the lower North Shore. Fish coming through the Strait of Belle Isle seemed to be blocked. When Atlantic salmon migrate, they swim close to the surface. The presence of ice confused or cut them off.

Sea ducks returning to their nesting grounds along the Labrador coast and farther north into the Davis Strait were stopped cold. We saw thousands of them along the coast. Every rock island, shoal, and ledge was covered with eiders. In the stretch of eighty miles from Mutton Bay to Blanc Sablon there had to be hundreds of thousands of the waterfowl. We saw more whales than usual in the Gulf that year and assumed that their migratory path was altered by the ice. I could look out from Harrington Harbour and see a whale breaking the surface of the water on the horizon every five minutes. A polar bear was spotted in the Wolf Bay area. This is unusual but happens when a bear drifts down on a large piece of ice and then decides to go overboard and swim ashore.

The economic impact was immediate. The sea ice disrupted the ferry schedule between Blanc Sablon and St. Barbe's in the Strait of Belle Isle. Fewer trips affected commerce. The cod fishermen did not dare set their long line nets in waters where drifting ice could destroy their gear. Salmon anglers who frequent the rivers on the Lower North Shore in late June and July told me that they did not see a fish, let alone hook one, for an extended period of time.

The earliest documented writings of the North included exuberant descriptions of seas and rivers teeming with cod and Atlantic salmon and extraordinary numbers of waterfowl and caribou. All of that was about to change. The coast could readily absorb fishing to sustain the small-scale local economies, but more and more commercial boats entered the waters to purchase barrels of fish from local fishermen. Overfishing, lack of foresight about a finite resource, and mismanagement on a global level contributed to the collapse of the fishery. New technology, modern inventions, and natural events such as temperature change further depleted these riches and put at risk a way of life. The disappearance of wildlife long taken for granted caused deep concern to the people living in this part of the world. If conditions persisted for years, the very existence of the small villages whose entire economy depended upon fishing would be in question.

The decline of the caribou herd was particularly devastating. The Quebec Lower North Shore caribou herd held approximately 20,000 animals in 1960. Just ten years later, the herd was down to a fragile 5,000, and by 1976 the herd had nearly completely disappeared. They were simply overhunted. Travel in the hinterland increased by ten-fold in the fifteen-year period between 1960 and 1975. Hunting parties of twenty to forty men, all on snowmobiles that were faster and more powerful than the first Ski-Doos in the early 1960s, outmatched the speed and agility of the caribou herds. The snowmobile was a real game changer in hunting prey. With more powerful snowmobiles, local people went deeper into the bush and further from their villages in pursuit of the animals. The caribou did not have a chance. Instead of just shooting the two allowed by the government, these hunters often shot as many as they came across and then alerted their relatives and neighbors to retrieve the carcasses. As was historically the case, nothing was wasted. The caribou skin and meat were used in their entirety, but it was a numbers game. There was even use of chartered aircraft to carry hunters further into the bush than possible in the past. Over time, the North Shore caribou were quite literally killed off. Not enough remained to sustain the herds of the past. The large herds of the Ungava area were more protected by the vast northern reaches of Quebec and Labrador.

Traditionally, families on the Quebec North Shore were allowed to kill two caribou during the winter season for the meat. In the fall, most of the caribou were in the bush and it was very difficult for most coastal hunters to get into the bush at that time of year without the help of a float-equipped airplane. Innu and the coastal residents who routinely trapped in the hinterland might kill a caribou in the fall but most coastal people waited until late January, February, and early March. That is when the caribou came to the sea to feed upon the lichen and the moss on the exposed outside islands.

I went on my first caribou hunt with Bob May in late August 1961, in the Ungava area. Bob's wife, Jean, was an Inuit. The May family operated a salmon camp during the summer months on the George River, 500 miles from Harrington Harbour, and in the winter they lived at Fort Chimo. I took Bob back into the hills to hunt a caribou. We landed on the lake and walked for two miles while Bob periodically stopped to peer through his binoculars at the barren slopes. He spotted a caribou and gave me my first lesson on the proper way to stalk. It was important to be downwind of the caribou because the herd would move away quickly if the animals picked up the scent of intruders.

When the caribou was killed, Bob promptly began to "paunch" and clean and dress the animal, cutting it into quarters and placing the pieces into rubber-lined laundry bags stuffed into large knapsacks. He put the heart and liver aside and left the innards on the ground as food for other wildlife. We then started the two-and-a-half-mile trek back to the airplane. That caribou was one of the heaviest loads I ever carried over rough ground and my back ached by the time we reached the plane.

When we arrived back at George River, the Inuit who lived there swarmed the airplane. I suspect they realized we had caribou on board because the floats of the airplane sunk deeper into the water than when we left for the hunt. The knapsacks were plucked from the plane and carried to the canvas cook tent. By the time I reached the cook tent about twenty minutes later, after tying up the aircraft to fuel drums and securing it for the night, caribou steaks were sizzling in butter in the frying pan.

In the winter on the Quebec North Shore, the caribou was handled differently. The caribou was loaded onto a komatik after the hunt to haul the meat from the bush to the village. Those families who were able to kill their quota of two caribou often kept the carcasses frozen outside the kitchen door until ready for use. Then an entire caribou might be moved into the kitchen and placed next to the stove to thaw.

The children sometimes climbed on the backs of the frozen animals and "rode" them until the caribou thawed enough to be butchered.

The caribou was the primary source of winter meat and protein for the indigenous people of the North, but it was not the only source for the French- and English-speaking families. Those families also relied upon seal meat, willow ptarmigan (a white partridge), and rabbit for their winter meals, along with salt cod or fish frozen from the summer. Some of the fishing families would order salt beef, chicken, and eggs from the last freight boat to make its way down the coast before the ice locked up the sea.

I came up empty-handed most of the time on the few caribou hunts in which I participated. I could see that an airplane and speedy snowmobiles changed the balance between man and beast. These modern modes of transportation gave men a great advantage and made the caribou easier prey. It troubled me.

Widespread use of snowmobiles and outboard motors on boats also contributed to the decline of the seabirds. When I first flew over the coast, I was entranced by the sight of thousands of seabirds, and within twenty years, I began seeing only about 30 percent of the numbers that I had first observed on the coast. In the early 1960s, travel at sea took place in a 26- or 28-foot boats that moved at 6 to 8 knots. Within a few years, twin 40-horsepower engines could move a 16- or 18-foot boat at speeds over 30 miles per hour. The offshore islands became more accessible within a remarkably short period of time because of improvements in outboard motors. Sea ducks in molt, barely able to fly, are helpless to hunters bearing down on them at such high speeds. Repeating shotguns with magazines holding five shells replaced the single- and double-barreled guns of the old days. More firepower and more speed proved to be a lethal combination for the sea duck and seabird populations. It was not at all unusual to travel at 40 to 70 miles per hour just on a regular jaunt between villages. No animal—caribou, fox, or wolf—caught out in an open bay or lake can match the high speeds of modern machinery. Government regulation and management of natural resources can be problematic and difficult to enforce in such remote areas. And the government efforts faced a cultural barrier with the people living on the North Shore. For years, many residents of the North believed that the natural resources were inexhaustible. I have great respect for the traditions and lifestyle of the people of the North Shore, but seeing one species harvested beyond a level of sustainability convinced me that dramatic steps needed to be taken to prevent these resources from being depleted. The survival of wildlife is intrinsic to the lifestyle and culture of the region.

Getting any of the local people to accept harvest limits in order to allow wildlife to survive in numbers sufficient to sustain the various species was extremely difficult. There is a suspicion and resistance to outside intervention. But more important, unrestricted fishing and hunting was a way of life so embedded in the culture that it was almost impossible for people to understand or appreciate the need for quotas and regulation. Moreover, all of these people needed the protein from salmon, caribou, and ducks in their diet, and they did not see their activities as problematic.

The Canadian and U.S. governments, through their fish and wildlife services, have been banding migratory birds for almost a century. Bands provide important information on the migratory routes of waterfowl. For example, I found that bands collected from the legs of black ducks on the Quebec North Shore resulted from the banding on the Eastern Seaboard of the United States, known as the Atlantic Flyway. The majority of my Quebec North Shore friends were reluctant to report band recoveries because they were concerned that they might have broken game laws, particularly those related to open and closed seasons.

In 1965 I made it clear that it made no difference how or when the tags were obtained. The government simply wanted to have information of date and place of collection. I decided to make an urgent appeal for band information. I bought a map of the Eastern Seaboard, encompassing the Atlantic Flyway stretching from Florida to the Labrador coast. The map was then mounted on a board; a pin was used to mark the place of banding and a red thread connected to the place of recovery.

In this way ten banding sites in North Carolina, Maryland, and Massachusetts were connected with recovery sites on the Quebec Lower North Shore from Kegaska to Blanc Sablon. The map and board fit through the door of the Helio. I carried the map to churches and during the announcement period displayed the map and pointed out the amazing connections. It did not take long for increased levels of recovered bands to be reported.

My engagement in conservation activities came about in part through my own observations as I flew over the region and witnessed over the months and years the impact that man was having on the wildlife. I was particularly interested in the black duck and the Atlantic salmon, but the change in other forms of wildlife was just as telling. I once could see hundreds of caribou from the air if I flew thirty miles inland. Today, it is possible to fly over the same stretch of land and not spot a single animal. The loss of wildlife threatened a traditional way of life on the coast but also acted as a kind of canary in the coal mine, an intimation that man was the most effective and least restrained predator.

Sport fishermen and hunters have long been at the forefront of con-servation. Their love of fishing and shooting is intimately linked with their love of the outdoors and the wilderness. President Theodore Roo-sevelt, a passionate hunter and great lover of nature, emerged as one of the most prominent conservationists of his era. His administration at the beginning of the twentieth century was responsible for a major expansion of national parks and forests, an effort that historians agree saved enor-mous and precious pieces of land for the public to enjoy for generations.

I first became involved with the Atlantic Salmon Association, later renamed the Atlantic Salmon Federation, an international non-profit organization created in 1948 to protect the Atlantic salmon and its hab-itat, through my father-in-law, Dana Storrs Lamb. Faith's father was a remarkable man. He was a hardworking stockbroker and longtime part-ner in an investment firm on Wall Street. He was also an ardent con-servationist and skilled angler who wrote nine books on angling and the outdoors, including *On Trout Streams and Salmon Rivers, Where the Pools are Bright and Deep, Some Silent Places Still, Woodsmoke and Water-cress,* and *The Fishing's Only Part of It.* He served a one-year term as pres-ident of the Angler's Club of New York and was a longtime director of the Atlantic Salmon Association. He came from a family long interested in conservation and education. His great grandfather, Augustus Storrs, with his brother Charles, donated 170 acres and $5,000 in cash to the state of Connecticut in 1880 to create the Connecticut Agricultural Col-lege, which became the University of Connecticut.

I met and became great friends with many anglers through Dana Lamb. All the anglers loved the outdoors and many brought their financial resources and connections to bear in what remains an ongoing effort to keep the Atlantic salmon from becoming extinct.

In a letter I wrote to a friend in New York in February 1977, I wrote:

> It is impossible to address all of the mistakes that have been made by white men in the North, but those of us from the outside must daily recite to ourselves the pitfalls of well-meaning do-gooders. I know that we often err, but we desperately try not to be patronizing in our dealings with the people of the North. We would like to give them a chance to develop themselves. We know that there is absolutely no way that we can build a fence around them. The young men on the whaling ships out of Newfoundland in the nineteenth century went off to foreign ports and brought back new and strange ideas. The same thing is happening today, and with graver consequences.

While I recognized the impact on the anglers, I was primarily concerned about the impact of environmental and wildlife changes on my parishioners. The cod and lobster fishing families faced particular challenges in those years.

Anglers in Canada and the United States joined together in 1972 when the Atlantic Salmon Association and the International Atlantic Salmon Foundation merged and became the Atlantic Salmon Federation. They shared similar experiences and concerns. Neither the salmon nor the various international commercial fishing companies paid any attention to the boundaries of nations and these sport fishermen recognized that they would be more effective if they worked together and combined forces. I served on the board of both organizations and have remained affiliated with the merged organization for my entire life.

The Atlantic salmon is a magnificent example one of the great mysteries of nature. These anadromous fish spawn in the freshwater rivers of Canada (by that time, a combination of development, pollution, and dam construction had effectively wiped out the Atlantic salmon population in Maine rivers) and then swim down the river and deep into the sea to feed for a year or more. After reaching maturity, they swim back to the spot where they were born to reproduce. Development, monofilament nets at the mouth of a river, construction of a hydroelectric power plant or dam, pollution from industry, and overfishing can wreak havoc with this age-old cycle. A study conducted for the Atlantic Salmon Federation in those early years found that 90 percent of the total salmon catch was taken by 15 percent of the fishermen, virtually all commercial fishermen. Fly fishermen and other sport fishermen accounted for approximately 85 percent of all fishermen, yet they took only 10 percent of the fish. Many followed the "catch and release" policy, tossing back the fish they caught. Moreover, the commercial fishermen were not making much money for their hard work and effort. A commercial fisherman might fetch $2 a pound for an Atlantic salmon. By contrast, the anglers' considerable expenses in travel, outfitting, and guides amounted to more than $1,000 per fish. Something needed to be done but there were no easy or obvious answers.

The purists in the angling and environmental community wanted to ban commercial fishing. Commercial fishing expanded and became mechanized and far more efficient after World War II. While I certainly did not support the enormous international commercial fishing boats, the new monofilament non-biodegradable netting, or the floating processing plants indiscriminately scooping up the treasures of the ocean, I did support the local fishermen. A total ban would hurt the small fishermen and their way of life.

For generations, these fishermen had lived off the sea. They were not responsible for the depletion of this remarkable asset. Indeed, they were among the victims. I argued their case in the counsels of the angler board meetings for years. Somehow, we needed to find solutions that protected the fish but also protected these small fishermen and their traditional livelihood and way of life. These North Shore fishermen were never just another "user group" to me. I knew them as individuals, friends, and parishioners. I knew firsthand how precarious their finances were and worried about the long-term survival of these fishing villages as much as I worried about the survival of the Atlantic salmon.

I could not know it at the time, but as the years passed and talented young and visionary environmental educators joined our staff, these concerns became one of the driving missions of the Quebec Labrador Foundation.

CHAPTER 12

QLF Grows Up

M Y LIFE has benefited from a certain amount of serendipity. My schooling, family background, and childhood exposed me to relationships and a world that was very different from the world I came to love on the Quebec Lower North Shore. Old friends, relatives, classmates, and colleagues became benefactors, supporters, and champions of many of my projects. I felt compelled to do what I could to help my parishioners and friends in the North and to preserve the magnificent wildlife that made the region so special. I also had great confidence in the innate ability of the people of the North Shore. Given the right tools and leaders, I was convinced they could adapt to the radical changes taking place in the outside world and in their own environment that affected their traditional way of life.

The Quebec Labrador Foundation had modest aspirations when first established. I initially wanted to provide fun, recreation, and opportunity, and create magical summer memories for the children. But while QLF was running summer athletic activities for the children, an international environmental movement was building strength throughout the decades of the 1960s, '70s and '80s. Propelled by a sense of urgency and a deep concern for the fate of the natural world, this growing environmental movement opened up opportunities for QLF that I never anticipated.

After I left Choate School and made QLF my primary job, I suppose it was inevitable that I would begin to combine my concerns and interests under that one QLF roof. I realized that raising awareness among the people of the Quebec Lower North Shore of the precariousness of the wildlife and their habitat could not happen overnight. In order to preserve the natural environment that was so important to their lives and culture, they would need to realize that they needed to make changes in their own hunting and fishing practices. I hoped to make this easier for them.

We zeroed in on education as the best way to develop a broader idea of conservation throughout the community. If the youngsters developed environmental awareness at an early age, then they were more likely to grow into adults who would be willing to make adjustments in behavior. Given that the children were already having such fun each summer with the volunteers, I reasoned that they could become co-workers in the environmental effort and learn to protect their precious natural world just as easily as they learned to sail and play baseball. We taught seabird ecology and carefully showed that collecting too many eggs would result in too few birds and eventually lead to a dramatic depletion of the seabird population. These lessons were not dry classroom exercises. The children learned in the field where they examined bird nests, saw how carefully they were constructed by the birds, and tracked the progress of the birds from season to season. The children were not only thrilled to learn about the life span and habitat of these birds but also became invested in the health and well-being of the seabirds.

Dr. Wilfred M. Carter, the longtime executive director of the Atlantic Salmon Federation, and I talked about the need to address the ongoing problem of poaching, the polluting of streams and local over-netting at the mouths of the spawning rivers. A 150-foot net set at the opening of a river caught enormous numbers of fish of all species each time it was lifted from the water. The Atlantic salmon were particularly affected because of their instinct to return to spawning grounds to reproduce. Wilfred was a highly disciplined, very proper Canadian who devoted his life to preservation and protection of the Atlantic salmon, and we became fast friends. We realized there was a need to address the conduct of fisheries at the local level and we agreed education was the answer. After some debate, we decided to locate the first program on the Tabusintac River in New Brunswick. I knew the river well and had first fished there in 1955.

We modeled the new environmental camp on the summer recreation programs being operated by QLF. But instead of hiring high-school students, we brought in college and graduate students as instructors. Unlike the high-school summer interns who used to pay for the honor of spending a summer in a remote fishing village, many of these older students eventually became paid employees of QLF. The organization was already moving from an all-volunteer effort into a more professional operation.

In the mid-1970s, QLF made two key hires that would propel the evolution of QLF into an international environmental conservation and education organization: Lawrence "Larry" Morris and Kathleen "Kath" Blanchard. Dr. Morris began to work for QLF during the summer of 1975 while he was working on his doctorate in Natural Resources Management at Cornell University. He used his work at QLF as material for his thesis and became a full-time director of the Living Rivers Program, the first environmental education camp at Tabusintac, New Brunswick, and later the first director of the Atlantic Center for the Environment, the structure we established to manage all of the environmental programs at QLF. As of 2014, almost forty years later, Larry is still at QLF; he became president in 1988. Dr. Blanchard is an internationally recognized expert on community-based approaches to seabird conservation and endangered species recovery. She worked for QLF as a senior employee for 25 years and later as a senior consultant. She played a pivotal role in the development of our seabird program and our approach to conservation in rural areas of eastern Canada.

At QLF I was surrounded by enormously talented and gifted people, such as Larry and Kath, who cared about every detail. They not only shared my concerns about the wildlife but also respected the people in the local communities and their traditions. I often say that I may not have been smart enough to do this on my own, but I was smart enough to give Larry and Kath the freedom they needed to create compelling and effective programs.

QLF has been at the forefront of many of the most significant trends in environmental preservation of the past forty years. We developed a working prototype of community-based conservation before the term existed. We were among the first to recognize the need to operate programs that spanned national boundaries and QLF, almost from the start, was a bi-national program involving programs in the United States and Canada. Eventually, the QLF community-based model would travel to other nations and continents.

When QLF introduced its community-based programs, most environmental efforts were top-down operations with orders and laws issued by someone remote and powerful, usually the government. This sort of approach is rarely effective in the long run. In rural areas people tend to resent and eventually ignore such edicts from the outside. And, as I noted earlier, enforcement of wildlife regulations is almost impossible in remote regions. Our programs were different. We started at the community level with children. Children can be powerful motivators for their parents. Anti-smoking campaigns, for example, that focus on children have proven to be effective in convincing many adults to quit smoking cigarettes. It is hard to ignore the passionate and persuasive powers of one's own children. Similarly, the children of the North Shore absorbed the lessons taught by Kath and the people she directed. Rather than teach the children what not to do, Kath and her team led the children and their families on excursions to the seabird colonies, where they observed the behavior of birds up close and learned about the harmful impact that human actions can have on breeding birds and their offspring.

QLF was always focused on education. We never engaged in the public and dramatic protests of other environmental organizations. While there is certainly a place for environmental activism and I would never judge another organization, I was far more comfortable taking a more conciliatory and longer range approach. I believe that this approach is also more effective over time. If fishermen, hunters, and industry can be persuaded to make permanent changes in behavior, then the wildlife has time to recover and will ultimately thrive in a more pristine and stable habitat.

The children who participated in the first Living Rivers Program in Tabusintac, New Brunswick, came from rural Maine, New Brunswick, the Quebec North Shore, and Labrador. We took them to visit paper mills, nuclear power plants, and hydroelectric power plants and dams. They saw with their own eyes and experienced firsthand the impact of development and industry on the Atlantic salmon and other indigenous species. The QLF programs were always designed to nurture community leadership. Our hope was that the young participants would not only learn but would also become role models for others. Many of these youngsters did emerge as community leaders.

After the first year, we began to draw adults in from the fishing communities to talk about issues related to the rivers and the watershed. QLF's education deliberately emphasized watershed and rivers rather than the Atlantic salmon. The anglers who organized the first efforts to protect the habitat of the Atlantic salmon were mostly successful businessmen from outside the region and, as a result, Atlantic salmon preservation efforts had the reputation of being championed by an elite group. By talking about the health of the rivers and watershed, we related the preservation efforts to something that affected the quality of life of the local people who likely had little in common with the sport fishermen but certainly cared deeply about the local waterways and wildlife. Yet it was the money of these salmon anglers that financed the first residential camp in the first Living Rivers Program. My many friends in the angling community were generous and, I hope, gave us the benefit of the doubt that our approach would prove successful.

Sport fishing had never been a threat to the Atlantic salmon. Despite the numbers of Canadian and American anglers, they each caught a handful of fish, not the hundreds and thousands captured by commercial fishing interests. I realized I could be a matchmaker. I could help identify clients through my connections in the Atlantic salmon community and help my parishioners with the leasing rights and licenses needed to set them up in business as outfitters and guides. I worked closely with my friend Leslie Foreman in 1963 and '64 as he began to set up a fishing camp and outfitting business on the Kegaska River. In a letter dated April 6, 1963, I encouraged him to build a camp with a picture window as it would "provide the maximum amount of light in the cabin and also be fine for looking out over the Gulf." Les built a small house on a grassy hillside backed by woods overlooking the Gulf.

It is next to the mouth of the Kegaska River and sheltered by a string of muskeg-covered islands.

That summer I got heavily involved in heading off an attempt to take away Les's leasing rights on the Kegaska River. A well-connected and ambitious Canadian used his government contacts to go after the leasing rights that had been held by Les and his family for years. It took a lot of meetings and effort on my part to get the government officials to recognize that this was a grievous violation of the rights of a family that had lived on the Quebec North Shore and fished on the river for three generations.

I thought Les would be an excellent guide and outfitter, and I was right about that. He did so well that by January 1966, I returned a post to an angler who had asked me to set up Les as an outfitter, telling him that Les was completely booked with anglers for the 1966 fishing season. But I recommended that he go to the Old Fort River, just 150 miles east of Kegaska, and be outfitted by another friend, Sam Fequet Jr. "Sam has one of the best stretches on the North Shore, and has not even scratched the surface of his new lease," I wrote. "The trout fishing is excellent throughout the summer, and although the salmon are generally small, they are quite numerous."

Outfitting was a business that provided new jobs to many of the local fishermen, their relatives and their neighbors. In every fishing party, there was a need for one guide for every two anglers. The anglers needed lodging, so there were jobs entailed in building, furnishing, and maintaining the camps. And the anglers needed transportation and food, so pilots and other camp staff were involved in every trip. There is an economic ripple created by small business development of all types and the outfitting business was one way to help the coastal families earn enough money to stay in their home villages. Buzz Merritt, a New Yorker, wisely coordinated the logistics for the famous log camp on the lower stretch of the river.

In 1977 QLF did more important work focusing on seabirds with a wonderful program at the St. Mary's Islands on the Quebec North Shore, one of the most important breeding areas for seabirds in the Gulf of St. Lawrence. During breeding season, tens of thousands of seabirds come to the islands to nest and rear their young. At this time, the cliffs and rocky slopes are filled with razorbilled auks, common murres, Atlantic puffins, black guillemots and double crested cormorants (locally called "shags"), while the grassy and tundra areas come alive with nesting eider ducks and terns. Dr. Blanchard and her team of interns, working side-by-side with the people of the coast, were able to demonstrate that QLF's educational programs were an effective approach to restoring the seabird populations while still respecting the way of life of coastal residents. Over the course of twenty years, they documented positive changes in people's knowledge of birds and their caring actions for the seabird colonies. Gradually, we began to see concrete progress: the seabird populations started to recover and a new generation of residents developed great pride in what they had accomplished for the birds.

QLF benefited from the fact that environmentalism was on the rise and we were acutely aware that we were able to reverse a few negative trends because of fortuitous timing. In fact, we recognized that when we celebrated the 25th anniversary of the organization at the University Club in New York City in November 1985; the theme was "The Right Place at the Right Time." By 1985, QLF had expanded from a community program that ran summer programs with volunteers into an organization that stretched into Maine and New Brunswick, Canada. We broadened our scope and added year-round programming. This included arts education, environmental education camps, ecological studies, natural history instruction, and information exchange workshops. Our staff, particularly Larry and Kath, who were experts in wildlife conservation, participated in international conferences on human and natural resources.

We were very much looking ahead at that 25th anniversary celebration. My concern for the people of the North Shore remained very high. One of the written goals of the 25th anniversary campaign stated, "The inhabitants of the Atlantic Region must maintain their livelihoods in the face of endangered natural resources—the sea, the forest, the soil, and the inland waters. They must adapt their cultures to survive in industrialized societies without sacrificing their heritage. They need strong, skillful leadership."

By year 25, QLF had sponsored 1,100 interns and volunteers. Scholarships had been awarded to 400 young men and women. Most had returned to their communities as nurses, pilots, teachers, engineers, lawyers, scientists, and managers. I found this so rewarding. When I first arrived on the coast, most of those positions were held by people who were, as the local people would say, "from away." Sports clinics, water safety instruction, canoeing expeditions, and residential camping programs taught survival and leadership skills, built self-confidence, and nurtured the strong sense of community that already existed on the coast.

William Cohen, then a Republican senator from Maine, recognized the value of QLF's bi-national programs. "The similarities among North Atlantic regions on both sides of the Canadian-U.S. border are evident," he wrote, "and yet there are too few ongoing efforts to recognize and promote that association. As a Maine resident and senator, I am grateful to QLF for helping to link Maine to her northern and eastern neighbors through programs that heighten appreciation of the natural resources we share." QLF had an annual budget of $950,000 in 1985. We had many ambitions for the future. We came to realize that QLF represented a model of community-focused education that would work not just in the wilds of Quebec's North Shore but also in remote villages in other parts of the world. There is a universality to small, remote villages regardless of race, language, religion, or place. Modernity posed the same mixture of opportunity and risk to delicate ecosystems and to a traditional way of life.

By the 50th anniversary in 2008, we had awarded more than 1,200 scholarships and had an alumni of more than 2,600 volunteers and interns and 600 international fellows. The annual budget was $3 million. The organization had evolved in ways I never expected. In fact, so much change had taken place since I first flew into the Quebec North Shore and created the organization that the staff could talk about "Old QLF" and "New QLF." The evolution was not seamless, but one project seemed to lead to the next. QLF remained true to its original vision but expanded far beyond the villages of the North Shore.

I had watched the International Grenfell Association adjust to changing times. The operational costs and many of the services that Sir Wilfred's organization provided for decades were absorbed by Newfoundland's Department of Regional Affairs, but the International

Grenfell Association maintained a vital role in the medical arena, and their positive influence endures to this day. I knew that QLF needed to be flexible and nimble and willing to adapt to new challenges and changed conditions if it was to remain relevant. With each decade, the changes taking place in the world, particularly changes in communications and technology, posed new threats to the Quebec North Shore but also presented new opportunities. Today the Quebec North Shore is no longer the isolated region it was in the 1960s. Satellite technology and the Internet and other innovations in communications allow a fisherman in Kegaska to communicate with someone half a world away in seconds.

The Atlantic Center for the Environment became our internal structure for all of the conservation and rural development programs that we subsequently operated. Programs that respected local traditions and practices were needed in other places. We eventually operated conservation and sustainability programs with local non-governmental organizations in the Caribbean, Latin America, and Europe, particularly Central and Southeastern Europe. Today QLF is described as an NGO with a regional heart and a global reach. We helped create the Port Honduras Marine Reserve in Belize to restore depleted fisheries and thwart poaching. In Muscat, Oman, increased tanker traffic and pollution had a disastrous impact upon local fisheries. Our exchange programs focused on addressing these concerns to not only save an important economic business but also preserve the way of life of the fishermen and their families. We supported the work Helen Hays of the American Museum of Natural History did in Punta Rasa, Argentina. For 38 years, Helen Hays had banded common and roseate terns on Great Gull Island in eastern Long Island Sound. With our help, Helen extended her research to South America to collect vital data on the migratory patterns of the same birds.

QLF was asked to sponsor international partnerships because of our success in working at the community level while also conducting programs that crossed national borders. Prior to the fall of the Berlin Wall, QLF was asked to introduce central Europe to the work of North American NGOs, which showcased the talents and role of the private sector. After the wall came down, QLF helped fledgling democracies harness private enterprise to conserve and manage areas that combined great natural beauty with local industry. In 1992 QLF was invited to run exchanges with conservation leaders in the Middle East, primarily because of our experience working across international borders. In the Caribbean and Latin America, QLF helped promote historic hemispheric connections through environmental exchanges and workshops. The notion of stewardship and the belief that man has a responsibility to protect and preserve the natural world and wildlife governed all of these efforts.

One of the signs of our maturity as an organization was our substantial alumni. The thousands of volunteers, interns, employees, and supporters are one of our proudest legacies. Their combined experience, commitment and expertise have enormous value. We decided to draw upon that web of talent with a Global Leadership Network that would provide consulting services to deal with complex conservation issues that cross national boundaries.

We had gone a long way since I mused about how I might teach swimming to the children of the North Shore and arrange for them to further their schooling with scholarships as I flew from Choate School. I never imagined the evolution or the impact QLF would have over the course of fifty years. For me, the most important work remains the scholarship program that continues to this day.

CHAPTER 13

Turn with the Sun

I HAVE BEEN lucky in my lifetime to be able to follow my dreams. Yet the enduring thread through all the decades has been connection to family. From my early days as the second youngest of seven children, I have cherished my role as brother, then father, uncle, and grandfather. I have delighted in the gathering of family and the opportunity to share activities I love. I flew to so many of my daughters' sports games in 69Easy that one team claimed the yellow floatplane as their mascot. My three daughters were natural athletes, so I had ample raw material for coaching track and field, lacrosse, fly-fishing, skeet shooting, pond hockey, waterskiing, canoeing, mountain climbing, sailing, touch football, and flying a floatplane. Family gatherings were characterized by games, pranks, and antics, along with whatever sports suited the location. The arrival of grandchildren added to the fun. We had traditions and pranks associated with each holiday. At each Thanksgiving touch football game, I walked out with a crutch, feigning injury, and then ran from the sidelines to complete a play. At each Easter egg hunt, I carried the biggest wicker laundry basket to make the children laugh, and at Christmas, I created a tremendous stocking for myself for the same effect. At night I told Grandpa Trapper stories (earlier called "Uncle Bobby stories" when told to nieces and nephews), childhood stories such as "Boker and the Rat," "The Chocolate Cake," and "The Fake Mouse." I drew up fabricated punch cards with activity lists: (1) ride on a komatik pulled by '64 snow machine, (2) duck hunting on the Essex marsh, (3) boat ride, and so on.

I enjoy seeing my grandchildren taking their wit and wisdom, skills and interests in new directions. There is some continuity and overlap with coaching, working with environmental non-profits, humanitarian work, comedy and media, and outdoor leadership, but they are taking these pursuits to new levels. Several worked for QLF on summer programs or with the staff in Ipswich. QLF has always been a family endeavor. My daughters played and worked in QLF summer programs, Kerry as a co-pilot for many years, and one son-in-law, a QLF alumnus, is on the Board of Directors.

Family created the balance and pulls of a busy life, and my wife, Faith, was our anchor to windward. She was an integral part of all that I did, from establishing Bert and I to founding the Quebec Labrador Foundation and the deep and lasting connections with the people of the North Shore and beyond. After 45 years of marriage, Faith died of cancer. She was strong, kind, and giving to the end. She embraced adventure from that first canoe trip and walk through the cathedral in Quebec City, and remained unflaggingly supportive and encouraging. Faith loved the people of the coast and they loved her. With blue jeans, a backpack, red bandana, and old tennis sneakers, she visited every day that she was there, bringing her happy presence and caring spirit. Her passing marked the end of an era.

While my spirits have never flagged, the ailments that accompany advanced age limit my mobility and sometimes compromise my independence. But the richness of my memories warms me during the cold Canadian winters. I close my eyes and remember flying 69Easy. I hear the steady *whirrrr* of the engine and see the sun glint off the sparkling sea below on a perfect flying day. An old friend in his boat spots the bright yellow airplane and whips off his hat to wave an enthusiastic greeting, and I tip my wings to acknowledge him. When the yellow floatplane splashes onto the surface of the water, I crack open the side window and the intoxicating and distinctive scent of salt air rushes inside; I hear the gulls calling nearby and the gentle wash of the surf against the floats.

Harrington Harbour grows larger and brighter as the plane taxis into the cove. I remember that remarkable feeling of flying like a bird over wild places, and I once again experience that sense of peace, fulfillment, and overwhelming joy.

I have lived long enough to see dramatic change and transformation. The harshness of the North Shore was eased by the introduction of electricity and other amenities of modern life. I played a part in bringing the first radio-telephone system to the villages on the coast in the 1960s. Martha Love, one of the founding board members of the Quebec Labrador Foundation, donated $10,000 in 1962 for the purchase and installation of a Marconi High Frequency Radio Telephone System from Sept-Iles to St. Paul's River. There was no landline telephone service on the coast then. A shaky crank-up telephone system linked a few families locally, but the main way to get a message farther afield was by telegram and that system could be unreliable; a single telegraph wire ran along poles that had been in place for years and a storm could easily bring down the line.

The Marconi radio was brilliant in its reliability and simplicity, only needing a generator or batteries to operate. We designated an operator in each village and set up a regular system of two calls each day at 8 a.m. and 5 p.m. Some of the operators kept their radios on all the time but others just turned it on twice a day to preserve battery strength or husband the gasoline needed to power the generator. This high-frequency, or shortwave, radio marked a dramatic improvement in communication between villages. If someone had an accident in Kegaska, Les Forman would report it at 5 p.m. and the news went up and down the coast from Father Burke at St. Paul's River to Riney Robertson at La Tabatiere to the Bryan family at Harrington Harbour. That reliable system of communication caused morale to soar, particularly during the cold winter months when it was difficult to travel and visit. The residents of the region felt more connected to their friends and relatives in other villages.

Eventually, the telephone came to the region. While some old timers never really became comfortable using the telephone and limited their conversations to short telegraph-like pronouncements, others spent hours on the phone catching up. The phone unquestionably helped family members and friends stay in touch and was another important way to relieve the isolation of old. The first phones on the coast were the local crank-up phones, and the classic oak box wall phones provided village service. The number of rings on the crank-up phones identified the recipient of a call. I remember an elderly lady in Alymer Sound who had number seven so a call for her was seven separate rings. However, she invariably picked up after one or two rings to listen to other people's conversations. She stayed on the line, her heavy breathing audible in the background, as the intended recipient took the call. After some time listening to her neighbors' conversation, she might querulously inquire, "Did you ring seven?"

Although the radio and later the modernized phone improved communication between the isolated communities, nothing was more welcomed or more enduring than personal contact. When I first flew into the villages up and down the coastline, children raced to the shoreline to watch the yellow plane touch down on the harbor waters. The arrival of any visitor was a significant moment, and the arrival of the minister in a plane was especially exciting. I always felt it was part of my job and responsibility as a minister to lift the spirits of my parishioners. I could express myself in the simplest way, through face-to-face contact with families during pastoral visits. This proved to be my true calling.

When I first came to the coast, I vowed to visit every single dwelling on a regular basis. It was an ambitious goal and it shaped my life. I tried to visit as many families as I could on a given day. If weather or daylight caught me far from home, I found a place to stay. It was never difficult. The instinctive generosity of the people of the North always assured me of a warm bed and hospitality to rest overnight.

When heavy fog kept the plane idle, I visited in Harrington. There was no such thing as the five-minute visit. It would not do to show up and exchange greetings and leave after some small talk. Visiting in those days had the formality of a long-established ritual, and each visit lasted for an hour or longer. One thing that has never changed in those isolated villages is that no one locks a door. Visitors drop in at any time, and no one knocks. One just walks up to a house, opens the door and enters. This universal practice gave me pause in my first years on the coast. My own background and training caused me to worry that I might be interrupting or disturbing someone by just opening the door without notice. Yet in all those years of visiting I never once felt unwelcome or intrusive. This says a great deal about the warmth and openness of the people of the North and a deep culture of genuine hospitality.

When visiting I would open the door and call out, "It's Mr. Bryan coming in," or shout out the name of the person I was visiting to give them some notice. Many of the fishing families went to bed early at night, as early as 7:30 p.m. In the early years there was no electric light to read by, no radio to listen to, and no television to watch, so people turned in early. They also rose early. For cod fishermen, it was not unusual to get up at 2 a.m. to be out on the sea by 3 a.m. Many times I would realize that the family had gone to bed and call out, "I can come back tomorrow," as I heard a mad scramble inside to light a lamp and find clothing. Invariably they would call back, "No, no, no, Mr. Bryan." And moments later, the family would be rushing down the stairs with broad smiles welcoming me into the kitchen or sitting room. We always said a prayer or sang a hymn. During visits, we discussed the weather, the state of fishing, or a recent seal or caribou hunt. The teakettle would soon be singing and a plate of cake or cookies would be served. In homes where I may have gone fishing or hunting with the man of the house, they often suggested we share a "touch" of gin. Gin was the drink of choice. The bottle would come out and the fiery gin was served in little shot glasses. At community celebrations, particularly wedding suppers and dances, someone was always standing by the door with a pint of gin to offer to the guests who went out for a breath of fresh air. I eagerly joined in on occasions that I wasn't flying or on church duty the next day. As is quite common in cold weather climates and isolated communities, there was a lot of drinking on the coast.

Every family had an old well-loved Bible or much-worn copies of the *Book of Common Prayer*, the traditional Anglican prayer book that includes all the traditional rituals and prayers for services and Holy Communion. In recent years, the Church has updated the liturgy to keep relevant with changing tastes, but the old timers on the North Shore preferred the old ways and, to be honest, so did I. They often read the service, including the parts intended for the priest, along with me. The people on the coast referred to services as "prayers." No one would ever ask, "Are we going to have evening services?" The question was always, "Prayers tonight, Mr. Bryan?"

Holy Communion is one of the great sacraments in the Anglican Church. When I visited people, especially in isolated outposts, I knew that Communion was expected and desired. I had a portable Communion kit that included a chalice, a paten (the small plate used in the service), a small spoon, a supply of the thin communion wafers, and wine. The linens used in the service were perfectly laundered and pressed, white with a small red cross and always meticulously clean. Losing gear and equipment is inevitable in a small airplane, and the Communion kit rolled out of my floatplane more than once. The kit once tumbled out of the plane onto the floats and then plunged into fifteen feet of water. The water was perfectly clear and I watched with amazement as a big cod swam by and ate the little spoon. It looked intent upon eating the whole kit but someone poked the fish away with a long pole and another parishioner jumped into the frigid water to retrieve the items. One memorable time, the Communion kit and my gun barrel fell into the water in Labrador. An Inuit man in a sealskin kayak rescued everything for me.

The visiting took me to the 6 major villages as well as at least 25 other outposts with a family or two. I flew regularly to each of the three lighthouses. I flew to the simple summer houses where fishing families lived temporarily during the busiest part of the fishing season and to log cabins or canvas tents in the bush where hunters would gather for three or four weeks in the dead of winter. I held many services in the dim lantern light of a tent after the men returned from a long day of hunting caribou or moose. Sometimes the fishermen pulled several boats together and we prayed together in the gently bobbing seawaters. There were communities that did not technically fall within my diocesan responsibilities but I visited them regularly because of Quebec Labrador Foundation programs. Over the course of my career, I logged more than 19,000 hours and came to know the way from Ipswich, Massachusetts, to the farthest reaches of Labrador, Newfoundland, and the Quebec North Shore like the back of my hand. There were places so small or insignificant that they were not marked on any map but they were part of my flyway. After years of flying, I could skirt around a bank of fog, spot an obscure inlet, and once again know exactly where I was.

The people of the Quebec North Shore were deeply spiritual. In times of grief, they needed the solace of prayer and a comforting presence. They often asked profound questions that have troubled human beings since the beginning of time: Why did God allow this to happen? Was this God's will? Whenever there is a grievous accident, a survivor will invariably say that "God was with me" or "I was saved by God." There was a deep fatalism that was a core cultural touchstone on the North Shore. They expected life to be unfair, difficult, and harsh because it had always been so. They knew bad things happen to good people and they accepted that as a fundamental part of life. When someone died, they would say: "It was his time."

I respected that sense of destiny but I also wanted the people of the North Shore to understand that human beings have choices. A fisherman could make a choice about taking extra safety precautions and stashing a life jacket with his gear before heading to the open sea. There was always a choice of the route to take over land or sea. As a boy, I read and re-read an adventure story published early in the twentieth century. In *Ungava Bob: A Winter's Tale,* by Dillon Wallace, the hero tries to take a shortcut across the ice with his dog team and winds up adrift. Months later, after many adventures in the wild and a time under the protection of an Inuit family, he makes a joyous return to his family and home having learned that sometimes the longest way around is the safest way home.

Dr. Gordon Thomas and I discussed the will of God many times. As one of the few medical doctors in the region, Dr. Thomas saved many lives through his skill and dedication. Sometimes, however, his best efforts came up short. Medical care had just come too late, for example, or the patient was simply so ill or injured that nothing could have made a difference short of a genuine miracle. Gordon Thomas was a deeply spiritual man. He once wrote:

> The problem of illness in children has always remained with me as a great puzzle. Some people are fatalistic while others say it is the will of God. I do not believe it is God's will that any should perish,

either physically or spiritually. We are all victims of our humanity and subject to the laws of nature, of human weakness and human pathology. What God does is give us strength to overcome and face the difficulties of life and its illnesses with hope and confidence.

Tragedy is as much a part of human life as joy, something the people of the North Shore knew better than most. They drew great comfort from their faith that God was standing by them during the great trials of life, and I drew upon certain prayers over and over again because they resonated with the people. One was: "Oh Lord, thou art one who does not need us but who will not be without us. Thanks be to thee who by thy spirit comest to be with each one of us, our Friend, our Guide, the Lord of Life."

Friendship and family were also a source of great strength and joy. Church services, community events, winter carnival, and visiting brought individuals and families together with neighbors in a way that helped them endure the long winters. Joy and fun are fuel for the human spirit, and the people of the North had plenty of both.

Modern life has lost the stillness and silence that remained a part of life on the North Shore longer than it did other places. Without the quiet and time to contemplate and experience that special connection with nature, much is lost. Of course, some assert that while many have fallen away from organized religion, spirituality is still a vital part of most people's lives.

A prayer I wrote and used frequently in my pastoral ministry went this way: "Forgive us for we readily accept the comforts of that still small voice and neglect the challenge to which it calls. Thou art the one who speaketh to us from stillness and silence. Enable us to wait upon thee that we may be renewed in strength and able to meet the duties and difficulties of life with humility and confidence."

The presence of running water, electric lights and heat, television and radio were all welcome innovations. Yet the resilience and independence of the people became somewhat compromised by the modern innovations. When there was no electricity, families used wood to keep their homes warm in the coldest times. I spent a week at Harrington Harbour in 2002 when an ice storm took out electricity for a week or so.

In 1960, I would have been fine because of ample supplies of wood even as the temperature dropped to twenty below zero. But in 2002 it was difficult because we had come to rely so heavily upon electricity. We spent the week in our winter clothes indoors day and night and were still cold. Food supplies grew short because the big transport planes could not fly into the region with provisions. Back in 1960, every family would have set aside enough food for the winter in advance and no one would have run out of food in a single week.

The people who remain on the coast retain a special affinity to nature that I share. The longest flights I made in the region were over open water. About ten times a summer I would cross from the Quebec North Shore to Anticosti Island and then fly over to New Brunswick and the lighthouse at Miscou Island on the northeast tip of New Brunswick. After crossing Anticosti, I still had sixty miles to go from the southwest point of Anticosti to Miscou. Over the open water there were no navigation aids so I used a compass and the directional gyro, but one day I became disoriented. I could not see anything to give me my bearings. I could only look down at the water and try to keep the plane level. Then I spotted strings of gannets in flight below me. The gannet is a white seabird with a six-foot wingspan. The birds are remarkable. They live for twenty to forty years. The largest gannet colony in North America is located on Bonaventure Island in the Gaspé Peninsula. One of the striking characteristics of these seabirds is that they return to the same nest site year after year. I realized the gannets were beginning to make their way at the end of the day to nesting sites on the cliffs of Bonaventure Island. So I followed them. They might fly 100 or 150 miles to feed but they always return to roost in their nests at the end of the day. It was still light, and I could see the gannets easily, in groups of ten or fifteen birds flying about twenty feet above the water. I was flying the Helio and was able to slow down my airspeed to easily jump from one company of birds to the next, all flying straight back to Bonaventure. As soon as I got within sight of Bonaventure Island and the tip of the Gaspé Peninsula, I knew where I was and was able to fly the final 35 miles safely to Miscou.

Travelers have used the sun, moon, and stars for navigation since ancient times. The North Star has guided the path of travelers for thousands of years. As a bush pilot in the North, where there were few manmade landmarks, I might rely upon the course of a riverbed, stands of trees, or the flight of birds to mark my progress. But mostly I relied upon the sun. I rarely flew after dark. A perfect day for flying was when the sun rose brilliantly from the east. In the far north, where the arc of the sun lies toward the south, the sun appears to move from the left to the right. Years before the ubiquity of global positioning systems, I used the sun to get my bearings. If in doubt, I turned with the sun. When flying into the sun, this meant turning right, and turning right became something of a tradition. Old ship captains adhered to the tradition with a superstitious commitment that was almost comic. If the winds were making it difficult to turn right, I would watch ships at Kegaska going through all sorts of gyrations trying to turn right as the wind blew them the other way. For me, flying out over the Gulf, turning right with the sun was always the way to find my way home.

Afterword

WHILE THE Great Depression had effectively halted development plans for Tunk Lake in Maine, it continued to be a desirable place for recreation development because it remained so close to its original pristine state. The vulnerability became apparent nearly thirty years after the 1957 death of Admiral Richard Byrd. For decades, the Bryan and Byrd families were among the few to maintain camps on the lake. The Admiral's heirs could not agree on the disposition of his estate, so it was not until 1983 that his son Richard E. Byrd Jr. sold the lodge and land. The new owner intended to build condominiums on the site; fortunately, the location was listed on the National Historic Register and a court order prevented him from proceeding with the construction. When Wickyup Lodge burned to the ground in 1984, he was charged with arson. The man, who was using an alias, had increased the insurance on the lodge shortly before the fire, and maintained that his dog started the fire accidently when it knocked over a kerosene lamp. The court disagreed and he went to prison.

The Admiral's son, Commander Richard E. Byrd Jr., was a kind and intelligent Harvard-educated naval officer who became reclusive as he grew older. He was an extraordinary man who, in our youth, was a great friend to me and my siblings. I presided over his service at Arlington National Cemetery on October 14, 1998, after his death at age 68.

My brother Jim and I kept close tabs on all development plans for Tunk Lake and immersed ourselves in the task of preservation with passion and perseverance. Back in 1976, my sister and brother-in-law Hazel and Ernie Tracy had granted a conservation easement on their six-acre shorefront lot to the state of Maine. Their action began years of family effort that led to agreements between individuals, the state, and non-profit institutions that eventually protected Tunk Lake forever.

While I experienced some close calls and frightening moments as a bush pilot over the course of my long career, one of the most traumatic incidents took place in July 1995, on my floatplane ramp at Harrington Harbour, even though no one was injured. That summer, my trainee and helper was Tobin Peacock. Tobin was sitting in the right seat next to me and his brother Tom, a QLF swimming instructor, sat in the jump seat behind him. Wiley Reynold's eighteen-year-old granddaughter, Christina Bennison, sat in the rear seat. She was happily anticipating her first flight in a floatplane.

The engine roared to life and I eased up on the brakes and taxied down the ramp. Four feet from the end of the ramp, I pulled the plane to a halt, and, with the prop barely kicking over, allowed the Cessna to continue to roll on over the edge. I had followed this procedure thousands of times over the years. It allowed me to ease the floatplane into the water where I could accelerate again and prepare for takeoff.

But this time was different. As soon as the nose wheels dropped off the end of the ramp and the wheel struts became fully extended, the left bow wheel hooked on a rock. On that day, the tide was at the lowest level of the year. There is only three feet of ledge at the end of the ramp and normally the plane would clear the ledge and ease into deep water. This time the plane stopped abruptly; the momentum flipped the floatplane onto its nose and then quickly over onto its back.

It happened in a flash. I immediately shut off the magnetos and electrical system, but in those few seconds, I found myself upside down with water pouring into the cabin. Tobin and I had rehearsed emergency procedures many times. He reacted promptly. As the plane was flipping over, Tobin asked his brother Tom to open the door. Within moments, Tobin and his brother were out the door. I remember seeing Christina's blue jeans disappear through the right-side door. Knowing the three passengers were out was a relief, but I had to wait until the cabin was filled with water to gain enough buoyancy to relieve the pressure on my seatbelt. The water rushed in and I was completely immersed. I held my breath, unbuckled my seatbelt and, after a clumsy tank turn in the middle of floating fishing rods and canoe paddles, I righted myself and shot out through the right side door. The first thing I saw was Christina's radiant smile. My relief held no bounds. Local friends Wilson Evans, in his diving gear, and Larry Ransom, operating a forklift on the wharf, were principle in righting the airplane. Without them, and the numerous Coastal friends who came to help, the airplane would have been wrecked.

Later, the "what ifs" shook me deeply. Most significantly, I might have been responsible for the deaths of three remarkable young people. Personally, the accident represented a confrontation with my own mortality.

It is not easy to be a member of a minister's family. I was often away when my girls were young and I spent a great deal of time focusing on the needs of my parishioners. I have been fortunate to be married to remarkable women who shared not only my ministry but also my love of the North and my commitment to its people. After Faith's death, I married Patricia "Trish" Peacock, the mother of two QLF volunteers, Tobin and Tom, and chaplain at Bishop's College School for eighteen years.

When Trish first flew in Cessna N369E on the coast, she enjoyed being a passenger but soon became aware that it might be important for her to learn how to fly. She visited the local Sherbrooke airport and signed up to take the pilot's course at Paquin Aviation, where she ultimately completed her flight instruction and passed her flight test in a Cessna 172. A year later, in 2003, on Pushaw Lake, Maine, near Bangor, Trish trained for her floatplane rating. Her instructor, Kathy Hodgkins, was a pilot for Continental Airlines who flew Boeing 767s across the Atlantic. Kathy's husband, Tim, was an FAA examiner and co-owner of T.K. Aviation at Pushaw Lake. Tim gave Trish her floatplane rating test. In a short time, Trish made a transition to a 295-horsepower Cessna 185 fitted with amphibious floats.

I am grateful for the love and support of my three wonderful daughters who grew up on the coast—Sarah Bryan Severance, Kerry Bryan Brokaw, and Sandy Bryan Weatherall—and my grandchildren— Bryan and Ben Severance; Winslow, Roz, Will, and Shea Brokaw; Grace,

Hayden, and Carolina Weatherall, and my great granddaughter, Appleby (Bee) Marr Severance. The Nadeau boys who came out to schools in the United States are like sons to me, and treat me as kindly as they would a father or grandfather. Kirby Nadeau is a teacher and coach at Bishops College and meets me every Sunday for breakfast. We laugh and tell tales of days on the coast. His cousin, Tim, my standout co-pilot for many years, checks in regularly and keeps me laughing. Kirby's eldest brother Philip, the first boy from the coast to come out to study at Choate School, is now the President of the Canadian Board of Directors of the Quebec Labrador Foundation.

While I was the first flying minister on the North Shore, I was followed by others and must mention the Reverend Jim Young and the Reverend John Neal, who carried on the ministry in their own way and had their own amazing experiences and came to love the people of the North Shore as I did.

As I look back over those many years, I derive great satisfaction and joy from introducing those I love to the North. My brother Bill's daughter Ellen worked as a QLF volunteer in Cartwright, Labrador for four summers. She returned to Labrador to teach school and married Enoch Obed of Nain, Labrador. They had three children. Ellen Bryan Obed became an author of noteworthy children's books on the North, beginning with *Borrowed Black* in 1979 and including *Twelve Kinds of Ice*, which *Kirkus Review* described as one of the best children's books of 2012.* My sister Joy's daughter Beth married a fisherman from Kegaska, Enis Stubbert, whom she met while working as a QLF volunteer. They had three children, and now live in Ottawa. Beth taught school in Kegaska and won the prestigious Marshall McLuhan Award for Excellence in teaching in Quebec.

This book has been a joy to write, as I have been able to reflect on so many experiences, hearing the voices and seeing the faces of people I have loved. I am particularly grateful to my daughter Kerry for the time and care she took in editing this manuscript. I also thank and acknowledge the help of my daughters Sandy and Sarah and the many friends who helped prod my memory, particularly Candace Cochrane, Ed Miller, Rick Bullock, Kath Blanchard, and Larry Morris.

I feel more acutely the fleeting nature of my own life, but I take solace in my faith and in the conviction that I will never be separated from those I have loved. I cherish the friends I have made and the adventures we have had. So many people have touched my life, too many to mention here. My deepest thanks to all.

At the end of every service, I recite one of my favorite prayers from *The Book of Common Prayer*. That seems like a good way to end this book as well.

Oh Lord, support us all the day long, until the shadows lengthen and the evening comes, and the busy world lies hushed, and the fever of life is over, and our work is done. Then in thy mercy grant us a safe lodging, and a holy rest, and peace at the last. Amen.

*In 2015, after the first printing of this book, Bob Bryan's great nephew, Natan Obed, one of Ellen Bryan Obed's sons, was elected president of ITK (Inuit Tapiriit Kanatami), giving him the leadership of and representative role for the 65,000 Inuit of Canada's north. In the final days of his life, Robert Bryan was asked what he thought of his grandnephew's position. "I knew it," he said. "I knew it all along."

Such was his love and vision for the north. Such was his love and vision for young people. To see these realized in one of his very own family brings the final chapter of his life to a perfect close.

Acknowledgments

THE AVIATION stories resulted from logbook entries, journals and a vivid memory of experiences in the air shared by pilots and passengers who flew with me.

I was the first Anglican priest to pilot an aircraft on the Quebec North Shore in 1959. In 1964, the Reverend Jim Young joined the Anglican Church aviators, followed by the Reverend John Neal. They are both brilliant pilots and the stories of their lives and flying missions are legendary. It was a privilege for me to work with them. I hope one day they too will tell their stories.

Thanks to many aviators who have helped and influenced me over the years: Groever Loening, Admiral Richard E. Byrd, Endicott P. Davison, Crocker Snow, Andy Pew, Tris Colket, J. J. Frey, Ed Miller, Rick Bullock, Gus Bullock, Gordon Lamb, Lawton Lamb, Johnny May, Telford Allen Jr., Wiley Reynolds Jr., John Pratt III, George Baker III, Kane Baker, Sid Seed, Tom Green, Bob Wade, R. L. Smith, Roger Baikie, Bill and Ginny Cowles, Brud Folger, Randy Cox, Justin Lessard, Roly Ferguson, John Blick, Lou Hilton, Felix DuPont, Tim Hodgkins, Kenneth Hoffman, Dick Folsom, Bill Taylor, Curtis Blake, and my loyal crewman Gordon Kippen. These are just a few of the aviators who have helped in the past five decades.

With thanks to friends, engineers, and mechanics who kept N69E airworthy over fifty years: Enis Cribb, Les Welch, Gaby Blanchette, Bill Gallichon, Steve Hnadowitz, Leroy Meuse, John O'Neill, Les Jones, Arthur Zolot, Mac Close, and North Atlantic Air personnel, as well as numerous other engineers and aircraft mechanics in the United States and Canada.

I was fortunate to have had special guidance from friends and associates who spent time with me on the Lower North Shore and encouraged me in my life's work: Sarah Severance, Bruce Severance, Kerry and Bayard (Bags) Brokaw, Sandy and Bobby Weatherall, Les Foreman, Clarence Rowsell, John Arthur, Kirby Nadeau, Philip Nadeau, Tim Nadeau, Garland Nadeau, Laurie Nadeau, Laurie Cox, Alice and Gary Lessard, Lloyd Jones, Jim and Sharon Ransom, Lloyd and Linda Ransom, Ruth Colgrove, Tom Colgrove, the Reverend Sidney Lovett, William Brokaw, Richard Berlin, Tom Matthews, Ed Woodsum, Peter Miller, J. D. Miller, Lee Wulff, Ted Rogowski, Bill Mapel, Henry Merritt, A. Lachlan Reed, Barge Levy, the Tilden family, Richard Cox, Kelsey Bush Nadeau, Nathaniel P. Reed, Peter Crisp, Wilfred Carter, Dugald Fletcher, Boker Doyle, John Scully, the Fred Moseley family, the E.O. Miller family, Tristram Colket, Curtis Blake, Bill MacEachern, John Bush, Jim Jones, the Reverend Kelly Clark, Hazel and Ernest Tracy, Bill Bryan, Bill Bryan Jr., James T. Bryan Jr., Jay Bryan, Dr. Fred Makrauer, Ellen Preston, Richard Warren, Joy Bacon and family, Ron and Riney Robertson, QLF associates (Larry Morris, Candace Cochrane, Tom Horn, Kathleeen Blanchard, John Rae, Stephen Molson, Ginny and Bob Martin, William K. Muir Jr., Bob Schmon Jr., Beth Alling, Frederick G. P. Thorne, Raymond Courey, Patricia Middleton, Forrest Mars, the Reverend Seymour St. John), and QLF Board Chairmen (Robert W. Martin Jr., Donal C. O'Brien, Endicott P. Davison, Donald K. Clifford Jr., Robert M. Schmon, Bernard Panet Raymond, John Houghton, Pauline Ouimet, James Levitt, and Jameson French).

With heartfelt thanks to my collaborators, Chris Black, who pushed me incessantly to move forward with my stories, and to my daughter Kerry who spent countless hours helping me write and edit this book. Kerry shared her vivid memories of the people and events of the North Shore and reminded me of details I had long forgotten. Kerry was backed up by my daughter Sandy Weatherall and granddaughter Grace Weatherall, both of whom helped immensely with the final edits and were an integral part of the writing team. Supporting me in getting the book to its final stage over the period of a dozen years were: Patricia Peacock, Tom Peacock, Nancy Malaquis, Karen Ross, Sonia Zalesack, and Jane Gauvin.

Archbishop Philip Carrington, the Right Reverend Russel Brown, the Right Reverend Timothy Matthews, the Right Reverend Allen Goodings, and Archbishop A. Bruce Stavert all flew with me. The Right Reverend Dennis Drainville was consecrated bishop after my retirement.

The Reverends Jim Young, John Neil, Ronald West, Curtis Patterson, Anthony Hitsman, Janet Smith, Gladys Morency, Geoff Piper, John Gibaut, and Paul Lampman were all particularly close friends in the St. Clements East area.

Without the tireless help of drivers Bill Boice and Nelson Bullard, accompanied by his wife Charlotte, the thousands of miles of shuttling across the border, and hundreds of other chores would not have been possible.

There have been more than one thousand contributors to the Quebec Labrador Foundation over fifty years. There were a number of contributors who made it possible to carry on some vital projects. They were: the Honorable Hartland Molson, Paul Desmarais, Forrest Mars, Dan W. Lufkin, David Rockefeller, Joe Bryan, Clare Tweedy McMorris, Russell W. Meyer Jr., Lawrence and Jean Morris, P. Chapin Nolen, Peter J. Sharp, Ernest B. Tracy, J. Anderson Pew, Bus Mosbacher, George F. Baker III, Tristram Colket, Robert and Ginny Martin, A. Lachlan Reed, and Curtis Blake.

With love and deep gratitude to my late wife, Faith L. Bryan, who gave so much of her life to the work of the Quebec Labrador Foundation.

Thanks to my children, Sarah, Kerry, and Sandy, and my grandchildren, Bryan, Ben, Winslow, Rosalind, Will, Grace, Hayden, Shea, and Carolina, who all call me Grampa Trapper.

Finally, to my wife, the Reverend Dr. Patricia Peacock who has been my companion in my final chapter and whose sons and grandchildren, and great granddaughter, Bee, bring me joy on their wonderful visits.

About the Authors

Author

The Venerable Robert A. Bryan was the founder and chairman of the Quebec Labrador Foundation. He was the first Anglican priest to minister to the parishioners of the Quebec Lower North Shore in a floatplane and ski-plane, and logged tens of thousands of air miles in the North. He was the Archdeacon Emeritus of the North Shore (Quebec) Anglican Church of Canada. In the 60's he was a teacher and chaplain at the Choate School. A graduate of Hotchkiss, Hebron Academy, Yale, and Yale Divinity School, he was a longtime member of the board of directors of the Atlantic Salmon Federation and a director of the New England Grenfell Association, the Seaplane Pilots Association, and the Waterfowl Research Foundation. Bob was president of the National Pilots' Association, special advisor to the Seaplane Pilots' Association, and a member of the 1954 Yale Class Council. He was a director of the Yale Hockey Association and a former trustee at Hebron Academy and St. Paul's School. Bob was the first American to receive the Order of Merit in recognition of his contribution to the quality of life on the Quebec North Shore. He was also the co-author, with Marshall Dodge, of the *Bert and I* humor albums and books.

Collaborator

Chris Black is a writer and communications consultant. She was a long-time political reporter for the *Boston Globe* and a White House and

211

Congressional Correspondent for CNN. She is a native of Woburn, Massachusetts, and honors graduate of Northeastern University. She lives in Marion, Massachusetts, on a tidal river with her husband B. Jay Cooper.

Editor

Kerry Bryan Brokaw co-piloted the float and ski plane with her father and worked in Quebec Labrador Foundation summer programs for many years. She soloed a plane on her sixteenth birthday. Kerry is a Harvard graduate and a Waldorf educator who lives in Ketchum, Idaho. She and her husband, Bags, raised their four children in Brooksville, Maine.

The direction and leadership of the Quebec Labrador Foundation became the responsibility of Dr. Larry Morris. I continued directing the work on the Quebec North Shore and served as the archdeacon of the Anglican Church. Larry expanded the work of QLF and the global reach. He became president in 1980 and continued as executive director until 2017 when Beth Ailing succeeded him as president.

Many thanks to Candace Cochrane, member of QLF staff and family whose extraordinary photographs of Newfoundland and the North Shore helped bring the Quebec Labrador Foundation to the attention of the world.

Richard (Rick) Bullock was another chief pilot for QLF. Every move I made with aircraft decisions was with Rick. His skill as a pilot, wisdom, and friendship were integral to QLF's work and to me.